Adopting Maternity

Adopting Maternity

*White Women Who Adopt
Transracially or Transnationally*

NORA ROSE MOOSNICK

 PRAEGER

**Westport, Connecticut
London**

Library of Congress Cataloging-in-Publication Data

Moosnick, Nora Rose.
   White women who adopt transracially or transnationally / Nora Rose Moosnick.
      p. cm.
   Includes bibliographical references and index.
   ISBN 0–275–97812–5 (alk. paper)
   1. Interracial adoption—United States. 2. Intercountry adoption—United States. 3.
White women—United States. 4. Adoptive parents—United States. I. Title.
HV875.64 .M66 2004
362.734—dc22   2003024227

British Library Cataloguing in Publication Data is available.

Library of Congress Catalog Card Number: 2003024227
ISBN: 0–275–97812–5

First published in 2004

Praeger Publishers, 88 Post Road West, Westport, CT 06881
An imprint of Greenwood Publishing Group, Inc.
www.praeger.com

Printed in the United States of America

The paper used in this book complies with the
Permanent Paper Standard issued by the National
Information Standards Organization (Z39.48–1984).

10   9   8   7   6   5   4   3   2   1

to community

Contents

Preface

I came to this work not as someone associated with adoption. Nor did I envision myself becoming personally involved with adoption at any time in the foreseeable future, even though I had always thought about adopting transracially. Most people writing about adoption, by contrast, are emotionally meshed in adoption either as birth or adoptive parents or as adoptees. I do not fit any of these categories. As an outsider, I am not an "expert" in the field—I do not hold insider's knowledge. Yet, during the course of this work the line between the personal and professional blurred. Barbara Yngvesson, in her work *Negotiating Motherhood: Identity and Difference in "Open" Adoptions*, writes of the fragile borders she negotiates as both an adoptive mother and a researcher looking into adoption. In introducing her work, she reflects on the slender distinction between her professional and personal selves. "The pages that follow reflect this movement and the boundaries that are continually set in place, disturbed, and transgressed by it—between life and work, between the people we study and the people we are, between the legal and the everyday, between legitimate and illegitimate families, and between adoptive parents, birthparents, and their children" (Yngvesson 1997: 33). I relate to her sentiment as someone who has become a mother, though not an adoptive mother.

I entered this project as "not a mother" and leave it as one. As I have journeyed through a mothering project, I have embarked on a mothering journey. As a mother, I am curious, more so than when I initiated this work, about how the scholarly arguments of feminists can pertain to a mother's life.

This written text is composed of many conversations. The essence of the work resides in the conversations I had with adoptive mothers. The work also embodies a conversation between the women's talk and the scholarly works that guide this project. Acting as a mediator, I juxtapose and compare the women's talk to views of selected feminists.

I constructed this project with certain feminist critiques in mind. I understood that White women confront an imperative to mother, whereas Black women, among others, encounter a public ethos that almost punishes them for mothering too many children (Abramovitz 1994, 2000; Gordon 1994; Silva 1996; Solinger 2001; Tsing 1990). Feminist interpretations of mothering imperatives vary, of course. Adrienne Rich, in *Of Woman Born*, eloquently conveys how mothering does not come to women naturally. Barbara Katz Rothman unravels the absurdity of women brutalizing their bodies with new reproductive technologies (NRTs) to gather a baby. Patricia Hill Collins (1991), meanwhile, maintains focus on the racial dimension of mothering standards. The above feminists, while attentive to different features of mothering, all uncover oppressive mothering imperatives. In response to such interpretations, Katz Rothman, among others, calls on women to quiet such pressures by not indulging in new reproductive technologies.

While I concur with Katz Rothman, at least theoretically, I found myself in a peculiar situation. In the processing of carrying out this work, I listened to heart-wrenching and grievous stories of infertility. I ached at the prospect of personally sharing this grief, and in projecting these women's losses onto myself, I felt the imperative to try my luck at fertility. I, too, strongly needed to become a mother fast, before my age would become a hindrance!

More than feeling the need to mother, I now understood the intensity of feelings and emotions that accompany becoming and being a mother—feelings and emotions that are not idle chatter, but express themselves through the hard toil of "mother work" (Ruddick 1997).

Commentaries on child-centeredness also hold new meaning for me (Hays 1996). In particular, I regard my children as priceless (Zelizer 1994) despite knowing that doing so comes at the cost of my own well-being since the woman is lost in the process of tending to the priceless child (Hays 1996). Arguments against child-centeredness also discourage women from monitoring themselves on the basis of expert advice (Katz Rothman 1994). Still, I watched my diet closely through pregnancy and continue to monitor my intake because I am breast-feeding. During my son's first year, I mothered, to some extent, "by- the-book" with parenting and medical books on my nightstand available as occasion and need arose. I watched with curious amusement as my husband periodically opened *What to Expect the First Year* to the "What Your Baby Should Be Doing" section of each chapter to compare our baby's progress with the experts' understanding of a baby's progress. We were relieved to know that he could do the things he should and were consternated when he could not do things expected of him. I cringe when thinking of the number of times I said, "according to the book," in an effort to boost the authoritative power of my motherly intuition. As a new mother, I also ran to the doctor more times than I would care to admit. I became, as Foucault (1979) saw, my own Panoptic institution—there was no need for physical structures to surround me.

My first year as a mother did not occur in isolation, but rather in relation to other mothers. And I continue to maneuver between two principal mothering worlds. I encounter "by-the-book" mothers who are proud that they follow imperatives set by the authorities. In the face of these mothers, I proudly assert that I defy expert standards (since the birth of my second child, I have ceased to consult manuals). Yet, I also come across "home birthers" who put me to shame because they did it all at home, avoiding medications and other medical interventions found in the hospital setting. These mothers use, with almost biblical precision, home health remedies and breast-feed until their children can talk. They criticize me for engaging the medical world too readily. Indeed, I don't say how many times I've gone to the doctor searching for answers instead of trusting my own intuitions. But I also recognize that the mother they would like me to be requires that I rarely leave my child.

I share my own mothering story to make a point—namely, that many of us, particularly when we become mothers, try to uphold a moral standard. The morals of some of the women I interviewed emanate from religious or even scientific traditions. However, others of us, although our sense of right and wrong may have religious roots, take instruction from secular, humanist, and political imperatives; for myself, these imperatives come particularly from academic feminists. Just like the religious person, however, I evaluate whether or not I am living up to expectations.

Against the backdrop of the above, the text that follows looks back. I look back at the words I wrote when commencing this project imbued by my feminist understanding. Most importantly, I renegotiate scholarly arguments through the lens of my own experiences and regard adoptive mothers. I ask, in particular, How do certain feminist standards and arguments apply to the daily and nightly realities of mothering?

Aside from the profound intersection between my day-to-day experiences and my academic work, several things need to be said about this project generally. This project is ambitious. I approached this work as an opportunity to examine the intersection between race, class, and gender; indeed, transracial and transnational adoptions by their very nature are particularly suited for looking at the relationships between race, class, and gender. Surely people who are involved in transracial adoptions confront, or at least engage, race in a manner that most of us who are White do not.

Adoptions also speak to class relations since the adopted child typically moves from less to more financially able circumstances. In addition, adoptive arrangements offer insight into cultural notions of the family and of women's positions therein—such that pregnant women who are not in traditional relationships are still constructed as less than ideal mothers (Solinger 1992, 2001; Yngvesson 1997).

In intersecting race, class, and gender, I broach many topics, including adoption generally, transracial adoption, transnational adoption, maternity, racism, and prejudice. Consequently, the scope of the work is multifaceted—at times race takes prominence, at other times maternity foreshadows race, and at still other times the bearing of feminist analysis predominates. The project, furthermore, is situated and located in the women's words both methodologically and insofar as the direction and tone of their words guided me toward new thoughts and topics. As a result, it must be repeated that this work is composed of several conversations.

Acknowledgments

There are many people whose assistance surrounds this work and deserves recognition.

Of course, thanks must first be extended to the adoptive mothers who willingly shared intimate pieces of their lives with a stranger carrying a tape recorder.

An assortment of other people deserve thanking. I would like to thank my dissertation advisor, Dr. Laurie Hatch. She was a dream to work with during the rigors and demands of the dissertation. More recently, she has continued to express a faith in my ability through laughter and good humor that encouraged me to make the dissertation a book. I am indebted to Mildred Vasan for not only taking an interest in my work, but for making this book a possibility and reality. Thank you. A thank-you must also be extended to Dr. James Sabin at Greenwood Publishers for the patience and good will he expressed to a mom with young children who happened to be writing a book.

Given my mothering demands, I know this work never would have reached completion had an assortment of "good" baby-sitters not entered our lives. I am, like most mothers, always searching for "quality and affordable child care." I am so fortunate to have found it in Mamta, Renee, Christa, and April.

Finally, there is my family to thank. I am thankful to have supportive in-laws, Ginny and Stefan, who make it possible for me to take the time to write a book. I am also lucky to have my mother, Ima, and my sister, Mia, in my life who are not just "family," but greatest friends and soul mates. I could not have managed this project without the help, support, and love of my husband, Ted. I am so grateful that he willingly spent hours of his limited work time to read and pour over the manuscript trying to make cryptic sentences sound less opaque. But more than providing editing support, he holds the patience and wisdom to ride the roller coaster of life well centered—he is essential to me. And I must thank my children, Louie and Helena. I simply never expected to love them and the world around them so fully. Lastly, my deepest gratitude goes to my father and brother whose love and compassion equipped me to face the world without them.

CHAPTER 1

Introduction

Contemporary adoptive families are increasingly not monoracial (Register 1991). In 1987, for example, a foreign child entered the United States for adoption every 45 minutes (Raymond 1993). More recently, in 1998, 15,724 international adoptees entered the United States (Pertman 2000). Shapiro, Shapiro, and Paret (2001) report that in 1999, 16,396 children were adopted from abroad, marking a 45 percent increase in four years. Contemporary adoptive families, then, are composed of White[1] parents raising children of a different race and ethnicity from themselves. Most often, the increased prevalence of such families is attributed both to the decrease in White women's fertility in this country consequent to their greater access to abortion and birth control and to White women increasingly choosing to parent alone (Altstein and Simon 1991; Hansen 1997; Solinger 2001). Given the negligible availability of White babies, adoption agencies and mediators guide White parents seeking to adopt toward special-needs children, who are defined as children connected with siblings, older than infancy, minority, or with physical or mental disability (Katz 1993). White couples seeking babies are thus confronted with two viable options—pursuing a domestic adoption of a Black and/or Biracial baby or seeking a baby overseas (Fulton 1995; Porter 1993; Shapiro, Shapiro, and Paret 2001).

Much is being written today about adoption generally, and about transracial and transnational adoption in particular. "How-to" manuals guide families through the lengthy and often grueling adoption processes (Gilman 1987; Kichen 1995; Knoll and Murphy 1994); adoptive families also use the Internet to share important "how-to" information about such things as how to fill out the forms required by foreign governments or how to know if an adoption agency is legitimate. A vast amount of the discussion about and information on this topic, moreover, addresses the question of whether such adoptions are good for the adoptive children and conducive to the formation of healthy racial and ethnic identities (Altstein 1993; Altstein and Simon 1991; Bartholet 1995; Curtis 1996; Hayes 1993; Herrmann and Kasper 1992; Hollingsworth 1997; Howe and Kennedy 1998; Lythcott-Haims 1994; McRoy and Grape 1999; Patton 2000; Simon and Altstein 2000; Simon, Altstein, and Melli 1995). This focus stems, in part, from the fact that the National Association of Black Social Workers (NABSW), over 30 years ago, loudly asserted that transracial adoptions are a form of cultural genocide. At the time, the NABSW took the stand that these adoptions were yet another example of racism because they represented Whites living out a rescue fantasy of saving Black children from bad homes. This proclamation that the NABSW made years earlier still continues to stir controversy.

Often writing with this proclamation in mind, increasing numbers of adoptive parents, mostly mothers, are chronicling their experiences through this largely unknown familial territory (Bates 1993; Gilman 1987; Knoll and Murphy 1994; Register 1991; Rush 2000; Thompson 2000; Wolff 1997). Relatively few of the confessionals available, however, critically scrutinize transracial and transnational adoptive families for the complex entanglements of race, ethnicity, class, and gender that unfold within them. In contrast, the present work aspires, through maternal narratives, to highlight how adoption reflects, reproduces, creates, and may even confront ideologies of race, class, and gender. As Patton (2000: 139) writes, "fictional and nonfictional representations of the issue of transracial adoption are sites of struggle over the social and political meanings of race and identity, gender and family, individuals and the role of the state." Specifically, I examine adoptive mothers' narratives to see how they negotiate the "sites of struggle" found in their very own families. In doing so, much is revealed about how these struggles are managed daily by mothers, as well as how mothers choose to portray the challenges they may face.

ADOPTION: REVOLUTIONARY PROGRESS OR REINFORCEMENT OF HEGEMONIES?

In *Birthmarks* (2000: 4) Sandra Patton argues "adoption is the terrain on which race, class, and gender are being contested." Patton examines transracial adoption policies for their ideologies and for how these ideologies are inscribed on individual biographies, in particular, the biographies of transracial adoptees. She reveals that, and explains how, adoption policies equate family with Whiteness and middle-class status. According to Patton, this biased equation has been played out in local and individual situations where, historically, adoption social workers have arbitrarily defined and categorized the race of Biracial and Black children to make them palatable to prospective White adoptive families. Social workers, she argues, would misidentify dark children's racial makeup to create the impression the children were lighter than they were in fact. This practice has left adoptees, in the end, without a cohesive sense of their racial "rootedness." It has instead made them acutely aware of how they have been "routed" into racial existence (Patton 2000: 62).

In a similar vein, Rickie Solinger's work, *Beggars and Choosers: How the Politics of Choice Shapes Adoption*, directly links adoption policies with the welfare of poor women. She looks at the relationship between the reproductive choices available to middle-class women and the reproductive vulnerability of poor women in particular. Adoption, in Solinger's estimation, "is an index of the vulnerable status of women in the birth mother's country" (Solinger 2001: 67). According to Solinger, legislative mandates support middle-class and White people in their quest to become parents while, simultaneously, undercutting poor women's efforts to raise their children. Poor women are encouraged to relinquish their children while middle-class women are helped to parent; policies are even promoted that subsidize fertility treatments for the middle class. Solinger (2001: 31) argues, further, that in the adoption transaction the birth mother is effaced in order to meet consumer demand. An example is the birth mother disappearing in the international setting. Policy initiatives, accordingly, in effect lessen the birth mother's grief in light of the grief adoptive parents may experience if they are unable to parent (Solinger 2001: 31). Solinger effectively uncovers the class biases of adoption policies and practices, which disparage poor and darker women as makers of bad choices in contrast to White, middle-class people who are portrayed as good consumers and, hence, as worthy of becoming and being parents.

Both Solinger and Patton challenge the popularly held notion that adoption is a universal good and argue, in contrast, that it often creates and recreates gender, class, and race-based hegemonies.

Amid critical discussions such as those of Solinger and Patton, there stands Adam Pertman's *Adoption Nation: How the Adoption Revolution Is Transforming America*. Pertman does not ignore some of the aforementioned problematic features of adoption. In the end, however, he argues that adoption creates positive, even "revolutionary" change. In his estimation, "adoption is reshaping what constitutes a normal family" (Pertman 2000: 222). He points to the number of people affected by adoption as one feature of the revolution. Increasingly, open adoptions also help shed the secrecy that has historically marked adoptions and, in so doing, affect greater public acceptance of families created by means other than biological ones. According to Pertman, the increased number of transracial and transnational adoptions symbolizes racial progress as U.S. society becomes more accustomed to racial diversity. The fact that gays and les-

bians are becoming parents through adoption further highlights the growing public acceptance of the idea that families can take diverse forms.

Of course, Patton and Solinger question whether revolutionary change
is unfolding by holding that hegemonic notions of race and appropriate
maternity are merely being reinforced under the guise of adoption as a
good. Gailey (2000) claims that individual adoption choices reveal weddedness, or lack thereof, to dominant ideologies. In the following chapters,
the question of whether transracial and transnational adoption practices
are regressive or progressive is addressed through maternal narratives.
Of particular relevance to this book is the question: Do White adoptive
mothers, in their own estimation and in their narrations, resist hegemonic
notions of race, class, and maternity? In the chapters to come, the women's
portrayals of infertility treatments, adoption processes, birth mothers, and
others' responses, among other topics, are documented in order to uncover how and if these women daily confront and reconcile questions of
race, class, and gender.

As may be clear from the above discussion, adoption, transracial and
transnational adoptions in particular, are a hotly contested phenomenon
today. One thing Pertman, Solinger, and Patton would all agree on is that
the adoption landscape is riddled with contradictions. Families talk about
adoption more openly than they did previously. Virtually all of the women
with whom I spoke had created photo and memorabilia albums about the
formation of their family to share with their children and others. More
and more families, furthermore, are participating in open relationships
with the birth mothers, a trend that may signal acceptance of the proposition that biology need not define a family.[2] Judging from my interviews,
the women believed that biology is not the sine qua non in this regard,
even though sometimes they encountered others' sentiments that insinuated biological connections as the ideal. One woman shared with me
that she overheard a friend of her daughter's apologize after learning that
her daughter was adopted. Indeed, adoption continues, partly, to be associated with sorrow and loss.

An assortment of other questions and contradictions surrounding adoption surfaced in the women's narratives. For example, even given greater
openness, do birth mothers, as Solinger claims, remain silent and effaced?
Historically, adoption has involved the transfer of children from less to
more financially secure homes. Does adoption promote the belief that
middle- and upper-class status is a necessary condition of good mothering? At the same time that the poor woman may be effaced, middle- and
upper-class gays and lesbians are gaining status as parents through adoption. In the United States then, is there growing tolerance that families can
take various forms?

The existence of White families, including gay families, with children
of another race that most likely live in predominantly White communities,

may challenge racial (and heterosexual) dogmas that dictate monoracial families. Through the visual displays these families present, Whites may become more accustomed to racial and ethnic diversity.

A further matter of particular importance to this work is the question, How do adoptive mothers characterize adoptions and their own positionality? Do these women perceive themselves to be part of revolutionary change, as Pertman describes. Do they conceive of themselves as existing in a web of relations that hurt the birth mothers or as simply carrying on their lives? Through maternal narratives I examine how crossing racial lines to mother a child darker than oneself influences a White mother's understanding of herself as a mother (Twine 1999). Visual differences between the White mother and her child serve as a constant and public reminder that the child has a birth mother different from her mother (Gilman 1987; Register 1991; Twine 1999). One mother of Korean children, for example, shared with me a painful experience she had with some children at a public pool, who relentlessly asked her, "Are those really your babies?" "How can they be your babies?" Given that the White adoptive mother's status is often publicly challenged, I look at how these mothers engage and negotiate mothering standards and ideals that assume racial conformity between mother and child. I ask, in particular, whether a mother's conception of herself as a mother is less publicly and, hence, internally challenged if she mothers an Asian child (a member of an ideal minority) instead of a Black or Biracial one. Additionally, attention is paid to whether or not challenges to maternal identities lead to actions by adoptive mothers that resist racial and gender hierarchies. As I detail in chapter 5, I discovered that those women who recognized adoption and their own maternity to be a site of struggle were more inclined to translate the contradictions experienced into antiracist activities. These women, moreover, were more likely to be women with Black and/or Biracial children.

Given my interest in whether mothering experiences directly varied with the child's skin color, the women were categorized by the race of their child: White, Asian, and Black, and Biracial. I interviewed 22 White adoptive mothers. Seven women adopted White children; seven, Asian; and eight women adopted Black and Biracial children.

A MATERNAL FOCUS

As is clear from the structure of this project, its focus is decidedly on maternity. Interest in adoption both as a site of maternal struggle and a site of maternal possibility stems from selected feminist renditions of adoption (Gailey 2000; Solinger 2001). Indeed, Gailey maintains that "adoption provides us with a way of seeing how the major vectors of difference in the society—class, race, and gender—affect the meaning of motherhood" (Gailey 2000: 15). To reiterate a point made in the Preface,

my book is a conversation with both the adopting women and certain
feminist accounts of the women's lives. An important dimension of this
work, in other words, is its attempt to negotiate the disjuncture between
their lived experiences as articulated by the women themselves and feminist portrayals of their lives. Although this work is concerned with the
adoption debate, it perhaps more decidedly emerges out of selected feminist debates. After all, it has been feminists who have recognized the
power and insight that women hold as mothers, while also bringing attention to the strictures that motherhood places on women. It is to the
above thoughts and others that I turn to in this section. I begin with my
rationale for highlighting mothers.

I center my gaze on mothering and mothering conventions for a variety
of reasons. Mothers have not traditionally narrated their experiences.
Even today women are still more often defined in relation to children than
are men, as witnessed by the fact that infertility difficulties are typically
taken to imply that the woman is at fault (May 1995; Raymond 1993). As
a result, it is most often the woman who must endure medical procedures
in order to overcome a couple's infertility "illness" (Raymond 1993).
Women's daily lives, moreover, are more likely to be devoted to child care
responsibilities than are men's. Women overwhelmingly retain primary
child care responsibilities and are more likely to participate in second
shifts after returning home from work (Hays 1996; Phoenix, Woollett, and
Lloyd 1991). The assumption persists that motherhood is a natural stage
of a female's development into adulthood (Thurer 1994).

These maternal arrangements surface in adoptive families. In her
work, *Kinship with Strangers,* Judith Modell found that adoptive families
maintain traditional gendered familial relations. This situation has been
codified in adoption laws and policies that assume, as the renowned an-
thropologist Bronislaw Malinowski explained in 1936, that "adoption is
simply the substitution of one maternity for another" (cited in Modell
1994: 29). This sentiment was reinforced in my inquiries through the fact
that information and knowledge about the birth fathers was spotty at best.
As is true of all mothers, furthermore, most of these adoptive mothers
spent more time with their children than did the adoptive fathers. Similarly to other mothers as well, they often used their motherhood to build
alliances and relationships in the wider community; some of the women
led organizational efforts to set up support networks with other adoptive
families. It is often on the basis of motherhood that women have sought
solidarity and mutual understanding despite the divisions and perhaps
even oppositions between them (Kenison and Hirsch 1996; Naples 1998b;
Rich 1976).

Through the narratives of White adoptive mothers, insights can be gathered about their own feelings and needs concerning mothering— feelings
and needs that may or may not have motivated them to adopt. I attend

to the extent to which they accepted or, contrarily, resisted medical intervention in the hopes of attaining the status of mother. Equally important is the effort they exerted to attain the status of "good mother," which for the White parents of Black children often meant participating in classes on Black heritage. I also pay attention to how the women characterized themselves and other mothers according to standards of "goodness" and "fitness," in particular in relation to race, ethnicity, and class. For instance, I study how initial adoption choices such as choice of country to adopt from express racial and ethnic biases. A mother of a Chinese girl shared with me her belief that prenatal care would be worse in the United States than in China because of the fear that drug and alcohol abuse is prevalent among birth mothers in this country.

As indicated, the women's narrations of these and other matters are filtered through and analyzed via selected feminist interpretations of mothering and adoption. In particular, my analysis arises from a variety of feminist works that examine "the experience of mothering" as well as "the institution of motherhood" (Gilligan 1982; Phoenix, Woollett, and Lloyd 1991; Raymond 1993; Rich 1976; Thurer 1994). These feminists devote special attention to the display and exertion of power that is embedded in the institution of motherhood and to the varied ways power is experienced depending on a woman's race, ethnicity, and class standing. Such attentiveness to power emerges, in part, from Michel Foucault's insights into the intersection between power and knowledge. Before detailing certain feminist understandings, my outline of Foucault's thoughts on this topic follows.

In works such as *Discipline and Punishment; History of Sexuality, Volume I: An Introduction;* and *Madness and Civilization,* Foucault did not seek to predict the future or even to explain social processes. Through historical case studies, he instead viewed as problematic the linear as well as dialectical accounts of history and the assumed progress that results from the intersection of scientific practices and society. Centering his gaze on scientific practices, Foucault argued that the "knowledge" they gather is conditioned by power relations that structure the gathering process. Power, in his estimation, is not simply a relationship between the powerful and powerless. Power is not, for instance, embodied in the monarch who stands above the rest of society, but instead, it permeates every aspect of a person's life. It is like a net in which everything that exists in society is caught. In the context of prisons, moreover, Foucault attends to the growing encroachment of scientific knowledge that so disciplines prisoners that they monitor themselves and internalize particular self-definitions and paradigms.

Foucault's genealogy of madness in *Madness and Civilization* chronicles the process by which medical science transformed madness from a spiritual state of sorts to a disease. This book traces the historical transformation of "mad" people from individuals who spoke the "truth" into people requiring segregation, institutionalization, and study. During the Middle Ages, he explained, the mad were revered in the belief that they understood life in a way unavailable to the rest of society. With the rise of medical science, in the seventeenth and eighteenth centuries, madness was no longer conceived as a form of reason. It was conceived, instead, as antithetical to reason. The rise of the opposition between reason and madness was accompanied by the generation, in medical discourse, of new diseases. With the rise of medicalization, the "patient" came to be asked to confront his illness and transgressions. Confronting one's illness was made complete with the rise of the asylum. Here, the patient was wholly defined since the institution marked him as mentally incapable, and required that he look inwardly to combat his mental ill health.

Foucault's historical analyses provide a framework for thinking about the medicalization of mothering, which leads women to inspect themselves internally to assess whether they are living up to expert standards. Foucault, himself, showed little interest in women. He made small overtures to their situation in his almost passing remark in *The History of Sexuality, Volume I: An Introduction*, that at the end of the nineteenth century a woman overwhelmed by her passions was labeled hysterical. Despite his inattention, analyzing the intersection between power and knowledge is particularly pertinent to women and their lives (Abramovitz 1994; Fausto-Sterling 1987; Keller 1987; Martin 1987; Polakow 1993). Nearly two decades ago, for example, Emily Martin (1987) brought attention to the fact that medical language disciplines women into silence and passivity. With the professionalization of medicine, normal bodily processes such as menstruation and menopause became diseased states. A general Foucauldian approach unravels the power relations that have historically quieted women from talking as mothers, pushed women to mother despite misgivings, and monitored women's mothering capabilities.

Maternal Constraints

A Foucauldian analysis stresses, among other things, how scientific knowledge invades and forms the individual. In 1976, Adrienne Rich wrote of the institution of motherhood, that it, along with the institution of heterosexuality, "creates the prescriptions and the conditions in which choices are made or blocked; they are not "reality" but they have shaped the circumstances of our lives" (Rich 1976: 24). The power of these motherhood prescriptions often resides in their scientific provenance, as well as in their widespread application. Their pervasive application notwithstanding, scientific standards are experienced individually. Similar to Foucault's prisoners, women find themselves alone and isolated as they inspect their lives for possible shortcomings, for example, not wanting their children or mothering inadequately, as the case might be (Kenison and Hirsch 1996; Rich 1976; Ruddick 1994; Smith 1990). Introspection has also meant that women's maternal voices and experiences have been excluded as counsels in their own daily lives. Their lives have instead been held by others; they thereby hold themselves to mothering standards that are not necessarily congruent with their own understanding of themselves.

Women of color have maintained a unique relationship to scientific mothering evaluations: they have been evaluated in light of ideal standards that at the same time are considered to be outside of their reach. Historically, the assumption has been that Black women, are, among other things, of ill moral repute. The thinking was/is that they are unreasonably sexualized beings (Hammonds 1997; Solinger 1992). It is situated outside of the reach of mothering standards, however, that Black mothers traditionally have not mothered in isolation as is the case for White middle-class women (see Collins 1991, 1994). Yet, directives to White women about the imperative to mother, as well as about how to mother well, contextualize the Black mother's experiences. Indeed, it is by contrast with White women that it becomes clear that the imperative to mother is not applied to women of color as it is to Whites (Abramovitz 2000; Gordon 1994).

Maternal Constraints: The White Woman's Imperative to Mother

The intersection of scientific knowledge with power has meant that the imperative that White women, in particular, mother has remained strong. Rich recognized in 1976 that a woman must mother in order to attain a satisfactory state of femininity. Chodorow (1978) articulated convergent sentiments through her object-relations theory, which argues that women, in contrast to men, acquire their sense of self through connections with others. More recent works offer similar observations that women are expected to be society's public and private nurturers (Gilligan 1982; Gordon 1994; McMahon 1995; Phoenix and Woollett 1991; Ruddick 1994). If a woman's sense of self is gathered from caring for others, she may regard herself—and be regarded by others—as inadequate if she does not nurture intensively (Hansen 1997). Mothering and mothering well, as Woollett (1991) explains, offer a symbolic display of a woman's physical and emotional adequacy (see also Kitzinger 1978). Rich even argues that a woman's body is designated as pure or impure depending on whether or not she successfully mothers. Worse yet, she lacks femininity should she be childless (Remennick 2000). A woman achieves moral perfection through motherhood as she discards her needs for those of her children. Simply put, a woman's adequacy has been measured historically by her ability to bear children—whence the historical practice of regarding infertility as a rightful claim for divorce (Kitzinger 1978; Raymond 1993). Should she not have children, a woman is left with the sense that she is missing out and, moreover, not meeting the requirements of self-integrity (Hansen 1997; Remennick 2000). The powerful and oppressive nature of the above sentiments has been not only reinforced, but also even created by medical science and psychoanalysis (Chodorow 1978; Gilligan 1982; Phoenix, Woollett, and Lloyd 1991; Thurer 1994).

The maternal instinct (the fact that women mother naturally) was medically "discovered" and analyzed. Should a woman be unable to conceive, hysterical outbursts were thought to be a natural outcome (Foucault 1965). Her turbulent womb devoid of children, not her homebound isolation, caused her emotional troubles (Smith 1990). According to Enlightenment thought, her worth resides only in her almost mystical ability to have children, an ability which deserves male adoration and requires male control and inspection (Thurer 1994). The persistence of such thinking is demonstrated by its application to the contemporary prospective mother who undergoes fertility treatment. This "frustrated" woman is often characterized by medical expertise as too emotional to make rational decisions about her own reproductive capacities, negating the suffering her body endures in the hopes of snatching a baby (Thurer 1994). What is, perhaps, most distressing about medical prescription is the extent to which women, irrespective of their personal desires, follow "expert" advice to have children (Rich 1976).

Of course, some feminist writers and poets have challenged the assumption that a woman mothers instinctually (Gilligan 1982; Lovibond 1994; McMahon 1995; Phoenix, Woollett, and Lloyd 1991; Plath 1965; Rich 1976; Thurer 1994). Decades ago, Sylvia Plath and Adrienne Rich both vividly dared to express their dissatisfaction with mothering.

Raymond (1993) and Hubbard (1990) even claim that the rise of new reproductive technologies (NRTs) seduce women into thinking that they are supposed to exhaust all medical possibilities of producing a baby regardless of the physical as well as emotional costs to them and their bodies.

A PERILOUS POSITION: THE ADOPTIVE MOTHER

The above academic and feminist portrayals of maternal strictures can be extended to adoptive mothers. For example, both implicit and explicit judgmental sentiments about adopting mothers flourish in the adoption literature. Indeed, White adoptive mothers hold a perilous position in the transracial and transnational adoption triangle, as witnessed by the very discourse surrounding them (see Modell 1994).[3] Academic dialogues, moreover, characterize her, the White adoptive mother, as both victim and victimizer (see Raymond 1993).

The adoptive mother with fertility difficulties gains victim status in some feminist works (Hubbard 1990; Raymond 1993; Rothenberg and Thomson 1994; Rothman 1994b), in part because she often relinquishes her body to grueling and physically damaging medical techniques in a futile attempt to gather a baby. The medical enterprise engages and encounters her body as diseased, thus at the expense of her sense of self and body. Janice Raymond, in *Women as Wombs*, articulates the belief that new reproductive technologies represent "brutality with a therapeutic face." As a blatant expression of patriarchy, she writes, new reproductive technologies symbolize men's willingness to violate women's bodies, but not their own.

Although the White woman of resources, like her poor counterpart, is constructed as a victim of medical intervention, her victim status is limited. Raymond (1993) and Rothman (1994b) assert that by merely participating in new reproductive technologies, she has become too attached to the imperative to mother. By offering her body to medical science, she has abetted in the reinforcement and creation of images of the "fit mother" (Gordon 1990; Koven and Michel 1993; Polakow 1993; Raymond 1993). Fit mothers willingly undergo any and all tests and procedures necessary for becoming pregnant, and once pregnant they anxiously submit to tests to screen the fetus as to its healthiness and their own contribution to its well-being (Rothenberg and Thomson 1994; Rothman 1994b; Tsing 1990).

The imperative for women to mother at all costs is not, however, universally applied. Women of color and of the South are systematically and physically discouraged from mothering (Hubbard 1990; Raymond 1993; Solinger 2001). Black and White women on welfare in this country, as well as poor women of the South, are coerced into using birth control in the face of White, middle-class consternation that these women live outside of medical control (Abramovitz 1994, 2000; Hammonds 1997; Polakow 1993; Raymond 1993). The equation is rather simple—being poor and darker skinned is equated with bad mothering (Abramovitz 1994, 2000; Solinger 2001).

In the United States, the welfare industry was designed to aid "fit" and "good" mothers (Abramovitz 1994, 2000; Gordon 1990, 1994). Of course, the maternal ideal was White. White women of social standing upheld appropriate maternal habits. White, middle-class mother heroines prescribed mothering strategies that presumed a two-parent family with the father alone working outside of the home (Gordon 1990, 1994; Koven and Michel 1993; Naples 1998a; Phoenix, Woollett, and Lloyd 1991; Raymond 1993). Such a cultural ideal of motherhood disparaged and disregarded the poor, immigrant mother whose work outside of the home sustained her family.

White women of all social standings were also held to the standard of the fit mother. According to Rickie Solinger in *Wake Up Little Susie*, for instance, the White unwed mother during the 1950s and early 1960s was expected to hide her pregnancy in Florence Crittenton maternity homes until the baby was carried away to the fit adoptive family. Age and marital standing became measures of appropriate or inappropriate motherhood. At this time, young White unwed mothers who expressed interest in keeping their babies were medically labeled as hysterical and pressured into relinquishing their children, which social workers intoned they must nobly abandon to a loving family (see Jones 1993; Solinger 1992). Although they were noble for letting go their children, they were also bad girls who deserved discipline and disparaging lectures from doctors and nurses (see Jones 1993).

To qualify as a fit mother required, then and still today, not only appropriate racial, marital, and financial status, but also adherence to professional advice. The modern mother follows scientific guidelines, often offered by physicians and psychoanalysts, and "raises her child by the book" (Thurer 1994).

Experts have given women directions about how to mother, but this practice has constituted a legacy that disparages mothers as potentially damaging enemies of the child (see Thurer 1994). It is not only that she cannot mother well, but also that her interventions can damage the child (see Hubbard 1990). A Jewish mother, for example, overwhelms and smothers her children, while an Anglo mother remains too distant and uninterested (Hubbard 1990). Even discourse about the womb blatantly constructs the mother as a possible enemy of the fetus if she entertains harmful habits. Technological advances in prenatal care, for instance, relegate a mother to inappropriateness if she chooses not to have amniocentesis in order to evaluate the soundness of her unborn child (Tsing 1990). It has come to be assumed that medical science can help women to achieve the perfect mother status and overcome their natural shortcomings (Thurer 1994). In this way of thinking, within this discourse, women's insights as mothers were and are relegated to uninteresting chatter.

As stated, the White adoptive mother maintains an unstable position within some of the feminist discourse discussed above. Some of the feminists listed above (Raymond 1993; Rothman 1994b) charge her not only with following and propagating hegemonic understandings of mothers, but also with avoiding thoughtful contemplation of how the hegemonic "fit" mentality expresses itself in NRTs and adoption processes (see Hibbs 1991; Raymond 1993).[4] According to this feminist critique, the White adoptive mother ignores the wider political and social arrangements surrounding new reproductive technologies and adoption. She disregards the racial and class tensions between herself and women of color. The White adoptive mother unwittingly represents the belief that infertility is a "disease" found among White and middle class women (Abramovitz 2000). In contrast, poor, dark women of the inner city and Third World, so the portrayals continue, produce an overcapacity of children, much to White chagrin (Abramovitz 1994, 2000; Chowdry 1995; Escobar 1995; Gans 1995; Gordon 1994; Hammonds 1997; Marchand and Parpart 1995; Raymond 1993).

Given the White mother's battle with infertility, it is argued, she reaches out to the Third World desperate for a child without critically analyzing how that child reaches her loving arms (Raymond 1993). She blindly gathers "unwanted" babies. Solinger (2001) insists that the Western appetite for babies skews the market in favor of those who have money to spend, while discouraging in-country adoptions. Raymond (1993) argues that prostitutes and/or teenagers are paid to produce babies for a growing foreign market, especially if they can produce light-skinned offspring (Herrmann and Kasper 1992; Hubbard 1990). In the worst-case scenario, according to Raymond, babies are sought out by opportunists eager to capitalize on the booming baby industry.[5] Babies are even gathered after the ravages of war leave rape victims pregnant. Although Raymond's claims may be difficult to accept, it is indisputably true that, historically, foreign adoption and access to foreign babies tracks U.S. military ventures (see Fulton 1995). Following World War II, for instance, the majority of transnational adoptions were Biracial children from Germany and Korea (Altstein 1993).

Lurking behind accusations of naive adoption are harsher charges of racism. The White adoptive mother faces the indictment that she perpetuates racial biases by participating in transracial adoptions that privilege her as a fit mother at the expense of the Black families able to adopt (Abdullah 1996). The White adoptive mother qualifies as fit by virtue of her skin color, coupled with the fact that she rescues the child from the biological mother who is understood to be neither morally nor financially capable (Raymond 1993; Silva 1996; Solinger 2001). Perhaps, most offensive to Hubbard (1990), is that these adoptive mothers may well express eugenic sentiments when they show preference for lighter skinned and flawless babies (Hibbs 1991; Hubbard 1990; Raymond 1993; Rothman 1994b).

The White adoptive mother's claims to motherhood only grow more problematic and complex at home. In the White community, where she and her children likely reside, she may be regarded as failing to meet maternal ideals, and, at the same time, as someone who is saintly for mothering less than "perfect" children (Register 1990). She challenges the imperative to mother racially "sound" children (see Hubbard 1990; Twine 1999). Her mothering crimes are publicly scrutinized because they are obvious, given that her children look overtly different from herself (Twine 1999). At the very least, these women are mothers who do not conform to mainstream standards (Ragoné and Twine 2000)

Her rightful claim to motherhood may also be contested by her adopted children themselves (Raymond 1993). Drawing from an example used by Raymond (1993), Korean-born, and U.S.-adopted Mi Ok Bruining has, as an adult, publicly condemned transnational adoptions as exploitative and racist. "Children of color are the commodities and products and victims of ownership and living human property, and this process is being disguised as the desire to parent a child" (Raymond 1993: 150).

As is obvious from Bruining's statement, the White mother who adopts transracially or transnationally faces a wide assortment of challenges. This book questions adoptive mothers for how the challenges of gender, race, and ethnicity shape their understanding of themselves as mothers. In particular, I am interested in how an adoptive mother's identity as a mother varies depending on the race of her adoptive child. "Identity is a social process bound by space and time" (Allen 1994: 90). Identity, and maternal identity in particular, is gathered from medical prescriptions, images in the media, others' reactions, one's understanding of oneself as a woman, and so on (Bassin, Honey, and Kaplan 1994). Are, moreover, these maternal self-images generated, I ask, from feminist discourse attentive to adoption? With this question in mind, I consider the applicability of the above feminist characterizations to the women's words. Most of the women interviewed tried to normalize their maternity. The feminist claims detailed earlier, for the most part, were simply not a part of their daily experiences, nor did these claims provide the narrative framework the women used to speak of themselves and other mothers. The feminist effort to reach for possibilities, however, can be applied to the women's maternal talk by looking for ways that their adoptions confront and alter gender, race, and class hierarchies.

ADOPTION, MATERNITY, AND POSSIBILITIES

Frances Twine, in "Transracial Mothering and Antiracism: The Case of White Birth Mothers of 'Black' Children in Britain," recognizes that mothers who are not in monoracial families "need to constantly prove their maternal fitness" (1999: 10). She proposes that for these mothers "maternal competence is tied to their ability to contend with family's racism" (1999: 4). Twine thus claims that these mothers engage daily in antiracist work—for example, when they confront family members' racism that goes unnoticed in much feminist discourse because most such discourse assumes that families are monoracial.[6]

Larissa Remennick, in "Childless in the Land of Imperative Motherhood," seeks to unravel how Israeli women who face infertility contend with the stigma of being childless by asking whether there is a point at which the women resist the negative label placed on them. In the process, Remennick questions which actions or inactions qualify as resistance. She asks, Do internal conversations a woman may hold with herself count as resistance, or does resistance require outward displays that reject the strictures of pronatalism? "Resistance is when stigmatized persons reject popular ideas regarding their flaws" (2000: 837). In the end, Remennick asserts that resistance requires speaking up and acting out as opposed merely to coping with stigmatization.

Like Remennick and Twine, I look at ways that the women resist to outwardly challenge racism, for example. In the interviewees' narratives, I attend to whether or not they tie their own lives and troubles to larger racial and gender concerns. Nancy Naples (1998a), for instance, found that women activists in the inner city extended their maternal work to the larger community.[7] Although I use my own, and one drawn from Naples, understanding of resistance, I also look to the mothers themselves for instruction as to how to define resistance.

Maternal Strengths

Thinking about maternity as a site of resistance and possible action reflects feminist discussions that celebrate and do not disparage motherhood. Most of the previous discussion of motherhood focuses on the oppressive and restrictive character of the institution and on how this character is played out and engendered in transracial and transnational adoption processes. I have chosen to accentuate feminist works that highlight maternal constraints. It should not be thought, however, that feminist works that celebrate motherhood do not exist (Dinnerstein 1976; Rich 1976; Ruddick 1994). In "Maternal Thinking," for example, Sara Ruddick eloquently articulates the profound knowledge that women possess as mothers—knowledge and ways of thinking that, she argues, are ideally suited for serving the larger public good. Ruddick tries to balance the explication of oppressive structures and institutions that shape motherhood with the power and joy that accompanies being a mother. My book tries to do the same. An effort of this sort, I believe, should start by confronting the literature that highlights the restrictions maternity places on women.

In understanding the private as well as public pains of mothering, the attempt can be made to enlarge the private as well as public space open to celebrating the virtues of mothering, as defined by mothers themselves (see also Kitzinger 1978; McMahon 1995; Rich 1976). The virtues of motherhood can also be drawn out by comparing women's understanding of themselves to selected feminist portrayals. Through such an exercise and with heightened interest in and concern for transnational and transracial adoptions, more effort can be expended on improving the "experience of motherhood" within the venue of adoption.

According to Rich (1976), the mothering experience, in contrast to the motherhood institution, offers women endless possibilities and heightened senses of self as both individuals and mothers. Rich notes that mutual understanding across differences of class, race and/or geographic location and display could possibly be fostered on the basis of mothering (see Kitzinger 1978; McMahon 1995; Rich 1976). Barbara Kingsolver (1996), an accomplished American writer, expresses a similar sentiment when she writes, "I can hardly count the ways that being a mother has broadened my writing, deepened my connection with all other women, and galvanized my commitment to the Earth and its fate" (Kingsolver 1996: 164). Indeed, it is bearing Barbara Kingsolver's sentiments in mind that this project is pursued. Likewise, Ruddick's understanding of motherhood enhances "the experience of motherhood." Mothering, in Ruddick's estimation, is an act of peace. "To become a mother, whatever one's particular relation to individual acts of birth, is to welcome, shelter, protect, and nourish birth's bodies and thus to undertake a work of peace" (Ruddick 1994: 44). It is hoped that through the insights offered by the adoptive mothers the peaceful nature of "mothering work" will be enhanced.[8]

CHAPTERS AHEAD

The aims of this work are multifaceted and most broadly include: to explore women's narratives to discover whether or not maternal identities alter depending on the race of the children; to examine whether or not those mothers who construct themselves as challenged are more likely to place their families within larger social contexts and, as a result, to resist; to explore whether or not the women describe themselves and other mothers, such as birth mothers, according to mothering imperatives and fitness standards; to relate the adoptive mothers' narrations to selected feminist discourse and determine, thereby, whether or not feminist accounts "fit" women's narrations of their lives. Fulfillment of the tasks listed above occurs throughout the chapters that follow.

In chapter 2, "Social Constructionism: Contextualizing the Context," the project is further explicated through a discussion of social constructionism, which is the theoretical framework this book uses to define race, ethnicity, class, and gender. This book also discusses how social constructionism likewise informs the research enterprise to reveal, for instance, the dynamic interviewing process, and the varied understandings of science brought to the interviews by the women and myself. Chapter 3, "The Process of Becoming a Mother," presents the women's talk that relates to becoming a mother, including infertility treatments and interactions with birth mothers. The women's characterizations of these and related matters are juxtaposed with selected feminist analyses of birth mothers and fitness standards. Chapter 4, "On Being a Mother," continues the procedure of Chapter 3 in presenting the women's words that bear upon their experiences as mothers. The women reflect on their own mothering capabilities and inadequacies in dealing with situations that their children present. In light of their narrations, feminist characterizations of fit mothers are applied to the women themselves. Chapter 5, "Location, Resistance, and Potentials" then assesses whether or not transracial and/or transnational adoption can be a site of resistance. As I detail there, the women with Black and Biracial children faced the most challenges, and some of these women translated the challenges faced into resistance. To understand this phenomenon, however, the "social" nature of this project must first be recognized and explicated.

NOTES

1. All racial labels are capitalized, i.e., "White," "Asian," "Black," and "Biracial." I do this because, like Lythcott-Haims, "I regard racial classifications as proper nouns in contemporary usage" (1994: 531). In doing this, I also intentionally accentuate the importance of race. With a similar intent, I use the term "transnational adoption" instead of the more commonly used phrase "intercountry adoption." This way, both terms, transracial and transnational, accentuate movement of children from one community to another.

2. It is often argued that informal adoptions performed in the Black community were always open and did not require laws or codification (Patton 2000; Solinger 2001). In the Black community, children were transferred into a continuum of care that did not negate the birth mother, but instead accentuated a community of care providers who may or may not be connected biologically. Codification of adoption might, therefore, reflect our cultural uneasiness with nonbiological families (Patton 2000).

3. Merry Bloch Jones, in *Birthmothers*, refers to the adoption triangle which includes the adopted child, the relinquishing mother, and the adoptive parents.

4. Merry Bloch Jones regards adoption as an ongoing living process. Adoption, in her perspective, does not begin or end at the point when the birth mother relinquishes or the adoptive family gains custody. Rather, adoption is an ongoing process. Indeed, Jones claims that 60 percent of the women who relinquish babies in the United States at some point search for their children (Jones 1993: 197).

5. Janice Raymond, *Women as Wombs*, discusses baby thefts as occurring specifically in Guatemala.

6. A question that arises from Twine's (1999) discussion of women who are the birth mothers of Biracial children is whether women who have been with a man of color, and are the birth mother to their children, are more attentive to race than adoptive mothers. One would suspect that they would receive more disparaging comments than adoptive mothers because they (the birth mothers) broke sexual taboos.

7. Of course, it might be easier to tie poor women than middle-class women to maternal activism and resistance. According to Naples (1998b: 23), "through the lens of maternalist politics, the specificity of low-income, working class, and non-white women's activism is rendered invisible." I ask, Do these adoptive moth-

ers, through their conscious motherhood, link themselves to other women and thereby challenge maternalist politics that have made poor women invisible? Effort is also made to recognize the unique, albeit often privileged position of adoptive mothers, and to examine how from this position, in their own characterization, they challenge.

8. Much discussion has transpired about whether women mother naturally. Are women natural-born mothers? The difficult dance that must be negotiated in this work is to avoid essentializing women as natural-born mothers while, at the same time, recognizing the power that women hold as mothers. Ruddick is often criticized for essentializing women as mothers and for not challenging gender hierarchies (e.g., Lovibond 1994). My work, unfortunately, may well contribute to the belief that women mother naturally, especially considering that most of the women constructed themselves in such a manner. Perhaps, if I were really to nonessentialize women, I would not dedicate this work to women who have exerted tremendous effort to become mothers. Through their insights, however, greater understanding emerges, and can be contrasted with women who, for example, have gone out of their way not to mother.

CHAPTER 2

Social Constructionism: Contextualizing the Context

In the previous chapter, the focus of this work, maternal narratives and their relation to identity, resistance, and feminist discourse, was introduced. In the present chapter, the contexts in which this project was pursued are examined and woven into the patchwork of the text to reveal that understandings of race, class, and gender, and the research enterprise itself, transpire in malleable social settings. The practice of attending to the dynamic and social quality of the research stems from a social constructionist perspective that alerts one to changing cultural definitions of race, class, and gender in society at large, within adoption discourse, and in the very local setting of the conversations between adoptive mothers and researcher. A "social constructionist" perspective recognizes, for instance, that our understandings of race emerge out of particular historical moments and amid unique configurations of social relations. Social constructionism, along with feminist research methods, also informs the research design employed in this study, one that relies on narratives, or women constructing their own lives, and asks how narratives mesh with notions of science and scientific practices that historically have not taken an interest in women. Indeed, my motivation for magnifying women's words comes from reflexive feminist research practices that, in this case, are contemplative about the women's words, the feminist renditions thereof, and the resolution of the two (Naples 1996; Naples and Sachs 2000; Reinharz 1992; Wasserfall 1993). A reflexive approach is "sensitive to issues of power and control in the research process," and in being such it discloses the context in which the words were gathered, analyzed, and relayed (Naples 1996: 3). Starting our reflexive walk through the women's words requires first defining social constructionism generally and then using a constructionist stance to define race, class, and gender. After this has been done, social constructionism is further used to detail the research context and expose contradictions between my understandings of science and the women's, as well as to question certain feminist research practices.

DEFINING SOCIAL CONSTRUCTIONISM

"Social constructionism" is a widely used, but ill-defined term. Indeed, social constructionism, by its very nature, is a particularly illusive concept because it can at once refer to both objects and ideas. Perhaps, a useful way to manage this difficult concept is to ask, Social constructionism is the appropriate framework to apply as opposed to what?

In this book, "social constructionism" concerns the ideas and practices associated with "race," "class," and "gender." Traditionally, "social" understandings of these concepts stood in contrast to either purely biological and genetic understandings of them or the belief that "the social order is merely an accommodation to the natural order" (West and Fenstermaker 1995: 30). According to a constructionist vantage point, "essential" qualities associated with races, classes, and genders do not originate from the "natural" or biological order of things, but emerge from the social realm. In their daily lives and interactions people create, recreate, and legitimate the conceptions of race, class, and gender that associate particular features with them. I stress, however, that this book, in using a constructionist framework does not seek to deny the significance of biology, but instead to attend to the social.[1]

From a socially sensitive perspective, then, we notice that the notion of race is an ideology and that its use is situated in particular historical and political moments, as well as acted out and created in local contexts. In the case of race, this is evidenced by the constant and ongoing process of racial (re)self-categorizing both in the wider society and in the transracial and transnational adoption context. A constructionist lens also reveals the ideological fervor driving class relations that perpetuates the belief that material well-being reflects a person's inner character (Roseheil and Mann 1996; Solinger 2001; West and Fenstermaker 1995). This is important because how the adoptive mothers socially construct the birth mother's class may reflect that, typically and historically, adoption involves the transfer of children from less to more fortunate economic circumstances. Do the adoptive mothers attribute the birth mother's willingness to relinquish her child to her lack of material resources? Do perceptions of the birth mother's class vary by race? Correspondingly, are character evaluations that are made of the birth mothers class-sensitive? As I detail in the following chapter, these mothers often spoke of "good" birth mothers who unselfishly relinquished their children. The language of unselfishness, however, was mostly applied to White birth mothers who relinquished White children—not to the Black birth mother nor to the White birth mother who relinquished a Biracial child.

With the above in mind, this work juggles the complexities of a constructionist perspective on two levels. The work recognizes that gender "is a routine accomplishment based in social and everyday interaction" (West and Zimmerman 1987: 125). But, more precisely, this study examines how the intersection of race, class, and gender as routine accomplishments surface in the adoptive mothers' narration of their lives—as well as, whether, and if so how, the ideologies of race, class, and gender surface there. Thus, I strive to show the relevance of race, class, and gender separately, but more fully how these "omnirelevant features" collaboratively and interconnectedly emerge both in the women's words and in their adoption contexts (West and Fenstermaker 1995; West and Zimmerman 1987). Lastly, it must also be acknowledged that the women's narratives are their "constructions" of their own lives. They consciously or unconsciously decided how they would portray themselves to a stranger tape recording their words. It is essential to keep this in mind because, to a certain extent, the women managed how they wanted to appear to me. The data gathered, thereby, reflects that I hold a relatively distant relationship with the women.

As mentioned previously, the following sections of this chapter use a social constructionist understanding to define the concepts of race, ethnicity, class, and gender in individual, as they relate to transracial and transnational adoption, and in relation to "social" interpretations of research.

DEFINING RACE, ETHNICITY, GENDER, AND CLASS

Race and Ethnicity

Most often, race is defined as a genetically ordained property. Traditionally, genetic traits have been aligned and associated with distinct races and peoples without recognizing the "variability" and "diversity" within the "races." According to Boyce Rensberger in his article, "Racial Odyssey," "the overwhelming evolutionary success of the human species is largely due to its great genetic variability." He continues, "the very notion of a pure race, then, makes no sense. But as evolutionists know full well, a rich genetic diversity within the human species most assuredly does" (Rensberger 1994: 40). Controversy surrounding the national census, for instance, reflects the "rich genetic diversity" among us and the lack of any "pure race." Of particular significance here, however, is the historical need to cleanly define the races and, correspondingly, the inherent values that surround racial definitions and categorizations.

Mary Maynard, in her article, "Race, Gender, and the Concept of Difference in Feminist Thought," observes that "common-sense understandings of 'race' have concentrated on such variables as skin colour, country of origin, religion, nationality, and language" (Maynard 1994: 10). Ethnicity, meanwhile, commonly signifies a group's way of life (Maynard 1994: 11). Certain researchers, including Maynard, do not passively accept such definitions of race and ethnicity.

According to Michael Omi and Howard Winant, in their book, *Racial Formation in the United States*, race is "an unstable and 'decentered' complex of social meanings constantly being transformed by political struggle" (Omi and Winant 1986: 68). Rather than being a genetically determined property, race is a social construct. Shelia Allen, in her work, "Race, Ethnicity, and Nationality: Some Questions of Identity," expresses well this thought. "Race and ethnicity are used as social constructs embedded in social relations, not unchanging characteristics involuntarily chosen" (Allen 1994: 101). Social constructs, thereby, are ideologies that develop from and are transformed in the social realm. Racial constructs, in particular, prove problematic for the values they express. Indeed, it has been argued that our racial system regards Whiteness as the norm, thus, ignoring White (skin color) as a racial category itself (Afshar and Maynard 1994; Reddy 1994). Along these lines, racial categories can be construed as arbitrary constructions that promote Whiteness at the expense of non-whites (Afshar and Maynard 1994; Reddy 1994). Omi and Winant (1994) argue further that focusing on race, in any context, promotes a racist sentiment because "race" accentuates presumed genetic absolutes and thereby denigrates cultural differences. In contrast, attention to ethnicity, although also a construct according to Allen, heightens awareness of cultural distinctions between people instead of highlighting genetic traits that assert dichotomous notions of Black and White.

The current work's conception of race and ethnicity is as follows. Race signifies a diversity of genetic traits (Rensberger 1994). This work concentrates on the social processes that create and project meanings onto genetic features. Genetically based features of our physical self are significant, but the meanings read into these traits are based in ever-changing and evolving social relations. The very concept "race" thus emerges as a creation of particular nexuses and relations of power. Likewise understandings and interpretations of ethnicity are created as well as altered in the social realm. From a social perspective it is possible to chronicle the historical evolution of an ethnic group in this country.

As noted, this work attends to the social and evolving meanings associated with being White, Black, or Asian and to the social import of the concepts of race and ethnicity. Specifically, the social relations behind the interpretation of racial categories enacted or lived by the women interviewed. I consider the social relations in which the women came to define race and ethnicity, if they do at all. Prominent among this is that the women enjoy the advantages of being White, but with adoption their privileged racial location may have slipped.

Adoption Literature and Race and Ethnicity

The women's understandings of race and ethnicity emerge then, in part, from their experiences with adoption. The discourses surrounding transnational and transracial adoptions disclose, to some extent, how race and ethnicity are defined within the context of adoption. The distinction between the two is usually confused. The very language used to describe these adoptions would lead one to believe that transracial adoptions involve race whereas the transference of "foreign" children to the West entails a cultural, i.e., ethnic adjustment. Specifically, domestic adoption of Black children by White families is characterized by its racial quality: "transracial" adoptions (Abdullah 1996; Bartholet 1991; Bayerl 1977; Curtis 1996; Davis 1992; Forde-Mazrui 1994). By contrast, the transference of nonwestern children from their country of origin to a family in the West is most often called transnational and/or intercountry adoption, regardless of the race of the children (Altstein 1993; Altstein and Simon 1991; Bartholet 1995; Gilman 1987; Herrmann and Kasper 1993; Simon and Altstein 2000). These labels create the image that transracial adoption predominantly involves children of races different from the parents whereas transnational adoptions involve cultural differences.

Given the above identifying markers, one would assume race and ethnicity are clearly separated in adoption discourse. Stark distinctions, however, between race and ethnicity are largely absent. Notions of race and ethnicity often emerge out of discussions about racism. As I mentioned in the previous chapter, the National Association of Black Social Workers (NABSW) long considered White transracial adoption practices as another instance of racism. In particular, the group asserted that many features of a Black racial and ethnic identity arise out of a history of racism, and with this being the case only Black parents are equipped to raise children of color (Harneck 1995).[2]

In light of past assertions made by the NABSW and others' interpretations thereof, heated discussions have transpired in both popular media and academic circles about whether or not such adoptions are acts of racism (see Abdullah 1996; Bartholet 1991; Hayes 1993; Lovett-Tisdale and Purnell 1996; Raymond 1993; Taylor and Thorton 1996). Opponents of transracial adoptions, in particular, most often use race, ethnicity, and racism interchangeably (Abdullah 1996; Herrmann 1993). They focus the debate on how racism affects the child's welfare (Herrmann 1993; Kallgren and Caudell 1993; Tisdale 1991).

White parents, however, counter that racial distinctions are more than anything else cultural interpretations that have historically ignored gradations of color (Lythcott-Haims 1994). Supporters of transracial adoption such as Forde-Mazrui (1994) even maintain that members of the NABSW are overly committed to racial dichotomies. Such supporters also point to longitudinal studies that prove Black children fare well in White homes. According to these studies, adoptive children develop sound racial and ethnic identities (McRoy and Grape 1999; Simon, Simon and Altstein 2000; Altstein and Melli 1995). While these proponents call for breaking down racial categories, they also are attentive to cultural differences. Forde-Mazrui, for example, maintains that a White family can raise a Black child to feel good about being Black without the child identifying with Black culture.[3] Bold claims are even made that Black children might overall be better off in White homes where they will be instilled with a White achievement ethos (Forde-Mazrui 1994).

This heated debate, with varied emphases on race, ethnicity, and racism, continues today given that 38 percent of all children in the United States without a permanent home are Black (Curtis 1996). Former President Clinton added fuel to the debate with his approval of the Multiethnic Placement Act of 1994 (implemented in 1996). This act removed "race," defined as skin color, from sole consideration in placing children for adoption. Some adoption social workers interpret this act as both an implicit and explicit attempt to privilege White families over Black ones as "fit" parents (Abdullah 1996; Goddard 1996).

Sandra Patton does not explicitly ask whether transracial adoptions are "good" for the adoptees in particular, but instead calls attention to public policies that bring transracial adoptees' racial identities into being (Patton 2000: 96). Through adoption policies we can see that the "changing understanding of adoption . . . coincides . . . with changing notions of race . . . class, and gender" (Patton 2000: 31). Adoption policies are not neutral, then, but implicitly and explicitly associate Whiteness with legitimacy. If adoption and adoption policies are taken to be sites of struggle, writes Patton, transracial adoptees must sort out their racial identities, and so their biographies are artifacts of this struggle.

Among other factors, many White families seeking to adopt turn to foreign opportunities in the hopes of avoiding such tense confrontations with race and ethnicity (Modell 1994; Shapiro, Shapiro, and Paret 2000). Unfortunately, White adoptive parents who shift to overseas opportunities avenues do not escape controversy stemming from race and ethnicity (see Trolley, Wallin, and Hansen 1995).

Critics of transnational adoptions are often more attentive to race than are its supporters. For instance, Valerie Herrmann and Barbara Kasper, in their work, *International Adoption: The Exploitation of Women and Children*, assert that adoptive families participate in and perpetuate the "trafficking" in darker skinned babies (Herrmann and Kasper 1992; Raymond 1993). More generous characterizations regard Western adoptive parents as simply disregarding the political and economic context within which they adopt (Raymond 1993). In either case, it is argued that these families ignore power differentials that privilege White and Western families over their poor, darker Third World counterparts (Herrmann and Kasper 1992). Not only do adoptive families participate in and promote racially based power disparities, but they disrupt communities that mark and delineate "a living line of culture" (Farrell Smith 1996: 17). The mass media have helped shape the public's understanding of international adoptions. Often in support of such adoptions, the media blur race and ethnicity into one configuration. The images that the media propagate, for example, characterizations both of the relinquishing and adoptive mothers that reek of ethnic and racial biases, have inadvertently and blatantly surfaced. The Third World woman's cultural practices are backward, according to this imagery. Her poor education keeps her from embracing modern birth control practices or from reproducing within her financial means (Chowdry 1995; Escobar 1995; Marchand and Parpart 1995). In contrast stands the White adoptive mother, who rescues children as she chases down babies in hostile environments in service to the child's interests as well as her own maternal instincts (Raymond 1993).

Supporters of transnational adoption, in most cases mothers, who have more intimate knowledge of adoptions than does the mass media, do not ignore racial and ethnic differences. Cheri Register, in *Are Those Your Kids?*, goes to great lengths to highlight the racial distinctions between herself and her Asian children. Several of the mothers I interviewed shared with me occasions when their children were coined "Chinks" by both children and adults in their communities. At the same time these mothers, unlike Register and similar to the proponents of transracial adoptions, denigrated the significance of race. They maintained that their children adjust well. Cultural camps teach Korean adoptees about their cultural heritage and background, for instance. These parents also claimed that longitudinal data reveal that adoptees benefit from the parents' conscientious parenting efforts. Studies show that international adoptees acclimate well relative to their nonadopted peers in their new countries (see Altstein 1993; Simon and Altstein 2000; Versluis-den Bieman and Verhulst 1995). Bunjes (1991) even found Korean adoptees to be more intellectually capable than their native Dutch classmates. It is often in discussions about intellectual capability that race and ethnicity collide. One mother of a Chinese girl explained to me that a friend assumed that "You are going to have a smart child." The mother's response went something to the effect, "She's being raised American, there is no guarantee she will be smart." These interlocutors worked from different points of references.

Whereas the mother believed that intellectual ability follows cultural standards, her friend assumed that race dictates intelligence.

As the above example demonstrates, ideas surrounding race and ethnicity depend upon the position and paradigm one supports. Of great import are the values expressed in these paradigms. As Patricia Hill Collins (1994) recognizes, the racial ethnic features of Asians are most often construed as ideal. Indeed, Collins contends Asians are upheld as the "model minorities." It may not be surprising that the racial quality of being "Asian" is often less pronounced than is the case for Blacks (Reddy 1994). Maureen Reddy, in *Crossing the Color Line,* argues that Biracial children are usually considered Black irrespective of their one White parent. In contrast, Asian children of mixed descent can discard their "Asianness" to claim the privileges of White identity.

Flexible Definitions: The Women Define Race

The dynamic quality of race entered the interviews. All the women interviewed were White. It was the race of the children that differed. According to the research design, the children were either White, Asian, Black, or Biracial. The White children were domestically born. The Asian children originated from Korea, except for one who was Chinese-born. Five mothers had adopted Biracial children, and four had Black children. The above categorization is no doubt accurate, but it ignores gradations of color that existed in the families.

Some mothers resided in multiracial families marked by White parents raising children of two different races. The research design did not include mothers with Latin and Indian, as well as Asian and Black children. The mothers with Black and Biracial children, in particular, defied clean racial categorization. Some of these families included two Biracial children, while others had one Black and one Biracial child. Complicating matters was that the mothers chose a variety of ways to categorize their children racially. Some mothers accentuated the Biracial quality of their children, as was true for Phyllis:[4]

I want him to understand that he's not just Black . . . not that I don't value, if he was just Black, but he's got more than just Black heritage in him. That's what the social worker said, "you have to raise them as Black." It's like why do you raise Biracial kids as Black? That doesn't make any sense to me at all. That's like reinforcing what White culture does to Biracial kids.

In contrast, Karen quibbled with the birth mother's claim that the child was Biracial in favor of her own assessment. "Now I don't know anything about her birth mother except that she was Black. She said Jessica was Biracial. Well, I see no White features in Jessica at all and if you get a

chance to see her, you probably won't see any either." Other women simply did not question their child's race. Rather, they assumed Blackness
either because the child's birth parents were both Black, in cases of a
Biracial child because they considered their child's Biracialness as irrele-
vant in a society that would define them as Black, regardless.

Variation also existed in whether the women considered themselves and
their families to be minorities. The numerical rarity of rainbow families,
one mother intimated, makes her family a minority. "I mean, we're kind
of an odd couple, anyway, a White couple with a Black child, you know.
It's a minority." A mother with Korean children described her family as
"different," asserting that her family resides in some gray area not associated with minorities: "Yeah, I'm not the minority, I'm the unusual. You're
not really a minority status, you're just really different, the purple family."
Deborah, like other women with Asian children, did not distinguish herself and her status as minority or not minority from her Asian sons and
their statuses. Only mothers with Black and Biracial children, and not even
all of these mothers, did distinguish themselves from their minority children. "Not being Black I feel like we can't do as much as we should,"
lamented one mother as she assessed strategies for "educating" her Biracial children. As evidenced by the women's very own constructions, the
suitability of placing these White mothers within discrete racial categories
is unclear.

Yet, while variability existed in how the mothers viewed their own racial position in light of their children, distinct patterns in their narratives
emerged based on the child's race. As I elaborate in the following chapters,
by and large the mothers downplayed the significance of race. Race was
silent in the narratives of women with White children. By contrast, mothers with Black and Biracial children spoke of the racial concerns which
enter their home and family life, whereas women with Asian children
highlighted cultural concerns—not race—within and outside of the home.

Class

The fact that the women chose not to separate themselves racially from
their Asian children stems in part from their interpretations of class. The
privileges of White identity have translated historically into economic
prosperity (Omi and Winant 1993). Middle- and upper-class status is often
equated with Whiteness (Abramovitz 2000; Polakow 1993). Asians can
claim White privilege, in part, because it is assumed they are "smart"
enough and work hard enough to achieve middle-class status (Collins
1994). In contrast, Black skin, as can be gathered from welfare reform
discussions, signifies poverty (Abramovitz 2000; Gans 1995; Rank 1994).
Class, incidentally, includes not only access to and control over economic
resources, but also cultural and lifestyle practices that either promote or

discourage class mobility (Lewis 1968). Sharp criticism has been launched at cultural analyses of class mobility by those who argue that darker skinned people are denied economic opportunities, and are not marred by character flaws that keep them from achieving economic prosperity (Abramovitz 1994, 2000; Gans 1995; Omi and Winant 1994; Phoenix 1996; Rank 1994; Solinger 2001).[5]

By and large, however, few critical discussions exist of adoption and class (Solinger 2001). Those that do exist analyze whether adoption practices promote a culture of poverty mentality that assumes the relinquishing family is financially and, hence, generally unsound (Raymond 1993; Solinger 2001). Of course, adoption usually involves the transference of children from poorer to wealthier homes (Altstein and Simon 1991). This practice is bothersome to Herrmann and Kasper (1992) for a number of reasons including the fact that it reproduces the implicit and explicit beliefs that the poor are not capable care providers (Polakow 1993; Solinger 2001). Solinger chronicles how reproductive choice language has transformed women's rights into consumer choices and, in the process, has disparaged poor women by characterizing them as bad choice makers who, according to the discourse, are responsible for their poverty—as opposed to public policies that have made it harder for poor, single mothers to make a living wage (Solinger 2001: 7).

With Solinger's argument in mind, I attend to how the mothers themselves configured class, observing, in particular, whether these women draw universal connections with other women based on their shared work as mothers irrespective of class differences. Such an interpretation comes out of Chandra Mohanty's work, *Women Workers and Capitalist Scripts*, which unravels the ideological frameworks that place women in comparable work globally. Mohanty focuses on "the ideological construction of jobs and tasks in terms of notions of appropriate femininity, domesticity, (hetero)sexuality, and racial and cultural stereotypes" (Mohanty 1997: 6). Here, I examine the ideological constructions the mothers use to explain motherhood generally and how conceptions of motherhood vary depending on such factors as class, race, and culture.

The Women Define Class

The understanding of class used in this work reflects the above discussions and the interviews. Education, occupation, place of residence, and recreational activities serve as criteria for analyzing the adoptive families' class. The relative class uniformity of the adoptive families stood out. All women were solidly middle class as marked by their educational achievement, with only one mother failing to hold a college degree and with at least 10 possessing post-baccalaureate degrees of some sort. They were housewives, professors, ministers, social workers, physical therapists, speech therapists, attorneys, computer analysts, nurses, medical technicians, and secretaries. Approximately 11 women worked full-time, eight worked part-time, and 3 were stay-at-home mothers.

Coupled with the mothers' education and work, I also used place of residence to measure class status. Seventeen of the 22 women were interviewed in their homes. All 17 lived in decidedly middle-class ones and some in upper-middle class ones. One would expect the group who adopted internationally to be a relatively affluent group, given the higher cost of such adoptions in comparison to domestic ones. I cannot completely ascertain relative affluence among the women as I did not ask for incomes or property valuations. The international adopters, however, more so than the others, lived in upper- middle-class areas. Some women with domestic adoptions also lived in similar neighborhoods, but this group was not as consistent. Only one woman mentioned financial difficulties as a problem for her family. Many mentioned costs as a limiting factor or, more accurately, as a consideration in adoption decisions.

Although the class similarities and differences among the adoptive mothers are significant, perhaps of equal, if not greater import are the class distinctions between the adoptive and relinquishing mothers. Solinger (2001) insists that poor mothers are disparaged because they themselves are not good consumers and cannot produce good consumers. Hence, poor mothers are marked as bad choice makers and ill-equipped to mother. In contrast, adoptive mothers, with buying power, are considered ideal to parent. Many of the adoptive mothers interviewed characterized the relinquishing women as members of classes lower than their own. Only one of the mothers, however, described the relinquishing mother as a "welfare recipient." This mother articulated the fear that her daughter might carry guilt given that she enjoys advantages unavailable to her biological mother and siblings. Much to my surprise, however, several of the mothers said that the biological family was middle class and held middle-class values. One mother even claimed that the birth mother was more affluent than herself.

Although I present the women's class and their description of the birth mother's class as definite, in actuality it was difficult to identify assertions of class free of race and gender considerations.

Class most often was mentioned in the conversations with mothers of Biracial children. The women voiced concern that their Black and Biracial children, by virtue of their race, might be associated with and/or choose to associate with children in lower classes. This took an odd twist when some of the women mentioned that their Biracial children could be mistaken for Mexican or Hispanic. Tera noticed, for example, that her daughter looked like she belonged to her Mexican friend's family:

It's funny. I've got a friend who's Mexican and she's got a four-year-old daughter, and we were out the other day with her. My daughter looked like she should have been her daughter. She's got the loose curls. She doesn't have the real tight curls, and they just all happen to be wearing the same color. It was really funny. My friend had on a purple blouse and her daughter had on a purple sweat suit, and then my daughter had on a purple outfit and it looked like she should have been right over there. So I wonder, with the growing Mexican and Central American population would people start seeing her, wondering if she's Mexican.

A question that surfaced for Tera and other women is, Is it to their children's advantage to be constructed as Latino? Their assessments seemed to be mixed and, what's more, to be based in class. Karen's narrative accentuated the issue. Karen felt that her Biracial son could "pass" as virtually any race even though the White birth mother had told them that the birth father was one of four Black men. Karen and her husband, however, not seeing any Black features in their son, conjectured that the birth mother had been with a Mexican migrant worker and chose not to volunteer this information as it might be to the chagrin of the birth mother's family. "I don't know, my husband has said to me that he thinks because of the area that there's a lot of migrant workers. He said that maybe she was with somebody and didn't want her parents to know. Maybe she just said that the father was one of four Black males. I don't know. I can only believe what she said." This complicated situation shows several things. Throughout the conversation, Karen was proud of her child's "Brazilian" good looks. Yet, she and her husband understood that it might be worse for the White birth mother to admit being with a Mexican migrant worker than to indicate that the birth father was Black. For the other mothers, the scenarios were not so complicated as they did not question the racial makeup of their child. They did, however, consider their child in relation to Latinos, with the assessment that Latinos may be positioned lower down the racial hierarchy than Blacks because of their association with poverty.

Gender

In this work, I listen to the evaluations and judgments the women associated with class, race, and ethnic identities. Of greatest relevance to this project is the confluence of race, ethnicity, class, and gender. "Race and gender, however, do not intermesh in some readily comprehensible or simple way," but instead "interrelate in highly complex and contradictory ways" (Afshar and Maynard 1994: 6). The intersections of race, ethnicity, class, and gender are often lived and experientially understood through mothering.

As with race, ethnicity, and class, gender is often given a simplistic definition as the cultural traits and practices associated with the biological sexes of male and female (Allen 1994; Reddy 1994). Critical assessment of this definition is necessary. According to Allen (1994), for example, "gender" as a concept only came into existence to include women. Men are considered nongendered entities to which women are contrasted. Gender, like race and ethnicity, can be interpreted as a pejorative social construct.

Of course, many feminist writers have brought attention to the power embedded in distinguishing female from male (Fausto-Sterling 1987; Fox Keller 1987; Martin 1987). Emily Martin, in *The Woman in the Body*, argues that medical science constructs the male as the representative of normality and reason, and whatever is not male is abnormal. Rich (1976) even boldly asserts that "the woman's body is the terrain on which patriarchy is erected" (Rich 1976: 38). Normal female bodily processes, consequently, are regarded as abnormal and unreasonable transgressions from male soundness (Ehrenreich and English 1973). This means that menstruation, pregnancy, and menopause are constructed as illnesses requiring medical attention and control.

Adoption Literature (Dis)Regards Gender

Unfortunately, the adoption literature infrequently critically analyzes "gender," even though, for example, cultural expectations for women to mother constantly surface in adoption dramas (Raymond 1993; Yngvesson 1997).[6] With this in mind, gender focuses on the gendered cultural values associated with mothering and mothering well. This means discovering how adoptive mothers interpret standards that assume women mother biological children, and do not cross racial boundaries to mother.

As might be expected, given the literature's relative inattention to gender, the intersection among gender, race, ethnicity, and class is equally bypassed. This is true despite the fact that, as Reddy alerts us, gender, race, ethnicity, and class are not experienced as additive features of a person's life. Rather, they are social conditions within which one lives. Most often feminist analyses that consider the intersection of race, ethnicity, and gender seek to include women darker and poorer than the standard middle-class woman (Collins 1991, 1994; Hammonds 1997). Collins, for instance, argues that private-versus-public distinction disregards the fact that Black mothers have always worked outside of the home. While wider feminist literature may be attentive to the intersection of race, ethnicity, class, and gender, as I said, the adoption literature, on the whole, is not (see Raymond 1993). Most often, race holds exclusive pertinence to the adopted child's development of an healthy identity, and if gender is considered at all, it is not simultaneously understood in relation to race, ethnicity, and class.

The Women Define Gender

Gender infiltrates every feature of this work since the research focus is mothers. The data gathered are essentially "gendered." Attending to maternity, as well as race and class, was predominantly my emphasis. I, for instance, introduced the term "mothering," while most often the women preferred to use the word "parenting." In the following interview excerpt, I asked a mother with Asian children to discuss times she felt adequate or inadequate as a mother:

Oh, I think every *parent* feels that, sure. Some days are easier than others just depending on what's going on in the family. I think that's the same. I don't think that the kids being adopted has [have] anything to do with that. Some days are just stressful, if people don't want to get up and you are like, "Hurry, hurry, hurry, we are going to be late for school." And afternoons are very hectic when all get home from school. They all want to tell about their day and they all have homework, you're trying to get dinner ready, especially if you have some place to be that night, so those times are pretty . . . but I think that's for everyone. There are differences in *parenting* a child of a different race, but they're manageable. It's just an extra step that you have to work through. And it's the same with adoption. You have adoption issues, and if you chose to adopt transracially then you have those issues on top of your normal *parenting* issues. It is hard. It is more of a challenge, but I think that it is all manageable and I wouldn't trade it for anything [my emphasis].

As can be gathered from the above example, I cannot even be sure that many of the women would consider their lives "unconventional," as I branded them. Many of the women, abstracted the political out of their family lives and normalized their mothering experiences as something not distinctly tied to their gender. Of interest to me, is whether thinking themselves as *parenting* further silences maternal, as opposed to paternal, experiences. For example, "parenting" language hides the fact that the mother may feel such ultimate responsibility for the child that she does not leave the house alone to run errands (Hays 1996). Instead, she makes arrangements for the children to leave. The father, in contrast, may withdraw not thinking about who will tend to the children while he is gone (Hays 1996).

Sharon Hays, in her book *The Cultural Contradictions of Motherhood*, speaks indirectly to "parenting" per se as it relates to women. She offers statistical support for the widely held supposition that women spend more time with children than men. In her own interview work, she found that although women expressed dissatisfaction and even resentment for bearing the brunt of child care, they were grateful for the attention their husbands did grant their children. Hays articulates several reasons why the women she interviewed chose to occlude their resentment through gratefulness:

First, many mothers love their male partners and therefore do not want to paint them in a negative way. Second, since women generally have the sense that most husbands do not help out in child rearing, they are genuinely grateful when their own mates help out in some way. Further, in the context of a society that has limited women's access to prestige, mother's special competence in raising kids provides them with a position of honor within the household. Finally, one needs to recognize that some of these women may fear their marriages will be threatened if they refuse to do the larger share of domestic chores. (Hays 1996: 107)

In many respects, the women in this work resembled the ones Hays interviewed, even though relatively few of these women voiced resentment toward their husbands. Some of the women intimated that men simply do not engage in all of the tasks of child care and were grateful that their husbands played with the children. It was also clear that these women, as a result, relished the prestige associated with their mothering capabilities, as evinced by their happily sharing that they felt good about themselves as mothers. Yet, this prestige and gratification did not come without its costs.

Most often, the women spoke of themselves as "she who shoulders the burden of care" (Bassin et al. 1994). Many of the women said they shouldered the care without looking at their position as distinct from their husband's; nor did they examine how they were positioned, by and in the larger social and political context. Kathy spoke for many of the women when she explained what it means to be a mother, "Oh, it's being responsible for someone else 24 hours a day, whether you feel like it or not, sometimes it's harder than others. When everybody feels good, it's fine." Kathy and many of the other women, while acknowledging the demands of being on 24-hour-a-day call, also said it was to their liking. Carol, for example, said about motherhood that "it is being totally responsible for another person, which is really cool and scary." It remains unanswered whether their husbands would characterize themselves as equally responsible.

While tempering the rigors and joys of motherhood, some of the mothers talked about their own need to be nurtured (Katz Rothman 1994). Sammie, for instance, asked, "Who nurtures me?" There were those women who also intimated or even said straightforwardly that they needed to be nurtured, but dismissed its significance by saying that the lack of it was not bothersome. Kathy dragged the kids to the doctor's office, even though she was sick herself: "I didn't have time to take me to the doctor because I had to take them [her children] to the doctor and it was sort of funny because the nurse said, "you look and sound worse than they do."

Mary, meanwhile, recognized that her identity changed with motherhood as she reviewed her day after returning home from "work":

Let me think what I have done for myself since I went home at three o'clock. I sat there and I thought about it. Well, I watched one minute of the basketball game that was all I had done for me. One of them [her sons] had an appointment. I had to take him to that and then help him with his homework. Just every since I've been home, it's just one thing after another. Fix dinner. Wash the dishes. My other son had a basketball game. Went to the basketball game. Then he had to have his uniform the next day, 'cause they were getting their pictures taken and I had to wash his uniform, dry his uniform, and hang up his uniform. Then had to get them upstairs and get their showers and get ready for bed and get them in bed, and that was it. From three o'clock that was all I did except walk in, stand there, look at the game and say, "Ooh, this is boring." And walk back out again, that was the only thing I had done for me. I hadn't read the newspaper. I hadn't done any of my paperwork. I hadn't looked at a book. I hadn't done a darn thing for me that whole time, so yes, my identity has changed.

Mary agreed that her husband could be characterized as a "parenting aide," but ended the above description of her day by asserting that it was not bothersome to her.

A good number of the women, like Mary, portrayed themselves as holding responsibility for the children, and for some of the women the demands of such responsibility necessitated that they themselves be nurtured. Parenting language hides this situation. This work does not do justice to those few women who were not in traditional relationships. These women worked more hours outside of the home and made more money than their husbands. A few of the women, moreover, were single mothers. Can use of the expression "parenting," then, signify progress? It is true that many of the fathers were portrayed as active participants, and also characterized as the children's playmates. Through parenting language, the women gave their husbands credit for their child-rearing work, even if it was not as extensive as their own such work. Perhaps these women, more so than myself, recognized men's position as fathers and their narrations might assist in making men more understood as fathers rather than solely as workers outside of the home. The use of parenting, then, might signify a movement toward the erasure of gendered expectations and toward a world in which men and women take equal responsibility for the children.

There are, however, contradictions and ambiguities surrounding parenting language. While use of parenting language might suggest that men and women increasingly are sharing child-care responsibilities, as evidenced by the interviews, ultimate responsibility for the children remains with the woman (Hays 1996). An emphasis on parenting language hides this feature of mothering. Parenting language may also have the added ill effect of concealing the power women gather from mothering work. Through their use of parenting language, these women, alluded to the cultural recognition and respect granted "parents" at the expense of

"mothers." The single woman raising children on her own is not characterized as a "single parent," but rather a "single mother." Popular notions
of the "single mother" in many respects valorize her as poor and unable
to control her children (Abramovitz 2000; Gordon 1990; Silva 1996).
Should she be described as a "single parent," in contrast, she may well be
constructed as the professional raising her children alone by choice or by
abandonment due to a husband's untimely death. "Parenting" garners
respect because those involved with parenting are doing a professional
job (Cassidy 1998). In this context, parenting language veils the work
women do and, in addition, disparages those not raising their children
by-the-book. Yet, at the same time, parenting language signifies the possibility of both men and women sharing "mothering work."

I have discussed parenting language to illustrate the social context in
which the narratives were pursued, gathered, and analyzed. By and large,
the women did not associate their maternity with larger gender concerns
as I do and, hence, their inclination to use parenting language. Yet, many
of the women were acutely aware that they maintained ultimate responsibility for their children.

A DYNAMIC ENTERPRISE: NARRATIVES

I chose narratives as the appropriate tool to gather adoptive women's
insights because narratives expose details and contradictions, as can be
seen in the case of parenting language. According to George Rosenwald
and Richard Ochberg (1992), narratives unravel the conflicts in a person's
life between self and others and between self and cultural conventions.
Narratives bear the mark of socialization. Of significance here was the
extent to which narratives relayed a mother's ability to contend with cultural standards of mothering that assume biological, as well as racial and
ethnic uniformity between mother and child. As Rosenwald and Ochberg
elaborate, narratives are highly effective ways for people to confront as
well as to invoke cultural norms, particularly for people who live unconventional lives. In this work, attention is placed on how mothers who
aspire to conventional standards negotiate their unconventional lives. I
had anticipated that "narratives lend themselves to analysis of the tacit
assumptions by which the narrators weave their stories" (Rosenwald and
Ochberg 1992). According to Rosenwald and Ochberg, narratives also produce "formative effects" through the very process of narration. This
means that stories direct lives. Yngvesson and Mahoney (2000) argue,
moreover, that authentic and congruent narratives or one's understanding
of oneself, provide an individual with a sense of self and wholeness. Rosenwald and Ochberg add to this thought that through the very act of
narration the narrator is offered the possibility of psychological, and in
some cases, political emancipation.

I do not aspire to emancipate. I borrowed from Rosenwald and Ochberg, however, an interpretation of narratives to conduct in-depth individual conversations and focus groups with 22 White mothers who had adopted within as well as across racial, cultural, and/or ethnic lines. My motivation for gathering the voices and experiences of White adoptive mothers stemmed in part out of my interest in challenging the knowledge industry to "start" its work in women's experiences and thereby alleviating the patriarchal stance so prevalent in the social sciences. Scientific imperatives that promote objective knowledge "mask" the gendered biases that drive the production of value-free knowledge. By reference to a Gary Fine quote, Nancy Naples articulates this thought well in her article, "A Feminist Revisiting of the Insider/Outsider Debate," "Gary Fine writes: 'Objectivity is an illusion—an illusion snuggled in the comforting blanket of positivism—that the world is ultimately knowable and secure.' Feminists take this critique further when they argue that a belief in the value neutrality of social scientific and other intellectual practices, in fact, serves to mask the relations of ruling embedded in the production of knowledge in the academy" (Naples 1996: 6).

Knowledge, Smith (1990), Collins (1991) and Harding (1991) implore, does not reside only in scientists in white coats, but also in ordinary people's lives. Feminist efforts in this regard strive to give voice to women who are often talked about but not listened to (Collins 1991; Gordon 1990, 1994; Mohanty 1988; Rich 1976). Mothers' voices, generally, have not been granted a place in public or scientific dialogue; rather, speculation and assertions about mothers have been generated without their input (Rich 1976). Even fictional works rarely use a mother as the primary narrator (Kenison and Hirsch 1996). I sought, then, to pursue Collins's (1991) humanist effort to expand knowledge to include mothers through interviews with White women who adopt transnationally or nationally.

Moreover, following Collins's challenge to conduct research with an ethos of care, I strove to provide all participants with the space to express themselves unhindered. Collins's ethic of caring "urges that research be carried out in ways that place utmost importance on allowing free and unhindered space for participants to speak, including emotions in the research enterprise and empathizing most completely with those with whom we converse" (Naples 1996: 10). I used an interview protocol (a predetermined list of questions), but the questions and the tenor of the research itself altered in accordance with the changing character of the interviews as this was instigated by the interviewees themselves (see Glaser and Strauss 1967).

Throughout the research process, new themes and concerns demanded alterations in the questions. Predetermined questions included the following: How did you choose to adopt this particular child? How do you see yourself as similar or different from other mothers, similar or different from other adoptive mothers who do not adopt transracially or transnationally? What is your impression of the birth mother? How might you be similar or different from her? Describe situations when you feel like a highly adequate mother and moments when you do not. What are some of the unique opportunities of mothering a Biracial or Asian child? If you could share any aspect of your mothering experience with other women, what would it be? If you could alter any element of your experience, what would it be? Despite the existence of a list of standard questions, the research design was flexible, allowing me not only to reflect on the information gathered, but to attend to the very nature of the research process itself (Naples and Sachs 2000; Reinharz 1992; Wasserfall 1993). I found, for instance, that many of the women expressed their devotion to God, which I had not anticipated. Thus, at the women's instigation I probed about their religious inclinations. In addition to incorporating new questions, I also reformulated old ones. I learned that many of the women could not compare and contrast themselves to the birth mother as they had virtually no information about her. When this was the case, I moved from asking, How do you think you are similar or different from her? to Are there times that you think about her?

Although I continue to remain deeply committed to the above design, difficulties accompany such a flexible model. For example, according to traditional scientific standards, it might seem troubling that the women defined the narrative space. Although I entered each interview equipped with a series of questions, the women decided the amount of time and attention they wanted to devote to each answer. This often resulted in varied emphases. Some women talked at great length about the adoption process, whereas others hardly regarded this aspect of their experience. The data, as a result, were not uniform as may be expected of survey research.

Of course, despite what might be perceived to be haphazard research, regularities emerged based in the narratives themselves. For instance, the two women who had traveled overseas to receive their children devoted more attention than the others to the adoption process and the trip abroad. In one of these women's stories I learned about "paperwork" a word noticeably absent from the other conversations.

Transforming incongruities, as in the above case, into "data" reveals the extent to which I proceeded from the data up. I let the women's words guide me. This way of going about research can be troubling not only to "scientists," but in addition to those interviewees who were accustomed to "normal science." Indeed, while I felt comfortable with this more fluid approach, some of the mothers were not. On several occasions, I was asked to provide a hypothesis and advised to narrow my research topic to assure scientific soundness. These women expressed their consternation that, for example, I had not initially formulated a definitive research question beyond the goal of comparing mothering experiences dependent on the race of the adopted child. Contrary to the scientific approach, I wanted the women's words to be the guiding force. As educated women, however, many of the interviewees were familiar with scientific standards, not my ideas, associated with survey research and the natural sciences. My inductive and qualitative approach was unfamiliar. Although I do not view these mothers' and my divergent understandings of science to be a barrier, I think it is significant to mention because my approach to narratives as a chance to confront science was just that, my focus. I was interested, among other things, in highlighting that gender and racial biases are hidden in scientific protocols. In contrast, the women generally did not question traditional notions of science and, believed in the felicity of objective results.

Steadfastness in my commitment to mothers, however, introduced a dilemma. Am I really letting the women's words speak first? Am I disregarding my own best feminist efforts to let the narratives guide me as I superimpose my own research agenda? Are the women's voices being erased? To a certain extent, this is the case. Many feminists (Gluck and Patai 1991; Mbilinyi 1989; Oakley 1981; Sacks 1989) urge researchers to attend to female interviewees through democratic practices. Scanlon (1993) and Borland (1991) describe specific ways of giving as well as taking. Lather (1986), as an emancipatory theorist, encourages the researcher to develop a partnership with female interviewees, which may entail coauthoring final documents such as this one.

While I respect the efforts listed above, I, like other researchers (Blee 1993; Reinharz 1993; Wasserfall 1993), question whether a democratic partnership between a female interviewer and female interviewee is always possible or even necessary in each research situation.

Taking instruction from this latter skepticism, I have chosen to contextualize the interviews and the accompanying data through critical reflection rather than to reformulate the research design to conform to the women's interpretation of the work in an effort to be truly democratic. By critical reflection I consider, among other matters, the power played out and negotiated in the research setting (Naples and Sachs 2000). I pursue critical reflection for two reasons. Regarding the research process produces data itself. Additionally, I am interested in contributing to the self-reflexive research effort in which so many feminists are engaged (Bowles and Duelli-Klein 1980; Collins 1991; Harding 1991; Naples 1993; Naples and Sachs 2000; Reinharz 1993; Smith 1990; Wasserfall 1993). These feminists recognize that through self reflection ethical concerns can be negotiated as well as incorporated into the written text.

To engage in reflexive research necessitates that the researcher, among other things, consider the interviewing setting as a drama that involves herself as one of the main characters. Smith (1990) and other writers (Blumer 1966) encourage the researcher to be attentive to herself as an active participant in the interviewing process. With this in mind, I am aware that my own personality, habits, race, and class influence what information is provided and the character of the stories told. My White and middle-class status made me similar to the mothers. One significant difference between us is that I was not a mother at the time. Only one woman, however, intimated this was a barrier, when she began her response to a question by saying, "See, you're not a mother." Most of the time, additionally, there were religious differences between us. I am not Christian, while the women overwhelmingly maintained strong ties to their Christian church. Other things we held in common such as an interest in becoming a mother. Several interviewees also had graduate degrees and, hence, were intimately familiar with the research process. The relative similarities between us made the possibility of becoming friends seem plausible. Oakley (1981) suggests that "good" qualitative research requires that friendships with the interviewees be forged. I do not completely concur with this sentiment.

Striking up a friendship in the research setting can prove challenging, and the attempt to do so can set unrealistic expectations (Blee 1993; Cotterill 1992; Reinharz 1993; Wasserfall 1993). Interview participants may well misinterpret a researcher's intentions as those of a friend's rather than those of a researcher's in which case it might not be until receipt of the final written document that the disparity between the researcher's and interviewee's understanding of the research setting become clear to the interviewees (see Borland 1991; Gluck and Patai 1991; Mbilinyi 1989). This is particularly the case in research where women share intimate pieces of their lives with a researcher stranger. One mother said to me, "You are so easy to talk to." With her impression of me as a sympathetic listener, she told her story with emotional vividness. While I no doubt sympathized, what may not have been completely obvious to her was that I also maintained critical distance.

Distinguishing the interview relationship from a friendship was difficult because of the similarities between us. Relatively little of the feminist methodological literature, however, focuses on interviewing strategies among women of like social standing. Much of such literature is dedicated to uncovering the power relations at work in conversations between women of different social standing. Gluck and Patai (1991) and Mbilinyi (1989), for instance, offer the researcher worthy advice about how to avoid exploiting poor women. Indeed, the methodological and epistemological assumptions driving much of feminist qualitative research prioritizes work with disadvantaged women. Collins (1991) aspires for social scientists to give voice to those who normally have not been heard, in particular, Black women and members of other minority groups. My past research foci on women on welfare and Black activists heeded Collins's instruction (Moosnick 1993).

Yet, unique problems and challenges are associated with interviewing women of like social standing, which go relatively ignored in methodological discussions. When I followed Collins's imperative in my previous research, for instance, I encountered women on welfare and Black activists who blurred the personal and political in discussing their lives and life histories. Generally, the adoptive mothers did not practice a similar narrative habit. As indicated, I sympathize with the desire to mother and the flood of emotions that accompany being a mother that these women expressed. But I, similar to the people I interviewed years earlier, am very attentive to race, class, and gender. While some of the women were equally attentive, a good many were not. Indeed, one mother reacted against the tendency of others to perceive her international adoption as a political statement:

There were times when I felt as though I was a poster child for world peace, and people assume that I was going to be politically liberal just because we've done this and people do make assumptions. I do get a little bit tired of being held up as a poster child for race relations. I just adopted these kids because I really wanted to be a mother. It's not a political statement. These are the kids. This was one of the easiest ways to adopt at the time. It was financial[ly] not a huge stretch. It was one of the least expensive, most streamlined ways of adopting. It was really more pragmatic than . . . and it was quick.

Many of the mothers agreed to share their lives with me simply as an opportunity to chronicle how their family was formed. One woman even asserted that she perceived me and my work to be good "PR" for adoption. My motivation obviously differs from these mothers'. Similar to Borland (1991), then, my research experience questions the appropriateness of making the personal political when the women come to the conversation with different motivations. By placing the women's words into a political context, the context the women introduced was lost.

Much of the above discussion is an attempt to negotiate the multiple and competing feminist directives at work in this research. On the one hand, there is the effort to give voice to those who are not normally heard, and to do so out of an ethos of care. Scanlon (1993) and Borland (1991), among others, even provide specific strategies for respecting the women interviewed and "sharing" power with them. Yet, while I attend to these women with an "ethic of care," I recognize that some of the feminist literature is critical of White, middle-class women who adopt (Herrmann and Kasper 1992; Katz Rothman 1994; Raymond 1993; Solinger 2001). Regarding giving voice, the voices that go neglected in adoptive arrangements may well be the birth mothers', particularly Black and international birth mothers for whom there is little written. In addition, there is a growing number of situations where White birth mothers tell their stories (Berebitsky 2000). So if I am to further Collins' humanist directive is my focus misdirected? Should I attend to the silent members of the adoption triangle? Perhaps, I am simplifying or being reactionary, because I do not think that Raymond or Collins would advocate not studying these women nor approaching them with care. It is certainly the case, however, that these women do not hold the unique perspective of outside knowledge as Collins had conceived it (Collins 1991). The challenge before me is to respect these women, while simultaneously understanding them through a critical lens. I bridge the two feminist impulses by recognizing the unique perspective of adoptive mothers whose lives and stories offer insight into the state of gender and race relations. In many respects, adoptive mothers represent traditional familial relations (Modell 1994; Yngvesson 1997). At the same time, they are people who have pondered normalcy rules that expect mother and child to match racially.

A complicated balance had to be negotiated between methodological expectations and actual research. Specifically, the researchers' and women's impressions guided the stories provided. I recognize that "interview data must be interpreted against the background of the context in which they were produced" (Hammersley and Atkinson 1990: 126). Part of the context included the academic understanding I brought to the interviews. Of course, I cannot completely grasp the contextual background within which the women spoke and lived. Most women were not so straightforward as the one who participated in the interview to enhance outside images of adoption. I cannot be certain what impressions the others wanted to relay to me. It was only in the focus group with three mothers with Asian children, for example, that jolting racial encounters not mentioned in the individual conversations came to light.

In this chapter, I have contextualized the data gathered by acknowledging that many of the women, unlike myself, came to the interviews largely inattentive to gender. Part of this disjuncture stems from my rootedness in academic feminist discourse which, by and large, the women did not share. Given my interest in selected feminist matters, I close this chapter by considering three unresolved methodological questions pertinent to feminist research methods; in so doing, I further contextualize the orientation of this work. These issues are: (1) Whether or not in-depth interviews that include emotions and that allow free and unhindered space for self-expression further objectify the subject or bring the "subject" into scientific conversations as subject; (2) Whether or not, similarly, critical "reflection" promotes the scientific effort to reach objectivity or intersubjectivity, or challenges; and (3) Does feminist research necessitate following a qualitative model? Let us consider each of these issues in turn.

Lurking behind this work is the unsettled question of whether or not giving voice and making women visible actually promotes humanism. Of course, there are virtues to women creating a place of their own through voicing their wants and needs publicly. But does making visible the invisible actually contribute to the enlargement of the Foucaltian Panoptic lens? Collins (1991), for instance, recognized the power Black women hold as people with unique perspectives. The Black woman tended to the White child in her work as an outsider within and then returned to her own children at home within the Black community: she thereby knew both worlds. Does not exposing her knowledge and the power that resides therein, diminish her strength? The invisible woman, whose position and knowledge goes unnoticed by science, holds power in her silence. Once she loses her invisibility, she is vulnerable to being made hypervisible. What I think must be acknowledged is that works such as this one that delve into a woman's intimate life and engage in "thick description" may objectify. The woman on welfare who agrees to share her story with the caring social scientist, for instance, may find that intimate knowledge of her life can either help initiate progress in her life or it can be used to further monitor her.

Equally unresolved for me is the question of whether critical reflection, which I employ and is an integral feature of feminist methodology, actually challenges science. Stephen J. Gould, in his premier work, *Wonderful Life*, asserts that reflexive science actually generates greater scientific and objective results than do the natural sciences because subjective biases are acknowledged and factored into the research conclusions. The reflective social scientist accounts for decisions made during the research process and, in so doing, exposes her biases. By contrast, the traditional scientist may not share such vital information and thereby ignore tacit motivations that influence outcomes. Gould leads one to believe that reflective "soft" science accounts are more objective than works that avoid reflection.

Lastly, pertinent to this work is the very basic question of what constitutes feminist methodology. Does qualitative work alone count as feminist research? A decade ago, Shulamit Reinharz, in her article, "Neglected Voices and Excessive Demands in Feminist Research," explores the assumption that qualitative work spells *feminist*. She writes, "Because feminist research stems from the critical distrust of earlier non-feminist research, and because much of this earlier work was conducted using quantitative methods, a symbiosis has occurred between "feminist" and "qualitative" in the minds of many people. Qualitative methods are thought to be the methods that protest against the status quo, just as feminism does more generally" (Reinharz 1993: 69). Reinharz, in contrast, through an analysis of varied feminist research, found plenty of feminist researchers employ statistical procedures. She, insists, therefore, that feminist statisticians' voices have been ignored and neglected by other feminists. In the past, I have equated feminist research with qualitative methods. Now, however,

I wonder whether I should move full circle and take the drastic step to promote quantitative works as truly feminist given that they provide information without too much intrusion? These quantitative works maintain, as feminist research does generally, a commitment to making women's lives known, but they do so without delving deeply into a woman's life.

These critical issues are part of the foreground and background noise within which the conversations transpired, the themes emerged, and the written text was composed.

NOTES

1. Although this work focuses on and is embedded in a "social" understanding of the women's words and in notions of race, class, and gender, I do not believe that biology and genetic features should be totally ignored. This work does not attend to biological interpretations of race. I think, however, that to engage biological and genetic theories fully the social context must also be presented. Moreover, because the biological story is often the first one told, I believe it is important to start with an eye toward "the social."

2. Sandra Patton, in her work, *Birthmarks*, offers an insightful analysis of the NABSW's 1972 position paper. She does not focus on the organization's proclamation per se, but rather on how that position has been distorted in popular adoption narratives. Patton explains: "The position paper's alleged assertion that transracial adoption was 'cultural genocide' has haunted the organization ever since; the association is continually castigated for this view and cast as villains in the popular narrative. In fact, the phrase did not appear in the actual position statement. While the NABSW is repeatedly cited as continuing to hold such a position, its stance regarding such placements has in fact changed since 1972. In the late 1990s its position emphasized the preservation and support of Black families. It stressed that more emphasis on family preservation could stem the tide of children in need of out-of-home care. When adoptions were necessary it stressed that every effort should be made to place children in homes of similar racial and ethnic backgrounds whenever possible, but that transracial placements were appropriate in certain circumstances. Its 1990s position stated quite explicitly that children should not languish in foster care unnecessarily" (Patton 2000: 155).

3. Shirlee Taylor Haizlip, in her book, *The Sweeter the Juice*, speaks of the arbitrary nature of skin color, race, and culture. She argues, in particular, that members of her own family, who are light skinned Blacks, were Black but became White. Later generations of this "White" side of her family were unaware of their Black background.

4. All names used are pseudonyms. They are as follows:

Mothers with White Children

Jan

Katherine

Judith
Susan
Joanna
Theresa
Eleanor

Mothers with Asian Children

Megan
Deborah
Pat
Kathy
Mary
Peggy
Andrea

Mothers with Black and Biracial Children

Leslie
Amy
Carol
Karen
Tera
Elizabeth
Elaine
Phyllis

5. In particular, writers like Mimi Abramovitz have criticized Charles Murray's interpretation of the poor, and poor women.

6. Many feminist writers link adoption with gender concerns by exploring the relationship between poor and middle-class women in adoptions (see Gailey 2000; May 1995; Patton 2000; Raymond 1993; Solinger 2001). Yngvesson, for instance, looks at open adoptions and how the birth mothers fare in these arrangements. Overall, however, the adoption literature focuses on the welfare of the child and, in the process, by and large overlooks the significance of gender, and for that matter, race and class.

CHAPTER 3

The Process of Becoming
a Mother

The previous chapter explored ambiguities and unresolved difficulties associated with feminist narrative practices, as part of the context informing this project. In the next two chapters, this methodology and related concerns form the background for introducing some of the themes that emerged in the individual interviews. These chapters are loosely arranged temporally as we follow the adoptive mother beginning with infertility treatments and concluding with grocery store conversations where complete strangers observe her and her child. The current chapter focuses on the route and process by which the adoptive mothers became mothers. Interview excerpts highlight the women's views of infertility treatments, adoption bureaucracies, birth mothers, and other mothers.

The mothers' interpretations are categorized racially since similarities and differences are explored between and among mothers with White, Asian, and Black and Biracial children. I found that race mattered to varying degrees depending upon the topic of interest. Mothers talked somewhat uniformly about their infertility and infertility treatments irrespective of the race of their child. In contrast, characterizations of and relations with the birth mother hinged on race. Race also proved relevant in discussions about the pace of the adoption process and other mothers. Accordingly, most sections of the chapter are structured around race, with initial attention given to commonalities among the women, irrespective of the child's race. Discussion then moves to racial details by examining distinctive features of White, Asian, and Black and Biracial adoptions.

Highlighting race and its significance in conversations about the process of becoming a mother, I also look at maternity itself by analyzing the women's words in light of selected feminist portrayals. I return to notions of mothering such as mothering imperatives and fitness standards that generated this project and relate them to descriptions of infertility treatments, birth mothers, adoption processes, and other mothers. I consider how certain feminist works that question and challenge imperatives to mother relate to the women's understanding of infertility treatments and birth mothers. My intention is to ask, Do the women impose mothering imperatives on themselves and other women? What's more, Do the adoptive mothers adhere to fitness standards that promote the idea that poor, single women are ill equipped to mother? In the adoptive mothers' estimation, does there stand a category of "other mothers" who are authorities on maternal matters? Lastly, through a discussion of the adoption process, I examine whether or not Raymond (1993) is correct in arguing that adoptive mothers ignore political matters.

To summarize, the tasks of this chapter include presenting selected themes dealing with how the women became mothers, examining the women's words from a racially astute perspective, and relating their thoughts to the feminist discourse that initiated this book. Let's turn our focus to where the interviews most often started, talking about infertility.

INFERTILITY AND DECISIONS TO ADOPT

"Motherhood is happy and infertility is sad."

"We were more interested in being a family than hanging out with a bunch of doctors."

Infertility figured into decisions to adopt for all the women but two.[1] These two women were unique in that one was a single mother and decided to adopt, while the other, married, did not know whether or not she could have biological children. Given that the overwhelming majority of women interviewed endured fertility problems, along with the fact that the feminist literature driving this work critiques the use of new reproductive technologies, I dedicate the current section to fertility discussions.

A defining feature of the mothers' fertility talk and my discussion thereof is the absence of race. This is not to say that race did not matter. Race, certainly, figures into popular notions of infertility given the widespread belief that Blacks do not experience infertility (Abramovitz 2000; Solinger 1992, 2001). The race of the child, however, did not influence renditions of infertility and treatments thereof. It could be said that there were no racial variations in fertility talk because the women were all White.[2]

I did not ask directly about infertility. The topic emerged naturally when I opened the interviews with the question, "What made you decide to adopt?" The women's "fertility talk" followed a vague pattern that entailed asserting a cause, recalling treatments, reaching a stopping point, and resolving infertility to enable adoption. Of course, women varied in how much and what they willingly shared. Some women volunteered that they or their husbands introduced the inhibiting causal factor. One mother joked, "My husband, he was just worthless. I mean, the fertility problems were mostly his." At least 11 other women willingly disclosed this type of information. In most cases, no cause could be medically designated. Reaching this medical uncertainty required, however, medical intervention. Women faced invasive procedures ranging from hormonal injections to laparoscopic surgeries. General agreement existed that these treatments were "awful," leading one woman even to proclaim, "It was the worst period in my life." The extent to which the women elaborated on their "awful" experiences ranged from some giving this a great deal of attention to others relegating it to unimportance. Tera spoke openly of feeling "whacked out" on fertility drugs:

The first drugs they did was something called Clomid and those are really bad. I was on really high levels of that, and that just made me pathological, sociopath[ic]. I don't know, it just made me totally, totally whacked out. Those are really bad and I just did those for a couple cycles, 'cause they didn't work. Then we went on to another drug and that didn't bother me at all except for some physical symptoms, but mentally it didn't, you know, do anything.

In contrast, the following mother quickly ended the conversation and bypassed an in-depth discussion, "Yeah, we did Pergonal a number of times and I had a laparoscopy, and we went through that whole scene."

Regardless of the amount of attention devoted to treatments and infertility, the women agreed that "infertility is bad." Disdain for infertility treatments crept into the narratives as women who spent years in "treatment" explained their reasoning for doing so. Had other options been available, Judith and her husband would have ceased treatments. "We just started looking into adoption possibilities and it was very bleak, and we would not have continued infertility treatment as long as we did had there been an adoption possibility." Women, in some sense, dismissed the length of time devoted to infertility treatments. Karen, for instance, stated, "All these years of trying, which wasn't that many years, but it was like seven or eight years." In a similar vein, Jan regretted that she pursued in vitro. "I mean, I had always said that I would not go through all this stuff, 'cause I had a friend that went through all the in vitro and all that kind of stuff and I said, there was no way." Despite her initial resolve against in vitro, Jan received the treatment twice and even contemplated a third try. Unlike Jan, however, most women proudly asserted that they consciously decided to exclude in vitro. Women and their husbands had to make financial choices and decisions, measuring the costs and benefits of fertility treatments in comparison to adoption options. But more than weighing the practical options available to them, women like Pat proudly announced that she and her husband never entertained the idea of in vitro. "Yeah, we went through probably a couple of years of all kinds of fertility stuff. We never tried in vitro or anything like that. We considered donor egg and decided at that point that it was just too expensive, that we had a limited amount of money that we could spend on [this] and we were going to put our money in adoption stuff. So that's what we decided to do."

Arriving at "a stopping point" where infertility treatments were no longer desirable occurred to these women at different rates. Some women chose to de-emphasize their movement from learning of their infertility, to encountering treatments, to adoption. In our conversations, Peggy, the mother of a Korean daughter, returned to her enthusiasm for international adoption, which kept her from experiencing the longing and grieving of other women. "I have a couple of friends right now that are going through the infertility thing, and just say that they can't go to baby showers. I just really never felt that way. I always knew that I was gonna have children and still able to be happy for other people and be around kids."

Other mothers with whom I spoke, however, did not enjoy Peggy's ability readily to discard her desire to have a biological child. Instead, they recalled longing for what seemed to come easily for others. Eleanor succinctly stated this sentiment: "We were happy, but there was just a void in our life, and it got to the point with me that I wouldn't even attend baby showers or things of that nature anymore because it would come to tears for me and it's not that I was envious of other people. I was very happy for them, but I just wanted to be able to do that, too." Unlike Eleanor, a few of the other women openly shared that they looked with envy at others, often younger women, who could have children with abandon. Sometimes these "other women" even were family members, as Carol, a transracial adoptive mother recalled:

There was just a lot of longing, you know, when we were going through the infertility stuff. I just felt like it was dragging on and on and on. You just question, "Why can't I have kids?" My husband has a niece whose had several abortions and has three kids out of wedlock and every time she gets a new boyfriend, she has a baby. "Why can't that be us?" "She doesn't have any business having kids." "How come we can't have kids?" You know, all that kind of stuff.

By saying "all that kind of stuff," Carol relegated her longing to the past.

The women mixed scientific, religious, and fateful language to understand and contend with infertility.[3] These women engaged science to a point and by accepting medical intervention expressed their belief in the efficacy of science. When science failed, however, some of the women looked back critically at their bout with infertility treatments and did so by intermixing religious and scientific language. Deborah struggled to negotiate God's will with scientific possibilities:

I guess the older I get the more I feel like it truly is a life and we shouldn't mess with what God's doing. I almost now think if I was going to that point again, I don't even think I'd go meet with the guy [the in vitro specialist]. I would have just said, you know, "This is the way it is," and I don't even know if I would have done the infertility that I did do, 'cause to me it doesn't matter whether it's a birth child or an adoptive. If it's not meant to be, it's not meant to be. If there was a specific problem or something that was found that could easily be corrected, maybe, but they never found a problem with us, so it was just kind of fishing in the dark.

She continued our conversation by reflecting critically on infertility treatments:

I really question how much people are told or if they're in a state where they are desperate and they don't hear it. The rate of ovarian cancer is increased with these infertility drugs, but people don't think about that. I think that's kind of scary, too. But we just took a real mild [approach]; I took Clomid and there are shots that you do. I have friends who are doing shots. Their husbands have to give them shots everyday and they go in every other day to have their blood monitored, and it can be real dangerous. We did six months and then I guess, after three trials they decided that maybe I had some endometriosis that might have been a problem, so they did a laparoscopy. I didn't have anything significant, so I went through a whole surgery for really no reason.

Other women who intermingled science and religion as they resolved infertility differed from Deborah in not necessarily coming to regard scientific interventions critically. Rather, they simply inferred that when science failed, God stepped in. Elaine said:

I always wanted a child and tried to have one biologically and it didn't work out. It seemed as though we were trying things that are sure to succeed and then they don't succeed. And I'm not especially fatalistic about it but it seemed that God was saying this is not meant to be. And there were so many children, I was so aware of so many children in need of a good family. And it just seemed that we were working so hard with science, against science to try to have a child biologically and it wasn't working, and then there are all these children in need and it just seemed as though it was ridiculous to continue to spend a lot of money and to do it. And the odds, as I was getting older, the odds were getting more and more against me in terms of becoming pregnant, and it just didn't seem to make sense to continue to try.

Here, Elaine interspersed fateful and religious language with science; science told her the odds were against her as she aged, and when she did not conceive with the aid of scientific intervention, God was the explanation.

After abandoning infertility treatments and scientific interventions to pursue adoption, many of the other women regarded their adoptions and, in particular, the children they did receive as almost ordained. Eleanor, a mother of a White child, expressed well the thoughts which others directly, as well as indirectly, voiced: "Well, there's an old saying, 'everything happens for a reason.' I believe that God leads people to be where they're at and I think that we're all here to help each other and I think our lives all touch each other. We say around here that we've never had any children, because God wanted us to be our son's parents."

Imperative to Mother

Above I introduced infertility talk as contextualized by the mothers' shared experiences as White women. In this section I consider how the women, as women who endured infertility treatments, made overtures to mothering imperatives as articulated by various feminists.

Selected Feminists on Infertility

Women, according to Chodorow (1978), gain their sense of selves through nurturing and in relation to others.[4] Should a woman choose not to mother, she experiences the feeling that she is missing out. Yet, the imperative for women to mother is not applied universally. White women are encouraged to mother at all costs, while darker skinned women are discouraged from doing so (Abramovitz 2000; Hubbard 1990; Raymond 1993; Solinger 2001). Driven to mother "at all costs," White, middle-class women willingly and eagerly indulge in infertility treatments, ignoring the wider implications thereof. Indeed, according to Barbara Katz Rothman, in "The Tentative Pregnancy: Then and Now," women who undergo infertility treatments are both victims and enablers. They expose their bodies to medical hazards and dangers; at the same time, through their participation they perpetuate the belief that Whiteness and financial security make a good mother.

Infertility: Feminist Portrayals and Women's Words

In *Beyond Mothers and Fathers: Ideology in a Patriarchal Society*, Barbara Katz Rothman (1994) unravels the multiple ideologies driving patriarchy, including those of patriarchy, technology, and capitalism. She explains, "The ideologies of patriarchy, technology, and capitalism give us our vision of motherhood while they block our view, give us a language for some things while they silence us for others." The ideology of patriarchy, in particular, places women in the position where they "bear the children of men" (Katz Rothman 1994: 141). The medicalization of pregnancy and childbirth, meanwhile, bears witness to the ideology of technology. Lastly, the ideology of capitalism commodifies both precious children and mothers. Those things we regard as precious become property.

The mothers had complicated understandings of infertility as evidenced by the interview excerpts. Deborah, as quoted earlier, came to regard infertility treatments as a "medical risk." Katherine, more so than Deborah, ridiculed the medical community for its thoughtlessness:

I think the medical community views infertility as an interesting problem that is worth researching, and the translation from research to dealing with people and dealing with their actual reactions to it has a wide gulf. Even though I understood it and I could have a sense of humor about it, I still could feel some resentment after an appointment at what a cad the doctor had been or the stupid things that he had said and very male-dominated field. They're really pushing for you doing the most extreme things, because of the research potential in that without really understanding the personal, ethical, emotional dilemmas that all of those things pose.

With sentiments like these, the women did not engage infertility treatments thoughtlessly. They instead reached a definite stopping point, which most often meant excluding in vitro. The feminist critiques of women who engage reproductive technology used in this work do not consider depths of participation and fail to take into account that, although some technological intervention may be acceptable to women, at a certain point it becomes undesirable. In many scenarios, adoption may well be the best alternative to suffering new reproductive technologies. Some of the women came to this conclusion after adopting. As adoptive mothers, they suggested to friends and others facing infertility difficulties that they bypass medical procedures in favor of adoption.

A variety of questions arise when thinking about the women's self-reported preference for adoption, as well as their relative participation in reproductive technology. Do women who are interested in adopting have a lower threshold for infertility treatments than women not considering adoption or vice versa? I found variation on this issue among the women with whom I conversed. I could not discern, however, whether women who eventually adopted darker skinned children ended infertility treatments sooner than those with White children. Quite unexpectedly, given my focus on race, a rough pattern instead arose suggesting that women who adopted physically needy children abandoned treatments sooner than others. Deborah brought this to my attention when I asked her to compare herself to other adoptive mothers. "I think the biggest thing is

being open to the physical, the special needs is the probably the difference."

Regardless of the child's physical well-being or race, the women chose
to denigrate their full participation in infertility treatments. From what I
can gather, they did so because of a variety of reasons, including an intolerance for infertility treatments—an intolerance that grew with the satisfaction gathered from adopting their children. Additionally, some of the
women seemed aware that devoting attention to infertility treatments
might relay to their children that they were not the family's "first" or
preferred choice.

Of course, these women felt a desire to have children and pursued this
with vigor, and it cannot be denied that many of the women spoke of
missing out. I heard sentiments such as "I couldn't go to baby showers"
or "I couldn't go another Christmas without a child." But, at the same
time, many of these women were professionals and put off child bearing
until their careers were in place. Many of the women also recognized and
felt that they did not need to be mothers in order to achieve fulfillment.
When I asked them whether they felt more complete since becoming a
mother, I received two types of responses. Some of the women unconditionally concurred. More often than not, however, they uttered something
along the lines that "complete" was not quite the right word—"enhanced"
was more accurate. Susan sounded like many of the other women when
she said:

I don't know if "complete" is the right word. I think it's [to be a mother] an
opportunity that like I said before, before we were able to adopt him, we had
really just sat down and said, "life can be good without kids, we'll just spend a
lot of time with our nieces and nephews and find other ways to devote ourselves."
I think we were prepared that we could have a really good life without kids and
be complete and happy but, it's an opportunity that I'm thrilled I had the opportunity to do. Because I do feel like it's added a lot of happiness and fun and nerves
and everything, so I guess instead of saying my life is more complete, I just say
my life is fuller, more full, a lot more fun . . . wouldn't trade it for anything in the
world.

I was somewhat surprised to hear many of the women, like Susan, quibble
with the intimation that completeness came with children. Of course, it
may not be such an unexpected response given that all of the women were
active people—with work both inside and outside of the home as well as
volunteer activities. Part of their active schedule, however, included nurturing work.

Considering that forming a family did not "come easy," some of the
women talked about finding ways to nurture outside of motherhood.
Work, in some cases, provided them with an appropriate outlet. Those

women with nurturing work considered themselves lucky, as did Sammie, a mother and teacher:

I think that I would have been fine to go through life and not have children, and just considered myself blessed that I had so many children in my life even though they were not my own. But there would have always been a sadness that I never had a chance to do it for myself, but I don't think I needed to be a complete person. I would like to have many, many children and have always wanted lots of children just because I enjoy children so, but I never felt like I needed them to feel as if I was a good person or a successful person or had led a fulfilled life. Looking back as an eighty-year-old, I could say, I always wished I had children of my own, but I actually had 263 and been an influence in their lives and that's something that many women don't get. If I was a bank teller that void might be even greater because I didn't have contact with children.

Other women who lacked contact with children in their work consciously sought to be around children, be it their nieces or nephews or children at a volunteer work. Eleanor ended our conversation with advice for others facing infertility, "I would just like to add, for people who can't have children to never give up and to always apply yourself to the area of children, work or volunteer wherever you can, because there's a special job for you." These women thus understood that nurturing was important to their sense of selves but also appreciated that "mothering" was not the only venue through which they could gather such satisfaction.

Of significance to me, in interpreting the women's infertility talk, is attending to a woman's need to mother and nurture. Did these women express an overwhelming need to nurture such that their sense of self would be depleted should they not extend themselves maternally, even though they said "completeness" did not accompany motherhood? I started this project thinking about the oppressive nature of the imperative to mother and attentive to social pressures to mother. Perhaps, with the insight gathered from the conversations, it is more accurate to alter my original focus away from the imperative to mother to the imperative to nurture.

Distinguishing the imperative to mother from the imperative to nurture is somewhat complicated given the overlap between them. Indeed, it is difficult not to define nurturing work in relation to and in juxtaposition with mothering. This is not to say that nurturing must only occur within mothering. Rather, it is from motherhood that understandings and interpretations of nurturing arise. Sara Ruddick, in "Thinking Mothers/ Conceiving Birth," offers some assistance in this regard when she speaks of "relational work," "Mothering—like, for example, teaching, psychotherapy, ministering, and any kind of caring labor—is a relational work in which others' response serve as an intrinsic and primary measure of achievement" (Ruddick 1994: 34). On the basis of the women's narratives, I would add that nurturing work offers gratification only if it combines almost unconditional giving with a sense of ownership—such that one gives and seeks responses from those with whom one identifies.

Given the difficulty of precisely articulating a definition of nurturing, it is equally a complicated task to interpret the imperative to nurture that the women voiced loudly. As I said, I entered this work thinking that "mothering" imperatives are restrictive and continue to believe this because all women beyond a certain age are evaluated according to whether or not they mother. At this point, however, I am equally attentive to how nurturing can boost a woman's feeling of satisfaction and gratification. I do not subscribe to the thinking that women are natural nurturers. Yet, it was clear that all of the women enjoyed and relished the intensive nurturing required of mothers and, moreover, vigorously sought the opportunity to nurture. Of course, it is difficult to know if nonadoptive mothers carry a similar resolve to nurture. In any case, the nurturing associated with mothering is no doubt unique given its accompanying rigors and gratification. I wonder, then, whether the feminist arguments in which I grounded this work dismiss the pervasive power driving some women to mother.

Adrienne Rich's premier work, *Of Woman Born* (1976), continues, effectively, to challenge the deeply held assumption that women are natural-born mothers and nurturers. She attends to the restrictive character of assuming that desires to mother come to women naturally. Although I concur with Rich on this point, I am struck by the deeply held and almost sanctified desires to nurture that these women expressed. Some of the women even characterized themselves as "natural-born nurturers" and alluded to their mothering desires as almost instinctual. Others spoke of coming to motherhood through some combination of natural instincts and societal desires. Given my focus on articulated wants and even passions, I appreciate, as did Sammie when she considered herself lucky to be a teacher and to have children in her life, that venues to nurture are rather limited. If these women could have satisfied their need to nurture intensively outside of motherhood, would they have done so? I cannot know the answer to this question. But I do know that some of the women, like Sammie, had nurturing work, but still sought to mother.[5] Other women who worked with children recognized both the enjoyment of nurturing at work and its limits (the children went home). The compartmentalization of work and home life does not promote enduring connections. A couple of the other women with nurturing work besides Sammie said that being around children and babies made their desire to mother stronger. Perhaps there are other factors that are equally important. The intensity of mothering work is extraordinary and the public recognition associated with and granted mothering efforts is singular.

Of course, the preciousness of mothering and nurturing is complicated by contradictions. Mothering demands ask women to act unselfishly and in other ways that directly contradict the requirements of the outside, business world (Hays 1996). Correspondingly, although being and becoming a mother enjoys a relatively high status in individual families and, perhaps, in church communities, a mother may experience a general decline in status since her mother work carries no monetary value (Crittenden 2002; Hays 1996). Also, while all women may encounter the imperative to mother, experiences of it vary by race (Collins 1994; May 1995). This surfaced in the narratives when, for instance, the women acknowledged that the adoption process involving Black children was relatively quick.

ADOPTION PROCESS

"A White baby will cost you this much, international this much, and a Black baby I can get real cheap."

"It's not easy to adopt. You go through a tremendous amount of paperwork and red tape."

Infertility talk, as noted, was marked by the silence of race. By contrast, the adoption process varied dramatically depending on the race of the child, such that White babies were understood to be the hardest babies to acquire and Black ones the easiest. Putting race aside for the moment, it is not surprising, given that adopting a child is a complicated process for virtually everyone, that the women, irrespective of the race of their child, were fateful and even religious about their adoptions. Prospective parents encounter extensive paperwork and a host of adoption workers who evaluate their parenting qualifications, among other things, as well as a sea of restrictions and requirements that limit their options. Many of the women almost portrayed themselves as participating in a game of chance, by luck hitting and missing adoption qualifications set by the state, private agencies, or international governments: "What people will do, you know. People will jump through any hoop that is put in front of them, and if you don't than you're not trying hard enough, and you must not want a baby enough."

Sometimes the greatest inhibiting hoop a woman and her husband faced was their age. Indeed, many agencies' or countries' image of an appropriate parent exclude the person over 35 years.[6] Elaine described the adoption landscape she faced as an "older" prospective parent:

We were too old and we got into this too late really, cause I was trying some fertility treatments and started late, and so we really got into the adoption business late. Then it takes a while to kind of figure out which way you want to go with the adoption, so we had some strikes against us in terms of age and that's why we could no longer go through an agency.

Coupled with agency-defined qualifications were additional limits and parameters specified by the prospective parents, as Elaine intimated when she said, "It takes a while to kind of figure out which way you want to go with the adoption." Preference for an infant was almost universal.[7] While the women shared in common their desire for an infant, they differed about what was acceptable regarding the medical condition and race of the child.

Negotiating the "acceptable" occurred in household conversations with husbands. Mary, for example, recalled the different preferences she and her husband voiced that dictated their adoption outcome:

I was saying maybe a child with a disability and he [her husband] didn't want that, 'cause, of course, that's not his thing. And he was thinking maybe an older child and I didn't want that, cause I'd had a lot of friends who had really bad experiences with that even when they were three or four. They've had so many bad experiences already that it's hard to get them through it.

At times, the mothers reflected on what they perceived to be the absurdity of "ordering" a child:

They had the home study and all, they asked questions—that was very interesting. She [the adoption social worker] filled a legal pad and we're sitting there going, "What do you feel about religion?" On and on and on, but then at the very end she said, "Well, what kind of baby do you want?" It's like an ordering. She said, "Well, would you want a child with any kind of defects or anything obvious?" Basically, our answer was we prefer to have nothing obvious at birth and that wouldn't have made no difference, but given a choice, I would choose a child that appeared fine.

Joanna, a mother of a White child spoke the above words. Tera, the mother of Biracial children said the following, "You just can't count it all out and just say, we're looking for this perfect baby." Discarding "perfection" was a narrative feature of women with Asian, Biracial, or Black children. Part of "counting it all out," however, included asserting racial and medical preferences.

Racial likes and dislikes influenced the adoption process itself since Black babies arrived with an unheralded speed unknown in the other type of adoptions. Meanwhile, international adoption agencies, along with the country of origin, specified who is eligible for children who do or do not require medical attention. All of the women understood that the hardest babies to acquire and to successfully adopt were White ones.

White adoptions happened through several sources, including agencies, lawyers, doctors, and friends. Personal connections that were less essential in the other adoptions also figured into the White adoption process. Connections and luck of the draw resulted in successful adoptions. For instance, doctors and friends knew of young women and patients who wanted to relinquish. Friends had daughters who became pregnant at 15 or 16 years and wanted to relinquish their child to others they trusted. This often translated into transferring children to others who were of the same religious orientation or the same ethnic community.

Movement of a child through a network of friends and acquaintances often meant placement within a similar community. A daughter of a long-time friend of Jan's, for instance, relinquished her child to Jan and her husband. Women like Jan, who, in large measure, worked outside of agencies to find their children, were rather spiritual about their good fortune. Katherine's adoption experience stands out as a case in point. Initially, she and her husband worked through an upscale California adoption agency that required them not only to travel to the agency, but also to provide a hefty down payment. With this agency they had to develop a "marketing brochure," as Katherine called it, to appeal to potential birth mothers. The agency appeared to be, above all, a business, and Katherine could not compete and, in hindsight, preferred not to compete. She felt that she and her husband were out of their league with this agency because its typical client was much more affluent than they. Much to Katherine's relief, their son came through another source, a doctor and friend who worked "strictly from the heart" rather than out of an interest in making money, "His [the doctor's] whole attitude about it was so joyous and so loving and so simple and no forms, no nothing, just a little conversation. No money, nothing and I thought, 'Wow, this is strictly from the heart.' And that's what it should be, I mean, that's what it is really about." Working in their favor was not only the doctor, but also their religion, because the birth mother wanted a family with her religious background, which they happened to share. Indeed, religious likeness with the birth mother was frequently cited as a reason why the birth mother chose to place her child with a particular family.

Because receiving a White child often hinged on chance, several of the women with White children considered international and domestic transracial adoptions before eventually deciding against it. In their minds, international adoption meant health concerns, and transracial adoption was simply not a viable consideration. Notice in the following quote that Jan assumes domestic adoptions involve White children when she alludes to the length of time to receive a child:

We went to the international orientation thing and after I took that, I was kind of excited and then I thought, "Gosh, that is an awful lot to go through with international." Oh, my gosh, they just know you frontwards, backwards and just actually even getting the child and possibly even going over there or having them brought here and all the troubles they could have. A lot of them normally come over with some kind of disease, you know, problems. And so I kind of just put it in the back of mind, and we really knew that domestically we probably weren't going to adopt, because, I mean, it would take years, years and to be honest, I was going to give up whether it was adoption, fertility, whatever. I was going to give up by the time I was 40. I wasn't going to do anymore.

Most often, the extended family's approval or the lack thereof interfered with the pursuit of domestic transracial adoption:

I think that it [transracial adoption] can be done very successfully, but I think that you would need a lot of family support especially and I think that if you can't get that, then it would be very difficult. You know, our final decision was determined by if we couldn't provide the environment that we wanted for our child, then maybe that is not the right thing for us to do. I think in our situation that [Asian adoption] would have been easier than Black because, like I said, our parents had grown up in that era and I just think it would have been real difficult for them and other members of our family. I think it would have been difficult really with any kind, but I think Black would have been the hardest.

Eleanor and others recognized that Asian adoptions would be easier. Some of the women with White children, however, obscured the distinction between special needs, on the one hand, and Asian and Black adoptees, on the other.[8] Joanna, for instance, "never thought about a child with a special need or the transracial":

We really did not and I've thought about that since you had called. I'm not sure why and I guess I felt at that point that we could just have a, we could just adopt a per . . . [perfect], you know, a child that could have been ours and we didn't consider, oh God, that sounds awful, I was gonna say anything less, but a child with a special need or the transracial. We just never thought about it, never thought about it and that would have been other issues to deal with obviously with family acceptance and all that.

Lurking behind the above quote was the sentiment that other types of adoptions are too challenging and, perhaps, even inferior. Later in our conversation as she spoke of the possibility of a second adoption Joanna said, "I think I'd like to have somebody else to turn my attention to. Of course, there are not very many options these days and the option of taking on a child with a special need, the temptation is there in a way, but I still just don't think I'm up to the challenge. I think it's quite a challenge." Admitting that one was not up for the challenge often was accompanied by slight feelings of guilt. Indeed, one mother remarked that others had been openly critical of her and her husband for choosing to pursue a White and healthy child. Susan even questioned whether or not her and her husband "were taking the lazy way out":

Hmmm, mmm, we thought about it [international adoption], but, I'm trying to think of the reasons we really didn't pursue it. I think part of it was just the commitment. We felt like that was an additional commitment, because beyond just being what it takes to be a family and raise a child, the additional responsibilities of learning a new culture and teaching them their culture and letting them know their culture and everything. Oh, I guess it sounds like maybe we were taking the lazy way out, I don't know.

With trepidation about other types of adoptions and limited opportunities to receive a White child, it might not be surprising that only one out of the seven women with White children had adopted more than one child. While reasons for this varied, three of these women mentioned that they could not ask for a more perfect situation or child. "There's never going to be another situation that could be as perfect as this one."

In contrast, five out of the seven women with Asian adoptees adopted more than one child. A couple of the women with Asian adoptees spoke of "perfection" in arguing that White adoptive parents are too "picky," as one of these mothers said. Peggy spoke her mind when she said, "I would think that people who've opted to adopt a local, White child that, I don't know this is my prejudice, that they're prejudiced and they're being selfish because most of those kids are going to get adopted anyway." Irrespective of motives or preferences, pursuing an Asian child took the mothers through a slightly different adoption route.

Asian adoptions involved agencies much more than friends, even though friends often triggered the impetus to adopt or provided information about a particular agency. The length of the adoption process depended on, among other factors, the international context and the corresponding agency's requirements. Around the time of the 1988 Olympics, for example, Korea closed and opened its doors depending on public sentiment of Koreans toward adoption. Indeed, the 1988 Olympics mark a watershed in Korean adoption. They were also a symbolic moment for Andrea:

Well, we got our child right around the time of the '88 Olympics. Oh, golly, there were some awful stories going around Korea that children were being sent to America for parts. Did you hear that story? That we actually had children that needed hearts and livers. And somebody made a movie about it in Korea and it became very popular. And it was a real crisis and they shut down the adoptions for a while. Crazy.

The unpredictable quality of international adoption can make it troublesome, according to Pat:

You know, that's the trouble with international adoption. It's just on and off and on and off, and that's a country's decision. It just always strikes me that it's really unfortunate for the kids that are waiting for a family to be in the middle of this kind of nonsense. But it happens. It happened recently. It sometimes doesn't happen so much that it's closed that they change the parameters so that certain kids are excluded and certain kids aren't. And that makes it really tough. I think that happens a lot more than people are aware. I hear that all the time. This country is closed for a little bit. This country is open. Even Korea for a little while, one agency was opened or closed and then they changed it. I mean you have to be someone who's involved with the process to really keep up from minute to minute as to what's going on.

Part of the problem is that countries do not simply close their borders, but alter the "parameters" and shift their policies regarding "special needs" children. A potential adopter must understand a country's definition of special needs and decide which problems are acceptable to their family. Andrea explained:

We were in the process of adopting as yet an unidentified boy from China. It would have been about a two-year-old boy, when I got a phone call from somebody I don't even really know. I'd met her at an adoption meeting once and we had talked loosely about special-needs adoption. She had a child with an extra thumb, and we were just talking about it and she remembered, and she found out about this agency that had this backlog. All of the sudden, they received many, many referrals for children with correctable special needs like ours and she gave me the number and I called them, and it was true. They had a lot of kids from Korea right then. I don't know why, but they'd suddenly been sent piles of referrals. Our daughter wasn't actually among those referrals. Those children mostly had already been placed by the time I'd called. But they sent me the referral to adopt a special-needs baby. They send you the list of horrors, I call it. And on the one side is minor horrors and on the other side is major horrors, and we checked off no to everything that looked like it would be permanent. You feel terrible doing that; you just know how many children you're saying no to when you're doing that.

Mothers, like Andrea, interested in adopting Asian children had to make deliberate decisions about the degree and extent of special needs acceptable to them. It was often the case that a family adopted one child requiring extensive medical attention and one child without such needs.

Despite committing themselves to Asian adoptions and often to medically needy children, most of the women came upon international adoptions by chance or by way of adoption restrictions. Only a couple of the women said that they had always envisioned adopting internationally, though not necessarily Asian or medical needy children. These women were the same ones who voiced a preference for a diverse family composed of racially different people and who traveled to receive their children. Virtually all of the women with Asian children, moreover, like the women with White children, understood Black adoptions to be the most difficult. Andrea, for example, described their reasons for not pursuing a transracial adoption, "We wondered about our [religious] community's reaction, and frankly that was why we went Asian instead of Black. Because I was somewhat keen on adopting a Biracial child or a Black child, but we thought that child might have a harder time in the community and we were pretty confident that our parents would have had a harder time; the grandparents would have had a harder time with a Black child."

Some of these women felt equally hesitant with domestic White adoption. Two women with Asian children were indeed critical of those wanting the "flawless" White child. But more prevalent than this sentiment was the intimation that White domestic adoptions often involve failed and shady transactions. Andrea succinctly stated this impression. "We weren't interested in private adoption. We wanted itemized bills. We wanted everything very above board and legally everything moving very smoothly." According to the mothers, the legal soundness of organizations such as Holt International, assured them that they participated in legitimate operations.

Mothers with Black and Biracial children never questioned the legal integrity of their adoptions. Instead, some of these mothers were uncertain, as they pursued adoption and weighed adoption options, whether or not Whites could legally adopt transracially. Similar to the women with Asian children, however, they did not enter the adoption process with a preference for a Black or Biracial child. Rather, circumstances led them to adopt transracially. The women mentioned looking into White, Asian, and South American adoptions before coming to domestic transracial. Leslie, for instance, said:

We qualified for Filipino, a child not younger than four and they kind of give you the worst-case scenario and it was like a four-year wait. And so we thought we will still try it, cause a lot of it has to do with your age and whether you have other children and like if you are divorced, some countries won't place a child in your home. So we said we can always change our mind, because who knows if we will ever get this child. And then when we met with the social worker at the adoption agency, we said to her, "Aren't there any children in this country that are available?" And she said, "Well, if you are interested in a Biracial child, I can pretty much guarantee you a child by the end of the year." And we said, "WHAT!" And you know at that time we thought, well if we are going for Filipino what is the difference of a Biracial? I mean to me they are the same race.

In the above narrative, and the one I have included below, these women, while they did not originally choose a transracial adoption, concluded that racial distinctions, while not insignificant, were not crucial to their final adoption decisions:

So when we talked about a baby and I did want a baby, they said in the State, at one point they told us that we would not stand a chance of getting a White baby. And so we starting thinking about a Black child at that point and they have a special training session for people who are considering a transracial adoption and we went through that and you get a good . . . They don't whitewash things. I mean, you get a real good sense of some of the problems and some of the difficulties in that. So we thought about it a long time. She was born and it turned out she was Black, and we were prepared by that time though it had been several years earlier that we had taken the training sessions, so we had done a lot of thinking about it. By that point, it [race] didn't really faze us one way or another.

What is certainly clear is that, unlike the other adoptions, once the decision was made to adopt transracially, the adoption process moved rapidly. Several of the mothers said something to the effect that their children were waiting for families, in contrast to White-on-White adoptions where parents awaited children for long periods of time. Karen recalled the adoption process that brought them their daughter, Jessica, "So we told the social worker to go for it. Well, that was June, we went down to see her again and she called me. Well, Jessica was born in the fall, and she called us in January about Jessica. I mean it happened that quick. If we had gone with a White child only, she told us that it would be two or three years." Quick adoptions and waiting children resulted in these women being contacted directly by social workers and friends to adopt other Black and Biracial children. Phyllis explained:

Through another network of families who have adopted Biracial children, we've turned down probably like six or seven babies just because timing wasn't right. Like one attorney said she had three at one time, I was like, "No, I'm not ready." But, anyway, this one couple called and said that this agency needed to place some babies and they weren't ready, so they called us. But actually at that time, we weren't ready, and so we called the agency and said that we were going to wait about six months, 'cause we wanted our child to be three before we adopted again.

These women also assessed other adoptions, Asian and White. In most cases, though not all, it was understood that Asian would be easier. Phyllis, however, was not thoroughly convinced:

I think that it [Asian adoptions] would be that they would have an easier time to some degree. But, see, like my mom is real racist against Japanese, World War II, and all those issues. I mean, she would flip. She would just like die. I know she would. And I don't know why people are so weird about that stuff, but she would flip. But my bet is that they have an easier time in terms of racial issues. But, see, if we adopted like that, our adoptions wouldn't be open and so we wouldn't have all these other benefits.

Regardless of the child's race, the end assessment was the same. The adopting women felt fortunate to have the particular children they did. Some of the women expressed this in a religious manner. Katherine reflected:

Well, the process of adoption is always a process and everybody always got a story. I mean that's the thing that I've learned is that, and, in the end, it's always a miracle and that was really true for us. I think that the decision to adopt is a decision that requires a tremendous amount of thought and planning and when it all falls in place, it is truly a gift from heaven and that's all there is to it. It's a Godly gift, because so many desperate events have to lock into place to make it happen.

Fate brought families together with children, one mother observed, for instance, that the day they filed their adoption papers was the same day her child was born. Even Elaine, who had endured a painful failed adoption, could look back upon the lack of success as the rightful outcome because, among other things, she had always longed for a daughter and the failed adoption attempt involved a baby boy.

The Political

For the most part, while the women placed a religious or fateful interpretation on their adoptions and the adoption process, they deflated the political. Recall that I based this work on the idea that White mothers who adopt transnationally and/or transracially maintain a perilous position. I came to this conclusion through the adoption and new reproductive technology literature, as well as through my own interpretation of adoptive arrangements that understood transnational and transracial family configurations to be political (Berebitsky 2000; Herrmann and Kasper 1992; Patton 2000; Raymond 1993; Solinger 2001). I supposed that adoptive families are more apt to be political because they have to contemplate social arrangements more than nonadoptive families do, as articulated well by Mendenhall et al.:

Adopting a child forces the family to deal with issues not usually required of biological families. For example, family members must subject themselves to careful scrutiny by adoption agencies. They must combat societal and their own reservations of "taking in" children who are often labeled "illegitimate" while (often) simultaneously dealing with issues of infertility. They must incorporate a child's birth history (good or bad) into their identity as a family and into the child's identity as well. (Mendenhall et al. 1996: 228)

Indeed, it is in a situation or family where social configurations are not taken for granted that the political can be engaged.

Selected Feminists on the Political

I define "political" to mean the intersection between subjective experiences and larger sociocultural matters that cause, reflect, and alter social relations and institutions such that individual racial experiences, for example, occur within and emerge out of the larger social milieu. This definition arises from Patricia Hill Collins (1994). She reveals that "mothering work" occurs within social cultural contexts, such that White, middle-class mothering experiences differ from those of African American mothers.[9] She says, "for women of color, the subjective experience of mothering is inextricably linked to the sociocultural concern of racial ethnic communities—one does not exist without the other" (Collins 1994: 47). I would argue that the larger "sociocultural concerns" of White communities also penetrate the subjective experiences of White mothers' mothering work. Of course, the White mother, unlike the woman Collins describes, is not concerned with the survival of her racial ethnic community. Still, by racially contextualizing the White woman's mothering experiences, Whiteness is no longer assumed. In relation to my own research work, I was curious whether the subjective experiences of the White, middle-class mother shifted when she mothered a child of a different race—did she now link herself to the sociocultural concerns of the racial ethnic community of her child (a question I entertain in the following chapter)? In the present chapter I discuss whether the White, middle-class mother tried to understand the larger political context through which her child arrived.

In *Women as Wombs*, Janice Raymond argues that adoptive families ignore the political and economic settings in which they adopt. Indeed, I found that most of the women did not politicize their families. As mentioned in the previous chapter, one mother, Andrea, even reacted against the imposition of political assumptions onto her family. Interestingly enough, Andrea found it objectionable that strangers supposed that she would be politically liberal because she adopted transnationally. Like Andrea, most of the women did not experience either the formation of their families or their family lives as political or even controversial. Rather, they thought of themselves as relatively "regular" or "normal" families, they thus readily discarded the political content of their lives. Considering the predominantly apolitical tone of these women's mothering, it would be easy to concur with Raymond's assessment. Yet, the analysis can be enlarged to consider how Raymond's characterization does and does not neatly fit the women's words, in relation, particularly to the adoption process.

The Political: The Women's Talk and Feminist Portrayals

While many of the women, particularly those who were religiously inclined, ignored the political poignancy of their lives, this was not universally the case. In some cases, the political could not be avoided because strangers brought political matters to the women's attention. It could be inferred, for example, that Andrea was all too aware of the political labels others placed on her family. She preferred to have the luxury afforded other White families who can easily bypass political expectations and challenges. Some of the other women, specifically the two women who traveled overseas to receive their children, found their familial mix desirable because they stood out. Their families represented diversity and progressive attitudes. Take Peggy. Concerning the addition of another child to her family, she said that she and her husband wanted a child from a different race to further the family's diversity: "Traveling to these different countries makes me just appreciate the diversity. And when we do think about a third child, it's like let's make it a totally different race and country so we'll have another excuse to travel and learn another culture and way of cooking." Most of the other women did not speak of their families as representing diversity. Yet, they signaled their awareness of the controversial and political character of their families without labeling it as such.

For instance, some of the women spoke about the ideology of capitalism, as characterized by Katz Rothman (1994). Conversations touched upon the costs and matching practices implemented by adoption agencies predominantly in relation to White-on-White adoptions. Recall that women who adopted Asian children noted that White-on-White adoptions could be less secure. The high cost of White-on-White adoptions, accompanied by the uncertainty of whether or not a child would arrive, was unsettling to these mothers. Deborah, for instance, felt secure in knowing that she chose to adopt through Holt International as opposed to a domestic White adoption service with its accompanying high cost:

And Holt now is just a huge international adoption agency. They're just very reputable and they really do just a good job for the kids. I never felt with them that I was in any kind of baby market. With the national stuff, I did because there are so many couples who want kids. Supply and demand is what it comes down to, and it has gotten just outrageously expensive. It's amazing to me that I can have a child come more than halfway around the world at less than half the price of a domestic adoption. You know, something's funny.

Several things stand out in Deborah's narrative. She almost saw herself as bypassing politically charged concerns because Holt International benefits the children. I heard this sentiment from other women as well which suggests that meeting the children's needs detours controversy. In the domestic context, however, Deborah related inflated costs to a booming industry for White babies. She does not completely ignore larger political contexts, but does not find them applicable to her own family.

Other women, even those who adopted White children, talked in a similar manner. They introduced politically uncomfortable topics, associated with the ideology of capitalism, but minimized the significance of these topics to their own situation. Katherine, recollect, felt uneasy with the California adoption agency that did not hide its interest in making money, especially given that her child eventually arrived through the help of a doctor who worked "strictly from the heart." Joanna, another mother of a White child, knew that the adoptive agency's practice of placing children with "good," financially able families might be to the chagrin of others. In addition, she felt uneasy when the agency's social worker asked her to spell out her likes and dislikes in a prospective child:

One of their [the agency's] selling points was that they . . . one way that they attracted birth mothers was that they placed these children in homes where they would have a good life. So they had some standards that direction, which some people may or may not agree with. They had the home study and all that was very interesting. I mean, she [the adoption social worker] filled a legal pad and we're sitting there going, "What do you feel about religion?" On and on and on, but at the very end she said, "Well, what kind of baby do you want?" It's like an ordering. She said, "Well, would you want a child with any kind of defects or anything obvious?"

While Joanna mentioned her uneasiness with the adoption worker's questions, the conversation then turned to the almost spiritual moments of her daughter's arrival, and thereby, deflated the poignancy of uncomfortable matters.

Deborah's, Katherine's, and Joanna's narratives directed attention to the underbelly of adoption—they spoke of adoption costs and, in Deborah's case, noted the hierarchy of costs based on the child's race. Katherine and Joanna, in particular, alluded to the birth mother and child as commodities. Perhaps indirectly, they recognized the odd placement of the birth mother, mediated by the adoption agency, as both a commodity and a seller in a seller's market (Solinger 1992; Yngvesson 1997). In this way they addressed the ideology of capitalism, but, as I said, they chose to minimize its relevance to their own situation. They struggled to narrate what Viviana Zelizer, in her book, *Pricing the Priceless Child*, perceives to be the inherent contradictions presented by placing emotionally priceless children on the open market.

In considering the theoretical arguments that drove this work, several things remain unresolved for me when analyzing the political or apolitical tone of the narratives. Most of the women had not encountered evaluations of the sort Raymond (1993) espouses that ground adoption in political arrangements. I struggle to analyze conversations where the participants, including myself, worked from different places. I came to the conversations motivated to enlarge the political quality of adoptions.

Many of the women, in contrast, entered our conversations to talk about their beloved families rather than the political relevance of them. Unlike Raymond's evaluation, however, this is not to say the political was non-existent or completely ignored in our conversations, but rather, was downplayed.

Still undetermined, and unaddressed by Raymond, is how to analyze adoptive arrangements that include a child with physical disabilities. Does adopting an older child or one with medical needs bypass political configurations? And if these adoptions are exempted from political consideration, does this not contribute to the mentality that these adoptive mothers are saintly for caring for "demanding" children?

THE BIRTH MOTHER

> "It was hard. There are times when you hate her, you love her. It's just, you know, nobody was rational."

While the women openly and, even at times, straightforwardly spoke of political matters in relation to the adoption process, this was less the case when they talked about the birth mother. This is not to say that political matters did not surface. On the whole, however, the women did not link birth mothers to larger trends and contexts as they did when discussing adoption costs. For the most part, birth mothers were talked about as individual people and not as a category of women who maintain the awkward status of being both mothers and not mothers, nor did the mothers link themselves to birth mothers in a larger landscape.

Through a textured weaving of fateful and religious language that by and large did not consciously entertain the political, complex portraits of the birth mothers emerged. Deep emotions surfaced toward her during the adoption process when, for instance, the possibility of a failed adoption threatened. Indeed, given that most of the adoptive mothers did not participate in open adoptions, the greatest direct or indirect contact with the birth mother occurred during the adoption process. Talk about the birth mother at moments defied racial boundaries, for instance, when they were characterized in like manners irrespective of their race. In most cases, however, the birth mother's race had a bearing on portrayals of her. Indeed, I struggle to neutralize the significance of race sufficiently to articulate similarities irrespective of race. It is commonplace, for example, for the Black birth mother to be much less visible and less willing to participate in open adoptions than the White birth mother. In any case, I begin by describing patterns that are not necessarily racially defined and then move to racially based interpretations of the birth mothers.

All of the women both recognized and talked about their relationship with the birth mother as an ongoing process (Jones 1993; Yngvesson 1997).

Even though most of the adoptive relationships were closed or semi-closed, mothers understood that their relationship with the birth mother does not cease at relinquishment, but instead comprises a nonstop play of interactions with periods of greater and lesser contact from the moment of relinquishment to that anticipated future time when the child may choose to find its birth mother. This was true even for the most distant of birth mothers on the other side of the globe with whom physical contact might never be possible; her symbolic presence ebbs and flows with the child's periodic questioning. Some of the women maintained contact, even if it was remote, with the birth mother by sending letters to the adoption agency to her. Others contended with her metaphysical presence as well as her physical absence and the possibility that she might never be found. Because most of the women did not have direct access to the birth mother, conversations touched upon the imagined time of meeting her.[10]

Renditions of "the moment" varied and did not neatly fit into the designated racial categories. Some of the women welcomed this time and expressed excitement at the prospect. Deborah looked forward to meeting her children's birth mothers in Korea—perhaps, more so than her children. "If they [her children] don't want to know, I shouldn't have the right to go do it, but I would be dying of curiosity. I want to know." Other women, meanwhile, simply gave it little thought as several women told me the birth mother only surfaced in unusual situations as in an interview setting:

I'm not constantly thinking about her. I think about her once in a while. I wonder what she would think of Amanda if she saw her now and things like that, but that's all. I wouldn't say it's a major concern or feeling. I mean, I'm sure she wonders about Amanda, but I'm also pretty sure that in time we are all going to meet. I just kind of feel that's inevitable and I'll deal with it then.

In subtle and not so subtle ways, some mothers dreaded the prospect. Joanna said:

I have to say in all honesty, just this morning on the *Today* show they had a little something about this adopted person, adult trying to find their . . . I kind of want to turn those down. I really don't want her [her daughter] watching a bunch a stuff about all that. I'm sure it's just something I'll have to deal with. But if she wanted to find out, I would support her in it.

Beneath Joanna's uneasiness with shows about adoption reunions lies the possible threat represented by the birth mother. Most of the women, however, did not verbalize such uneasiness. Undertones intimating the birth mother as a threat occurred in reference to Black and White birth mothers and did not afflict all women with these children. Only two women, both with Black children, explicitly said they felt "threatened" by the birth mother. As I explain in the following chapter, this is understandable given that both other people and their children had challenged them as the rightful mothers. One of these mothers, Elizabeth, shared with me an incident when her nine-year-old, along with a neighborhood friend, also adopted, decided that their mothers were really stepmothers. Her daughter came home asserting her mother's "stepmother" status and asking when she would get the chance to meet her "real" mother. As I consider in the following chapter, the children distinguishing themselves from their mothers is a feature of Black and Biracial adoptions. Before discussing such topics, however, let us further consider nonracialized descriptions of the birth mothers.

There were other common ways of talking about the birth mothers that did not articulate racial categories. When I asked the mothers how they were similar or different from the birth mothers, most cited their age as the defining difference. As Leslie said, "Well, age-wise very different, 'cause we are about the age of her parents, 'cause I guess her parents must of had her . . . I remember seeing those dates, 'Boy, does she realize how old we are?' " Most often, the birth mother was described as not having the financial resources to provide for a child. In one case, however, when asked about the similarities and differences between herself and the birth mother, one mother of Biracial children immediately volunteered that the birth mother was from a wealthier family than herself. Only one mother talked about the birth mother as someone living in poverty and on public assistance.

Generally, the birth mother was portrayed sympathetically. Susan, a mother of a White child, reacted against unsympathetic renditions of birth mothers:

I have a lot of respect for birth mothers because I think everybody's circumstances are different. Everybody's reasons are different. I feel like sometimes it's the selfish choice to keep the baby, not always, but I realize every situation is different. I mean, I've heard people say, you know, "Oh, I'd never give up my baby and I'd never give my baby up," but I also know the kind of life they can provide for the child can be pretty tough too.

Other women, like Susan, voiced respect for the birth mother's choice to relinquish. The women respected the birth mother also by remaining quiet—choosing not to share certain information about the birth mother in consideration of her privacy.

All of the mothers, irrespective of the child's race, had to strike a delicate balance. They have to think about how they portray the birth mother to not just others, but in addition, to their children. Women voiced hope that the birth mother had gone on to lead a happy life unscarred by her choice to relinquish, as did Deborah when thinking about her son's birth mother in Korea. "I use to pray for Tom's birth mother a lot the first year we had him. I kind of grieved for her."

While the general tone was of sympathetic empathy with the birth mother, there were moments of uncertainty. Mary, a mother of Korean children, articulated the belief that her children's birth mothers were brave for relinquishing but that she herself could not imagine doing so. "Yeah, I just can't image [relinquishing]. You know, they [the social workers] tell you all these things about how they're doing it for the babies and I still can't imagine. I just can't."

The most complicated portrayals of the birth mother arose in discussions about failed adoptions or the threat thereof. Failed adoptions were associated only with White birth mothers, both those relinquishing White and Biracial children. Tera expressed well the depth of emotions she experienced as she recalled the tense weeks after the birth of her child when the birth mother could not bring herself to sign the necessary legal documents to officially relinquish. "It was hard. There are times when you hate her, you love her. It's just, you know, nobody was rational." Tera's adoption proceeding ended in a successful placement. In other cases, failure occured. In these situations, the prospective adoptive mother tried to be understanding and sympathetic toward the birth mother while at the same time guarding her own interests. Deborah reflected on her experience with a failed adoption in which the child entered their home only to be removed a short time later. She tried to quiet ill thoughts that the birth mother possibly used them to pay medical bills, "I have that wonder about it [the failed adoption] being a scam, but I don't think that's what it was. I may just be naive, but I think that she really loved the baby. I know that she really loved the baby. So I know that the baby's going to be OK." Deborah resolved her trepidation through a sympathetic understanding of the birth mother's love for the child. More than through just a sympathetic understanding of the birth mother, many women related to her maternally.

Elaine literally felt herself to be a mother figure to the prospective birth mother. She cared and tended to the birth mother, taking her to doctor's appointments and buying her maternity clothes during her pregnancy, only for the birth mother to decide eventually against relinquishing:

I spent a lot of time with her [the prospective birth mother] and I felt like I was a mother to her. I really felt that's why I really couldn't be angry with her, and I don't think she used me. I bought her some maternity clothes and she offered to give them back to me, what am I going to do with maternity clothes, you know? But, I don't think she was out to use me. I know situations where people have felt used and I didn't feel used. I think she was just confused and emotional, and couldn't go through with it. I can understand that, you know, I could really, because I had grown to think of her as somebody who needed nurturing, because I had spent time with her, because I was concerned about her health, not just because I was concerned about the child she was carrying, but because I was concerned about her, too.

The extension of maternal feelings and thoughts to the birth mother emerged not simply when failed adoptions were recollected. A maternal voice was extended to White birth mothers more than to the other birth mothers because White birth mothers were more often physically and socially present, and because of their young age. One mother explained that she and her husband sought to find their child's birth mother after learning that she faced financial and emotional difficulties. Involved in an open adoption situation with the birth mother, Tera even regretted that she could not intervene on the birth mother's behalf as she watched her make unwise life choices:

She's [the birth mother] trying to get her life back together, which she's been trying to do that ever since we've known her. It's hard. You want to step in and just say, "Melinda, now, if you do this, if you finish college, you'll do better and if you dump Adam and quit this destructive relationship." He would hurt her and it was not a good relationship in any way. If you do that and do this, you want to just kind of step in, but you can't.

In most of the above cases, an adoptive mother extended her maternal self to the birth mother when she was within physical sight and this translated into her being White. Further inspection of the narratives reveals that renditions of the birth mother varied not only by her race, but also by the race of the child. Consider White birth mothers who relinquished White children.

Most noticeable about the White birth mothers with White children was that they were in some sense part of the same community as the adoptive parents. Often this was a matter of conscious design.[11] In five out of the seven White adoptions, the birth mothers chose the adoptive families. The adopting women had to win over birth mothers in order to receive their children, and often by stressing the similarities between them. They were connected through mutual friends or the assurance that their children would get a religious background similar to the birth mother's own. "She wanted a Baptist. She was a Baptist young lady and she wanted a Baptist family," Judith shared. Although the women might share perhaps a religious orientation, most of the women did not maintain ongoing, in-person contact with the birth mother. Only one mother in the group had an open adoption. The most common practice involved periodically sending pictures and letters to the birth mother through the adopting agency acting as intermediary.[12]

Three of the women with White children said that the birth mother was a high school student or, in one mother's words, "very young." Most often she was construed as a "student" who decided to relinquish in order to realize educational and professional dreams. One adoptive mother, Kathy, compared herself to birth mothers as follows, "I've finished school. I have a career. We have a stable marriage. I have financial resources. I have a support system. I have a husband. So in those ways, I think I'm different. I'm ready. I was ready to be a mom and I had achieved the personal and educational goals that I had set and I was ready to be a mom. So that's different." Commonly the White birth mother had no previous children, but in the adoptive mother's estimation would sometime in the future settle down to family life when financially and socially ready. As Judith explained, her daughter's birth mother now leads a productive life. "I know she's [the birth mother] married and has gotten her degree in elementary education, is very happy. And I'm sure will have a family before too long."

Perhaps the most interesting feature of their narratives was that this group of women used the word "unselfish" to describe the White birth mother—used much less frequently by the adoptive mothers with children of another race and with less regularity of the White woman relinquishing a Biracial child. Judith echoed these sentiments when thinking of her children's birth mothers:

I have wondered many times if I had been in their shoes, would I have had the courage to do what they did, because what they did was unselfish. I think that I would tend to be selfish, and I've asked myself many times with tears rolling down my face, as they were babies, if I knew that handing this baby over to somebody else would truly, truly be the very best thing for them, would I do it? And I've not answered that question because I truly couldn't know until I was in that position. But they have to be very loving, warm, caring individuals.

This thankful rhetoric reflected a number of things that included the value placed on White babies and the undeniable difficulty to receive such babies.

Portrayals of the Asian birth mother differed in part due to the simple fact that she resided at a distance, both figuratively and physically. Little information about the birth mother and parents was the norm. Some of the women cited this as an appealing feature of their adoptions, while others longed for more information. Despite a dearth of information, women with Asian children also voiced respect and gratefulness toward the birth mother. Megan, anticipating the birth mother's concern for her daughter's well-being, wished that she could allay her worries. "I wonder if the birth mother was remembering that this was the day that she had a daughter. I found myself wishing there was some way I could telepathically let her know that all of her dreams for her daughter were coming true or on their way to." Unlike the other the birth mothers, however, the Asian birth mothers were tied to their cultural contexts. The pressures of Chinese and Korean culture, forces outside of their control, pushed them to relinquish, as Andrea elaborated:

The social workers gave us stuff to read about the social pressures on unmarried girls who get pregnant and how adoption really is a good solution for these girls and their babies. Because they, at least at the time that our son was born, we knew that a child born out-of-wedlock probably won't get to go to school for very long, won't have any friends, won't be able to get a job, won't be able to get married if they don't have a family name. Family name and bloodline is very important in Korea.

The Asian birth mother became a culturally defined objective figure—this held particularly of Chinese adoptions where information was scarce. Megan could not even speculate where her daughter's birth mother fit on the economic scale, "There's no way to know where her family fit on the economic scale, because families that are very poor, but also families that are middle class are not able to keep their baby girls, so it doesn't necessarily mean that she came from a very poor family." The challenge for these mothers was to present their child's culture of origin with respect and reverence even when it would reject their child.

Respect for Asian culture and birth mothers, both Chinese and Korean, surfaced in talk comparing them to domestic birth mothers. The Asian birth mother was thought to have a better diet than the average American mother-to-be, both White and Black, and less likely to use drugs. According to Deborah, for example, "It was more important to me that the child had been well cared for. And there is not as much trouble with drugs with Korea. You know, care of the birth parent and that kind of stuff, it's not as much of an issue. And that was a concern of mine."

Virtually every mother discussed the possibility of meeting the birth mother at some point should their child express an interest in this. Future trips to Korea or China were almost a given. Of course, hopes for identifying the Chinese birth mother were virtually nonexistent given that she abandoned anonymously in a public setting:

The babies are taken usually to a public place where they're found quickly. They're taken to markets or train stations, bus stations, hospitals sometimes directly to the orphanage. They're left in places where they will be found quickly, but there's no record of it at all. Sometimes babies will have notes left with them with their birth date, or just sort of a plea to take care of my child. But there was nothing left, no note, I think with any of the babies in our group and they were left in all different places, but all public places. Yeah, that's one of the things about Chinese adoption and probably, I would guess, an awful lot of international adoptions is that there's no tracing the birth family.

Characterizations of the birth mothers in the Black and Biracial group also diverged from the ones presented of the Asian birth mother to some extent because she was not off in the distance. Indeed, three of the women maintained open adoptions with the birth mother. Birth mothers in this group were both White and Black. In some families with two children, one child had a Black birth mother and the other a White one. As I said above, ongoing contact with the birth mother varied by race, with White birth mothers more present than Black ones. In one family with two open adoptions, the child with the White birth mother knew his birth mother much better than did the child with the Black birth mother. It might not be surprising that, of the three mothers with open adoptions in the Black and Biracial group, only one of the birth mothers was Black. Many factors may account for the Black birth mother keeping her distance, including the birth mother not wanting to acknowledge that she relinquished—a practice not traditionally associated with the Black community. Racial differences between herself and the adoptive parents might also discourage frequent interactions.

Other curious arrangements emerged. The Black birth mothers were construed by the adoptive mothers as women already with children, whereas the White birth mother, as noted earlier, was usually understood to be young and to have become pregnant before she was ready to mother. With this in mind, the Black birth mother could perhaps be seen as in a financial bind; hence, little language of unselfishness was applied to her. One mother explained that her son's birth mother was a 30-year-old woman and that her child was the birth mother's ninth. Elaine talked similarly about the situation of her daughter's Black birth mother and why she did not think about her on a regular basis. "Well, I do [think about the birth mother]. I guess because she has five other children, I know she's got a lot on her plate as it is." Interestingly enough, however, the White young woman who relinquished Biracial children was also not uniformly characterized as unselfish. More often, she exemplified immaturity, as did the White birth mothers relinquishing White children. For Karen, the mother of two Biracial children, one with a White birth mother and the other with a Black one, stark differences between the birth mothers existed. Karen wondered out loud whether the White birth mother was coerced into relinquishing while the Black birth mother simply was not interested in raising children:

She was 19, so she wasn't a child, but I think she must of been like a college student . . . just very, very pretty. Oh, she was really a pretty girl. And very nice. I'm not sure that she really, really truly wanted to do this. Sometimes I wonder if maybe her parents didn't talk her into it. I don't know. It was just a different situation than with my other child. Everything about it was different. My other child's birth mother had already had three other children by different fathers. She didn't have any of the children. Every time she had the baby, she gave it to the father.

In light of Karen's and the other women's words that distinguish the birth mothers racially, consideration can now be given to selected feminist articulations about birth mothers.

IMPERATIVE TO MOTHER

Mothering Imperatives: Selected Feminists on Birth Mothers

According to Rickie Solinger (1992, 2001), treatment of and sentiments toward birth mothers expose cultural biases and values associated with maternity. In her most recent work, *Beggars and Choosers,* Solinger argues that motherhood has become a class privilege. This can be gathered not simply from popular discourse, but also from public policies that discourage poor women from mothering. Focusing more on class than on race, she maintains that poor women are not considered good citizens and, accordingly, are not viewed as able mothers.[13] For Solinger, by the way, good citizens in our society are ones who participate in mass consumption. She thus ties reproductive behavior to marketplace behavior. Because poor women are not good consumers and cannot produce good consumers, they are constructed and treated as though they are not qualified to mother (Solinger 2001: 223).

In *Wake Up Little Susie*, Solinger places current notions of maternity into historical contexts. During the 1950s, according to Solinger, a White, pregnant, unwed "girl" was cast away to hide her pregnancy and to relinquish her child to others who were more fit to raise it. By isolating herself and relinquishing, she could overcome the stigma associated with her "illegitimate" actions. In contrast, the unwed Black woman was disregarded since her babies carried little monetary value; consequently the need to isolate her was rendered unimportant. Although Solinger, in many respects, looks back at a time when unwed, pregnant, White women fled to Florence Crittendon Homes, the racially based sentiments she speaks of linger today; this is evidenced by the narratives.

Mothering Imperatives and Birth Mothers: Selected Feminists and the Women's Words

As noted previously, women with White children more often described the White birth mothers as unselfish than did the mothers with Asian, Black, or Biracial children. In characterizing them as unselfish, the women indirectly alluded to the positive value placed on White children, which pervades the adoption landscape. Joanna and Katherine, for example, spoke of practices initiated by adoption agencies to court and attract White birth mothers. In making it financially desirous for the White woman to relinquish, these practices perpetuate the ideology of capitalism. The sacredness and scarcity of the White child meant that the White birth mother avoided keeping the child or even from aborting. Judith thanked the birth mother for making a soulful choice and relinquishing, "She was in a very difficult situation and she withstood a lot of pressure, because she could have terminated the pregnancy. I think it was her religious convictions that would not allow her to do that and still feel comfortable with herself. Then again, it was partially her religious convictions and partially her life situation that made her feel that adoption was the best choice for her." Many of the women, regardless of the child's race, expressed thankfulness toward the birth mother. Yet, they did not necessarily use the language of selfishness and unselfishness in speaking of her. Indeed, as indicated, the White birth mother with a Biracial child was not characterized as acting unselfishly—this could be because the White mother relinquishing a White child had a choice, while the other birth mothers were thought to be in a bind.

Solinger's description resonates with this work. All of the birth mothers made sacrifices, but the language of unselfishness intimates that the White woman made significant sacrifices. Characterizations of the White birth mother reflect the adoptive mother's attempt to negotiate mothering imperatives with notions of fitness. Specifically, the adoptive mother recognizes that White women are encouraged to have valuable White children, but that only certain White women are qualified to rear the children (Solinger 1992, 2001). The White birth mother with the White child was unselfish in relinquishing, but she might not be equipped to be an able mother because of her age or financial standing, among other factors. Perhaps, then, it is misguided to say that the White birth mother with a White child experienced pressures to mother. Rather, the pressure was placed on physically having the child and handing the baby over to others.

Fit Mothers: Birth Mothers and Mothering Well

While confirming my understanding of mothering imperatives, the women's narratives spoke of fitness in a mixed fashion that supported as well as challenged my presumption. A general sentiment surfaced to the effect that there are ages too old and too young to mother. Often the women referred to themselves as too old and to the birth mother as too young. On several occasions I heard that, as they approached 40, the thought of becoming a new mother was unappealing. In contrast, the birth mother was often thought to be unready for motherhood because she was just entering her twenties or, if her age was not a factor, she was unmarried.

Although many of the women intimated that there are appropriate ages to mother, they differed in their emphasis on class. When speaking of the birth mother, some of the women insinuated that mothering well necessitates a middle- or upper-class standing. According to Susan, the birth mother could not keep the baby in part because she recognized her own financial limitations, "I've heard people say, you know, 'Oh, you know, I'd never give up my baby and I'd never give my baby up,' but I also know the kind of life they can provide for the child can be pretty tough too." As was the case of so many of the other women, Susan voiced respect for the birth mother's ultimate decision to relinquish in the face of others' consternation. As just mentioned, the women, particularly when discussing relinquished White children, struggled to resolve contradictions between their perceptions of mothering imperatives and notions of fitness. The White birth mother was "good" for having the strong constitution required to both have the child and to relinquish, recognizing that she was not able to mother at the time. One mother, Judith, resolved this tension by claiming that the birth mother, with increased age, financial and marital stability, went on to have a family of her own.

Meanwhile, the women with Asian, Black, or Biracial children made fewer overtures to the imperative to mother and instead, commented predominantly about fitness.[14] According to the women with Korean children, the Korean birth mother had to "fit" into the rigid Korean notion of appropriate mothering. Most of the women with Korean children believed that these women relinquished their children because the fitness standards in Korea are too restrictive [they gathered their understanding of Korean birth mothers from adoption social workers and agencies]. Because information about the Asian birth mother was limited, the adoptive mothers worked only in generalities. The imperative to mother was not invoked often in connection with the birth mothers of Black and Biracial children: the epithet "unselfish" was inconsistently applied to her. Rather, it was related, her ability to mother was hindered because of her age, education, financial capabilities, or commitment to other children. In their narratives, then, the women had to reconcile notions of fitness with images of the birth mother they provided to their children and others.

While the women had to negotiate their own renditions of fitness to others, they also had to circumvent popular conceptions of fitness. Some of the women rejected the proposition that good mothers and parents generally are financially secure. Carol, a transracial adoptive mother, quit her volunteer work at an adoption agency after noticing that other workers equated good parenting with high incomes. Deborah, a mother of Asian children, reacted to my probing about her children's birth mothers with a note of irritation that people assume the birth mothers are poor— to counteract such thinking Deborah chose to talk about birth mothers' personalities.

In thinking about notions of fitness and age-appropriate mothering, I was attentive to such facts as that a girl who gives birth in high school, without financial means might be socially ostracized. Additionally, I was curious whether becoming a career woman who delays motherhood negatively influences interpretations of the young mother. On the flip side, Do professional women who postpone mothering experience the negative effects of a work-oriented society that does not permit women to step aside to mother at a younger age? At the conclusion of this project, I also consider whether there really exists a more opportune time to have children. Certainly, as Kathy recognized, being ready to mother is important. Here, again, is Kathy's characterization of herself in comparison to the typical White birth mother, "I've finished school. I have a career. We have a stable marriage. I have financial resources. I have a support system. I have a husband. So in those ways, I think I'm different and you know, I'm ready. I was ready to be a mom and I had achieved the personal and educational goals that I had set and I was ready to be a mom. So that's different." Despite the virtues of stability it remains unclear whether a norm of mothering can exist without punishing those women who do not comply. Perhaps, a more opportune time to mother can exist, but be regarded as an ideal out of many women's reach. The narratives did not readily entertain these larger questions. Hence, as Solinger suggests, public policies should not punish those who do not mirror an ideal.

In any case, it must be recognized that all of the women, regardless of their child's race, had a difficult narrative chore before them in talking about the birth mothers. Given the current adoption ethos of the good birth mother, these women were required to understand and sympathize with the birth mother's position, who did something that many of them could not imagine doing—relinquish a child.[15] According to Barbara Yngvesson (1997), the birth mother may well represent chaos. She stands as a symbolic display of out-of-wedlock motherhood applicable to both the adoptive and nonadoptive family. Many of the women's narratives represented attempts to reconcile fitness and imperatives to mother in juxtaposition and in correspondence with "chaos." As suggested by Yngvesson, birth mothers appear "chaotic" because they defy wider notions and standards of maternal fitness.

OTHER MOTHERS

> "The Aunties would come around and try and talk to us a little bit about the babies or help us calm them down."

I have chosen to focus on the adoptive mothers' perceptions of the birth mothers to accentuate the relations between women and to consider how these relations varied by race. With similar intent, I dedicate this section to "other mothers."[16] This category of women emerged when I found that, generally, the women talked about other female care providers. Other mothers most often surfaced during the adoption process, when the adoptive mother was initially receiving her child. Regardless of the race of this other mother, she, unlike the birth mother, was a maternal authority, often providing advice to the birth mother and, in addition, to the adoptive mother. Because these women were of the same race as the adopted children, at times they were thought to be more capable mothers than the adoptive mothers. The nature and character of these providers differed according to the race of the child and the birth mother. In the case of the White birth mother, for example, her own mother cropped up in the conversation. In the international context, the female provider was the foster care mother or the anonymous woman off the street who provided unsolicited advice. The White mother of Black and Biracial children spoke, finally, generally of Black women who could provide advice on how to control Black hair, among other things.

If the birth mother was White and young, inevitably her own mother figured into the conversation. Her mother pressured her either to relinquish or not to. Of interest here is how the adoptive mother described her relationship with the birth mother's mother or, as she is often called, the birth grandmother. The birth grandmother was someone with whom the adoptive mother felt more in common than with the birth mother because, among other reasons, she was the same age. Phyllis, one adoptive mother of a Biracial child, initially conversed primarily with the birth grandmother while the birth mother sat quietly in the background. In the case of Jan's open White-on-White adoption, she and the birth grandmother, a longtime friend, in many respects planned the adoption:

My girlfriend told me that she was having, you know, problems and stuff, "so if you need anyone to talk to, I can listen." She told me that her daughter was pregnant and was only 15. And I said, "You're going to be a grandma." And we had looked into adoption by then. We had gone to international, whatever they call it, orientation, seminar, and she said, "Oh, yeah, but she's gonna give him up for adoption." They knew it was a boy. And once she said that, I said, "Oh my goodness, would she consider us as the adoptive parents?" And she got very excited about it and said, "Are you serious?" And I said, "Well, I am. I suppose I should really talk to my husband about it." And she said, "Well, I can I give you a call back tomorrow." And she talked to her husband and her daughter and I talked to him.

In the above situation, the birth grandmother facilitated the adoption; in other cases, she hindered the process. A successful adoption for Judith rested on the birth mother defying her own mother's desires:

Her mother had a very difficult time. Her mother did not want her to place the baby. I'm calling to see what's going on and they [adoption social workers] said that the mother was still there and that they had planned on not calling us until they saw that they were both leaving without the baby, because, they were real concerned. But she [the social worker] said, she thought that she was going to hang tough, but she really wouldn't be sure until they left without the baby. She [the birth mother] spent quite a bit of time with the baby and I have pictures of her holding the baby.

In the above scenario, the birth mother persevered or "hung tough" despite her own mother's pressures. In other cases, the birth grandmother contributed to the failed adoption attempt. Elaine recognized that she experienced a failed adoption because the birth mother chose not to go against her own mother's wishes:

She [the prospective birth mother] said she was going to keep it, because her mother had said to her that she would disown her if she gave up the baby. Her mother lived some place else and her mother obviously was doing nothing for her anyway and yet, her mother said she'd disown her and this was the most important thing. She couldn't give up this second child because her mother would disown her and, I mean, the girl was torn over it.

According to Elaine, the uninvolved mother carried too much influence. Tera also disapproved of the birth grandmother's actions, in this instance, with the birth grandmother's insistence that a Biracial child must be relinquished. "The whole racial thing . . . her mother [the birth mother's mother] had told her when our son was born that if he was White, we'd help you raise him, but you're on your own basically if you want to keep this baby."

As I said, characterizations of the White birth mother's own mother ranged from a co-planner or even friend to someone interfering. A couple patterns emerged: the birth mother's mother arose in conversation with some regularity when the birth mother was young and White; the birth grandmother exerted influence over the adoption outcome; and, by and large, the adoptive mother constructed the birth grandmother according to the adoption outcome.

The birth mother's mother did not figure in the narratives about adoptions of Asian children. Rather, foster mothers entered the narratives—a role broached by some other women, but more often by the mothers with Asian children, given that foster mothers were virtually the only other mother figures available to the adoptive mothers. As in the case of the birth mother's mother, characterizations of the foster mother varied. Andrea, for instance, expressed unconditional appreciation toward her son's foster mother, "He had a wonderful foster mother, a wonderful foster. We got pictures of her later. She had sent a gift and a beautiful letter for him, pictures of her crying the day, the last day she held him. She actually had him for most of that first year." Peggy, in contrast, who met her daughter's foster mother in Korea, found her attachment to her daughter disconcerting, "It was strange, because she had this foster mother. She had her from the time she was two months until she was four months, and she was heart broke. Usually kids stay a couple of months with her, and they're usually smaller. She [the foster mother] hardly wanted to hand her to me. I wanted to hold her and she's crying like no. It was kind of strange."

A more minor female care provider also figured into the mothers' stories: the female escort who traveled with the child from Korea to the United States. She, most often, was the person who first handed the baby to the awaiting arms of the adoptive mother. Mary relived the scene when she was first handed her baby and immediately felt herself to be the "appropriate" provider:

When he came off the plane with the lady who had been his escort, and she handed him to me and he was, "Whah," and he was soaked from head to toe. I mean, he didn't even have a diaper on, you know, those little diaper liners. He had one of those and rubber pants. Evidently, they just hadn't brought enough diapers with them and he was just absolutely soaked and crying and as soon as I changed him and got him dry, he just put his arms around my neck and laid his head down and it was just like I'd always had him.

In contrast, Elizabeth observed that her infant daughter simply looked better in the arms of the escort, whose skin color and physical build matched those of her daughter's.

Given that only two of the women with Asian children traveled to receive their children, most of these adoptive mothers encountered only the Asian female escort. The two women who visited the country of origin, however, encountered a cultural standard and ethos that permitted the woman on the street the liberty to volunteer her mothering skills to others. So-called "Aunties" helped new mothers at the orphanage in China acclimate to their children; women on the street offered unsolicited advice. The most striking example of this occurred when Peggy journeyed to Korea to receive her daughter:

We took the subway everywhere. We didn't take taxis, 'cause we were on a limited budget. And I didn't realize that the [foster] mother had long johns on, a T-shirt, a regular outfit, all these layers on [the baby]. I mean, in Korea the people don't open the windows on the subway even though it's hot. She was just screaming her head off. Finally, some Korean women just took her from me and they're peeling layers off and passing her and so the subways are like in New York when it's really crowded. And I was like, I'll never see her again and they were all trying to take the papers and blowing on her. That was kind of scary, because there for about ten minutes I had no idea, but when we were about to get off, I got her back.

In the cultural context of the relatively homogeneous home countries, there exists a familiarity whereby women have a sense of ownership for other children and count as "Aunties" to anonymous children on the street. Two women remarked that they had experienced similar encounters in the United States where Koreans felt ownership for their children. One mother spoke of Asian neighbors intimating that they were the rightful owners of her children. Strange scenarios emerged like the one Andrea conveyed where a Korean woman tried traditional Korean techniques on her son to calm him:

But then there was another Korean mother who when we first got our son tried to hold him the way a Korean mother holds a baby and tried to speak Korean to him, and he became hysterical and wouldn't have anything to do with her and would be comforted when I would hold him and that was very hard for her. She didn't understand how a Korean child would not respond to all the Korean things that she was doing. He was 11 months old then and it might of scared him.

According to Andrea, the interaction proved more uncomfortable for the Korean mother than herself. Most often, however, the Asian woman on the street or in the neighborhood in this country shows little interest in the adopted child, or, at least, her interpretations of the adoptive relationship can not be deciphered by the adoptive mother.

Women with Black children regarded the woman of color or the woman from her child's cultural heritage in a like manner. She was consulted for, among other things, advice on how to care for the Black child's hair. Some mothers pursued this voluntarily, as did Karen once she realized that the foster family did not know how to care for Black hair:

The people [foster parents], bless their souls, I loved them, the people that kept her, but they did not know how to take care of her hair. Well, she has that typical Black hair. Well, I learned right away what to do. But they didn't know what to do. They would wash it. They washed it and that was basically all they did, so when we got her, her hair was like one little fuzz ball. I mean it was really cute. It looked like a little Afro, 'cause she had a head full of hair. And they loved her. They gave her everything she needed. They didn't know how to take care of her and it was so funny, because I didn't know what to do either, but I had a girlfriend that I worked with who was Black and I called her long-distance and I said, "HELP! I've got to have help, you've got to help me, what do I do?" and she told me over the phone. We talked quite a bit just so that I could get use to taking care of a Black child, a baby. She said, she needs lotion, lots and lots of lotion, because their skin gets very dry and there's things you do for them that you don't have to do for yourself because I'm not Black. But I learned.

Not only did some of the mothers seek out Black women's advice about caring for the Black child, but, in addition, one mother, in particular, Elizabeth, anticipated that Black women would evaluate her mothering skills on the basis of her ability to control Black hair or to care for Black skin. Elizabeth kept in the back of her mind a friend's experience. At church, the friend happened upon a Black woman applying lotion to her Black, adopted daughter's body, while proclaiming in front of a crowd of other Black women that her mother should never let her out of the house looking so chalky. With this vivid image, Elizabeth vowed never to let her daughter leave home "chalky." Elizabeth's story exemplified how other mothers were largely constructed as fit mothers, particularly when they were of the same race as the child. Indeed, in Elizabeth's mind, these women stood ready to judge the mothering capacities of the adoptive mother.

"Other mothers," according to Patricia Hill Collins are "those who help build community institutions and fight for the welfare of their neighbors" (Naples 1998: 115). With this in mind, other mothers practice broad-based mothering as they offer maternal care to others without biological connections to them (Naples 1998: 119). In Twine's (1999) estimation, relationships with other mothers are an essential survival strategy for White mothers with Biracial children. In the women's narratives, other mothers fit Collins's specification, particularly if the women concerned were Asian or Black. These other mothers stood ready to intervene on the child's behalf and believed themselves able to meet the child's needs—perhaps even better equipped to do so than the adoptive mother. What is clear from the women's talk about other mothers, as well as from their narratives about birth mothers, is that the adoptive mothers' own maternal identities developed in relation to other women with whom they regarded as both able and unable to mother. The adoptive mothers' own maternal identity is explored in the following chapter.

SUMMARY

This chapter has provided thick description on other mothers, birth mothers, adoption processes, and fertility treatments. As should now be clear, maternal matters were organized around race. The racial perceptions described here, however, occurred on multiple levels. As a rule, blatant as well as subtle racial distinctions were categorized by reference to the adopted child's race. In those moments when the child's race did not matter, the adoptive women's did—White. Their infertility talk stands as case in point: The women's infertility talk was the same regardless of the race of their children because they experienced infertility and infertility treatments from the perspective of their White [and middle-class] statuses. As discussed, popular cultural notions of fertility fall along racial as well as class lines (Gordon 1990; Tsing 1990). The common perception is that Black women produce too many babies and Whites too few, unless, of course, the White woman is poor and on welfare (Abramovitz 2000; Gordon 1990; Silva 1996). This partly racialized understanding of infertility surfaced in the narratives when White birth mothers were described as unselfish for relinquishing whereas Black birth mothers were described as having their hands full with other children.

The thick description provided here, then, is filtered through not only the women's race, and the race of their children, but, additionally, the larger racial climate. To complicate matters, racial positions and perceptions were also filtered through my own racial (and class) lens. With this said, let us review and summarize narrative likenesses that reflect the women's common identity as White, middle-class, adoptive mothers.

There were numerous ways that the women narrated their walk through motherhood in like manner. As I have said, their fertility talk was not filtered through the child's race. All families had to find their way through complicated adoption landscapes eventually to reach a child. Many of the women, regardless of the race of their child, were also fateful and even religious about their child's arrival into their home. They spoke of achieving an "opportunity" to mother; the women were grateful to the birth mothers for granting them this "opportunity." And the birth mother's presence ebbed and flowed in these mothers' lives—even if, more often than not, because most of the adoptions were not open ones, reference was to the birth mother's symbolic presence.

These commonalities reflect the women's shared status as White, middle-class adoptive mothers. The virtue of thick description is that it offers details—details that highlight differences in narrative patterns based on the race of the child.

While the adoption process overall was complicated for everyone, it varied according to race. The adoption process moved much more swiftly for those adopting Black and Biracial children who were "waiting." Bureaucratic snags in the home country figured into the narratives of the women adopting Asian children. And connections and pure luck brought families White children. Racial distinctions also came out in discussing the birth mothers. As discussed, the White birth mother with a White child was unselfish for relinquishing, a descriptive adjective not regularly applied to the Black or White birth mother with Black or Biracial children. The White birth mother, in addition, was usually understood to be without other children. In contrast, the Black birth mother was believed to be tending to other children when she became pregnant with another. The Asian birth mother, meanwhile, was situated somewhere between the White and Black ones. The language of unselfishness was not applied to her with the same regularity it was to the White woman. She was not, however, constructed according to her fertility, but instead by reference to cultural constraints such as cultural taboos against single motherhood.

In looking back at the patterns that emerged from the racially categorized narratives, various ideas that generated this work were alternately challenged and reinforced. Unlike many of the women, I entered this project attentive to the political. Contrary to Raymond's (1993) perception, however, the women did not completely ignore the political. Rather, the women most often mentioned politically charged topics, like adoption costs, but then chose to depreciate its significance to their own situations. I also initiated this work thinking about the oppressive nature of mothering imperatives (Rich 1976). These imperatives surfaced in the interviews as something differentially applied depending on race. Yet, the work also uncovered that a focus on the imperative to mother was somewhat misguided as it relates to the adoptive mothers themselves. They spoke, instead, of an imperative to nurture and recognized the gratification that accompanies nurturing work. Associated with the imperative to mother are notions and norms of mothering well and fitness. These mothers, in their descriptions of the birth mothers, had to negotiate and reconcile notions of fitness with characterizations of the "good birth mother." No such difficult narrative tasks existed when the women talked about other mothers; these women, particularly those who were Asian or Black, represented the essence of good mothering and felt some ownership of all children from their racial/ethnic background.

Before, in the next chapter, regarding how the women viewed themselves as mothers it must be said that the patterns that emerged in their talk were not in black and white in character, but in shades of gray. While a qualitative research eye encourages the availability of patterns, it also makes them more evasive. Patterns emerged, but were accompanied by conflicting details. Most of the women, for instance, had not encountered the critical resolve of the feminist arguments that grounded this work. This being the case, many of the women diffused the political quality of their daily lives. Others, however, were acutely aware of the political issues surrounding their adoptions, and still others simply hinted at political matters when they spoke, for example, of the costs associated with adoptions. Such attention to and awareness of detail comes with both disadvantages and advantages. Focus on subtleties can make the act of writing difficult because conflicting details impede asserting patterns with confidence. Part of the problem is that while I, the writer, am aware of the context in which the women spoke, I cannot fully relay the narrative terrain in this document. At the same time, however, it is through a qualitative lens that complexities become visible. Attentiveness to patterns as well as to exceptions also expands the work to engage new questions not posed initially.

I indulge in the above brief discussion because, as I said, it exposes, to some degree, the context in which this chapter was produced. The ambiguities surrounding qualitative work color the following examination of women's talk about being mothers.

NOTES

1. I do not focus on the linguistic patterns the women employed to talk about infertility. But one pattern that is noteworthy is that the women would speak of infertility as both singularly experienced and jointly undergone with their husbands even when the treatments were endured only by the women.

2. Of course, as Anne Tsing recognizes in her work, "Monster Stories: Women Charged with Perinatal Endangerment," race and class have a bearing on social understandings of fertility. Tsing found that the criminal justice system has the habit of punishing dark, single mothers for not "caring" for the fetus, while ignoring the White, college student and mother who engages in the same practices. There is also the common sentiment that Black women do not battle infertility. I encountered this belief when an adoption social worker told me that she had yet to see an infertile Black couple.

3. I struggle to distinguish fateful from religious language and vice versa. It seems clear to me that some of the women used what I would call fateful language whereas others employed religious language. I vaguely differentiate between the two whereby the former signifies that something is meant to be, while the latter constructs something as meant to be because of God's will.

4. I use the "selves," in sense of selves, purposefully, because many of the women talked about having several identities. They were, perhaps, mothers first, but they were also teachers, ministers, wives, friends, daughters, and the like.

5. What is curious is that Sammie, unlike most of the other women, was in an extremely open adoption and characterized herself as almost a joint "owner" of "her" child.

6. China, in contrast, prefers adoptive parents to be in their thirties.

7. Variation existed in their preferences for type of infants. Some of the women only wanted the very youngest infants. One mother, for example, did not want a baby over three months old. In contrast, two women had adopted both infants and older children. Their children also differed racially. What is interesting is that one of these mothers said that the racial difference was less important than the age of arrival in her bonding experience.

8. It is not surprising that these women would blur the distinction between special-needs and transracial adoption given that the official definition of special needs covers both children who are not White and those with medical needs.

9. Ruddick (1994) uses the term "mothering work." In doing so, she points out that mothering is based in practices, not biological determinism. She explains:

> When mothering is construed as *work* rather than an "identity" or fixed biological or legal relationship, people can be seen to engage in mothering with differing expense of time at various periods in their lives and in various and often changing sexual and social circumstances . . .

She continues:

> Mothering *work* is no longer distinctly feminine. A child is mothered by whoever protects, nurtures, and trains her. Although it is a material, social, and cultural fact that most mothers are now women, there is no difficulty in imagining men taking up mothering as easily as women—or conversely, women as easily declining to mother . . . (Ruddick 1994: 35)

While I think "mothering work" is a useful term, I, like Lovibond (1994), think that rendering maternal practices gender-neutral does not go far enough in challenging gender hierarchies.

10. Four of the women maintained open adoptions with the birth mothers. Of course, open adoptions do not take one form, but vary in degree and extent of "openness"—often depending on an agency's preference (Grotevant and McRoy 1998).

11. In domestic adoptions the birth mother often chooses the adoptive parents. This requires the prospective adoptive parents to write letters to the birth mothers describing why they would make good parents. Katherine thought about the "bizarre" quality of the process:

> It's such a humiliating thing to have to develop a marketing brochure to say, "Please give us your baby." We did it. We had pictures made, and the whole thing. It's sort of prostituting yourself. "Please see us as worthy, we really are good people," and there's a sort of humble begging quality to this process that you don't know to expect. Of course, in the end, it's all worthwhile, I mean, you don't care, you'd do anything, but it's just this whole process that it's just bizarre. It's just bizarre.

12. Most of the women portrayed themselves, rather than their husbands, as maintaining contact with the birth mother. They were the ones who wrote the yearly letters or sent pictures to the adoption agency to eventually reach the birth mother.

13. Although Solinger's is a class-based analysis, she does make overtures to race. She argues that women's role is to produce good citizens, and this sentiment is not applied to poor Black women who have never been considered citizens (Solinger 2001). It would be interesting to consider her arguments in relation to middle- and upper-class Black women.

14. As stated, the women with Asian, Black, or Biracial children less frequently characterized the birth mother as unselfish than did the women with White children. As transracial and transnational adoptive mothers, they, like the other adoptive mothers, did mention that they were selfish in their need and desire to have children. This attitude deflates the thought that they are saintly for nurturing a "special-needs" child. These women countered that they were receiving selfishly as well as giving.

15. Of course, this was not true of all the women. Some of the women could imagine relinquishing if in a similar position as the birth mothers. And one woman shared with me that she herself had relinquished a baby.

16. *Other mothers* is a term that comes from Black feminists (Gailey 2000).

CHAPTER 4

On Being a Mother

Coming to understand yourself as a mother in relation to other women and mothers is no doubt a common experience for all mothers, as we live together and share cultural images of the ideal mother. Contextualizing oneself as a mother in relation to other mothers may be particularly pertinent to the White adoptive mother of a Black child who seeks out women from her child's cultural background for assistance and even approval. In this and other ways, adoptive mothers come to know themselves as mothers in like as well as different fashions as do biological mothers.

In the previous chapter, other mothers, as part of the context and landscape by which adoptive mothers became mothers, was one focus area. In the present chapter, we meet the women the moment that they become mothers and beyond. Conversation excerpts offer a window into the initial moment when the women come to regard themselves as mothers, into others' responses to them as mothers and to their children, into their impressions of their husbands as fathers, and into interactions with their children. As in the preceding chapter, topics are organized around race with initial attention given to likenesses across races of the children and subsequent attention to pinpointing racial differences. Also following the regime of chapter 3, the women's talk about being mothers is compared with the feminist arguments that generated this work. The questions posed in this chapter that stay attentive to selected feminist arguments include, How do fitness standards apply to the women's own narrative portrayals of themselves as mothers? Do they engage political concerns when they encounter racially uncomfortable situations that their children present? I begin with the women's talk about their initial step into motherhood.

THE MOMENT: "I'M A MOM"

"I just kept telling myself you really are a mom after all this time."

"It is just total responsibility for another life, which is scary and cool."

Adoptive mothers, I was told, are distinctive because they consciously pursued motherhood. Virtually all of the women, irrespective of race, recognized that motherhood was an achieved status or an "opportunity" obtained through great effort. Kathy, among other women, constructed her hard journey to motherhood as a positive accomplishment, one contributing to her status as a good mother:

Adoptive parents are able to appreciate their children in a different way than families that biologically have children because we go through so much to have a family. It really is a concerted effort. It's a lot of hard work, so I think that once we have our child in our home, we're not as likely to take that child for granted, and I think we realize how fortunate we are to have children. Sometimes I think when things come easy to you, you just might not appreciate it.

After waiting in some cases years to become a mother, the first moment the mother held her baby was noted as an achievement. When Megan talked about "the moment" she received her child in the orphanage in China, in the company of other prospective adoptive parents she said:

You could just cut that energy in the room with a knife, because I was the first one, and every camera and every movie camera was on. Everybody was just, "Huh," and so I walked up there, and the Auntie walked in with this baby, who was just kind of wide-eyed, looking like, "What is going on?" But they didn't let me take her immediately. They had to check her name and check my name about twice to make sure they didn't hand me the wrong baby and then have to undo things. So then finally the Auntie just handed her to me and I first take her. I have a great picture of "the moment," and she's just looking at me like, "So you're the one!" All of the sudden, from one minute to the next, you're handed a baby and it's official; you're a mommy.

Most women spoke of bonding and feeling a sense of ownership with their child immediately, as did Joanna, a mother of a White child. "From the very first minute I felt like she was mine from the very first minute when they laid her she was mine and she felt like mine." Immediate bonding with the child might be expected given that so many of the women, including Andrea, talked about longing for the time that she could assume the mothering role:

The only time my identity was messed up was the month that we didn't have Peter, right before we got him, because I was already in mommy mode in my head, but there was no child. I wasn't a mother. And once he came home, I felt finally I am now who I am. I remember once my husband kind of saying the same. He said, people would say doesn't this change you and it was more of a feeling that no, we are finally now this is what we always were, and we just now were able to do it. It was what was going on before that was wrong.

Although filling the mothering role was often something long awaited, factors like adoption policies, health of the child, history of a failed adoption contributed to the speed at which the mother felt herself to be a mother.

Bureaucratic protocols aided or hampered the pace at which a mother came to know herself as a mother of a particular child. Karen recognized this as she acknowledged that the agency's policy facilitated her feeling like a mother:

When you try to have children and it all fails, everything just fails and the doctor finally says, "Well, I really don't think you'll ever get pregnant even if you have the in vitro, even whatever else we can do, I don't think you'll ever get pregnant." It's like a big loss. It's just a big shock to you, and you think, oh gosh, you're never going to have kids. And then here is this baby laying in your arms. I just thought, gosh, you really are a mom! This really is your baby, because with this agency you do not get the child until those parents, if there is two parents involved, their rights are completely terminated. And I think that's what is so special is knowing that they, the mother or the father, cannot come back and say, I want my baby back. It's just knowing that, and I thought this really is my baby.

The combined effects of official recognition, along with the distance of the birth mother or father, contributed to Megan feeling secure leaving China with her child:

When we left China, this baby is mine; now we're headed home, it's mine. Yeah, when you take off, 'cause even though there's not anything anybody's gonna come back and try and reclaim the baby in these situations, and really all of the paperwork is just a process to go through, but still every step validates it a little more. Once you get her U.S. visa, it's a little bit more validated. Every document that you add to your pile that lists you as the parent.

Conversely, the threat of a birth mother or father or even the living memory of a past failed adoption hindered some mothers from fully committing to their child initially. After months Elaine finally decided her daughter was hers:

There was the three months in which she was not in our home; there were ups and downs there too. I wasn't as committed or connected to her as I was with the failed adoption, and it was because I had gotten hurt with that situation that I thought, well, this may not work out. She has to be in your home, I've forgotten what it is now, three months or six months before they'll even legally process the adoption, and I think I really felt at that time she was mine, but before the time the legal adoption came through I realized she could be taken any time. But I really felt at that point that she was ours.

Regardless of her child's race, adoption policies as well as a history of a failed adoption influenced when a mother felt that her child was her own.

Irrespective of race, the child's personality also contributed to the pace of the bonding process for most of the women. Mothers explained that they had different "bonding" experiences with their children, as did Mary:

Tim, immediately. John, it was harder because he was not a cuddly baby. He was a baby who pushed away from you and cried, and we didn't know what it was, 'cause he was so much younger. He was more than a month younger. Tim was three and a half months, and he was not even quite two and a half months, and we thought it would be simple. Tim was so easy. We just picked him up and he was ours. It was immediate. John, picked him up and he pushed away. Oh, it was a long time before you could even hold him without him pushing on ya. It was like, leave me alone, even as little as he was.

The description Mary provided assumes that personality differences between her Korean sons accounted for their starkly disparate reactions to her. Throughout her narrative, similar patterns in the children's personalities re-emerged despite the fact that her sons were preteenagers. According to Mary, Tim grew to be highly identified with America, while John showed interest in those things Korean.

Mothers who had domestically adopted both Black and White children also took clues from their children in developing a sense of ownership and attachment to them. The children's initial response to the mother influenced the bonding process. More so than with the other mothers, moreover, the birth mother figured into how and when the women, specifically those with White children, perceived themselves as mothers. Respecting the birth mother's wishes pleased these mothers. Judith was thrilled that she fulfilled the birth mother's wishes that her daughter would have a sister, "I see Tina being protective of Viki. It really warms my heart, because I think, OK, that's what the birth mother wanted. She wanted her to have somebody in her corner besides her parents. She wanted her to have that big sister watching out for her."

More than simply gathering satisfaction as a mother by fulfilling the wants and wishes of the birth mother, these women mentioned feeling relieved when the birth mother recognized them as the mother. Jan felt grateful when she overheard the birth mother telling the child to go to "his mother." Some of the mothers, meanwhile, who had no contact with the birth mothers, wondered out loud whether or not the birth mothers would approve of their parenting efforts. Katherine conjured up a whole scenario where she happened upon her son's birth mother:

I think OK, I'm in church. I'm going to look up one day and she's going to be right there, and I'm going to know it and she's going to know it's me. Or it will be the day that I'm sitting with Eric and he's being a holy terror and I'm really pissed and I'm ready to drag him out by his hair, and she's going to look over and go, "Oh no, what have I done?" Or I'm standing in the check-out line at the grocery and I'm writing my check and I look up and I know it's her. What do you say? That's the thought processes that I have that there will be this chance meeting.

Katherine's fantasy meeting with the birth mother expressed the feeling not so much that the birth mother would arrive looking to reclaim her child, but instead that she stood ready to evaluate Katherine's mothering skills. Yet, lurking behind Katherine's narrative were questions of ownership. Somewhat uniformly, the women came to feel themselves to be their child's mother as they developed a sense of ownership for the child. I found that the degree of ownership that the women expressed toward their children differed by race. Mothers, in particular, of Black and Biracial children voiced the sentiment more than the others, that they were not the exclusive owners of their children. Further, within this group, those women most willing to acknowledge that their children belonged elsewhere were more likely to work for racial change [a topic addressed in the next chapter].

A virtually unchallenged understanding of themselves as their children's rightful mother was most noticeable for the mothers with White children. As Judith said, "I know they are a part of me and I'm a part of them very much so. They're mine and I'm theirs." While similar talk came from the women with Asian and Black and Biracial children, there were some hints that their children were not exclusively theirs.

Some of the women with Asian children mentioned that their children arrived longing for their Asian foster mother, as mentioned in the previous chapter. Andrea vividly described her son's experience:

He went through a little bit of grief. He was with us two or three days. He was old enough to know the Korean word, Oma, mommy. And the first night that we had him home my husband pointed to me and said, "Oma, Oma." He just was, no, he buried his face in the carpet and moaned, he didn't cry, he just moaned. It was awful. It was really heartbreaking, because he had a wonderful foster mother. It was really hard and it was surprising. It took me two weeks to believe that he really accepted me as his mother. I think he came to that conclusion earlier, but at two weeks I had to give him to somebody and he went crazy. He wouldn't let me out of his sight and all the sudden I realized he wanted me. It took me two weeks to believe it. Up until that point I just sort of felt like his baby-sitter, like I was watching somebody else's kid.

An additional feature either contributing or hindering to a sense of ownership, not mentioned among the women with Black and White children, was the child's health. When Megan saw her daughter through a temporary illness she understood herself to be her child's mother:

One of the things they did in the clinic [the clinic in China] was clean out her ears, cause she'd either had that infection for a long time or had previous infections. It was just really awful holding her down. She was just screaming. I thought, oh, my gosh, this is so painful for me to have to hold her that I really felt like I was her mother, you know, seeing her through that. But every step of the way you get more and more attached. Then she would respond to my voice first, so you realize she's beginning to know that this is the person that's going to be there. I'm sure it's just like with a baby you give birth to when they actually hand the baby to you, she's a stranger, but still there's some kind of an attachment there and every little step is something more.

In the scenario above it could be construed that the illness facilitated a sense of motherhood because the mother was immediately required to care for the child. For Andrea, however, her sense of attachment was challenged when her daughter arrived with an array of medical needs:

The thing that I noticed in the airport was that her eyes were crusted shut from infection and that was just really scary. I mean, you're standing next to the baggage claim and they put this really sick infant . . . her skin was gray and she couldn't open her eyes and she clearly couldn't breathe very well, because she was making this horrible noise every time she breathed. And they say, "Well, have a good life." There was a little note that said, "We know she has a cold and her medicine accompanies her." There was no medicine there, and it was far more than a slight cold. It was rough.

A couple of weeks after the child's arrival, Andrea recognized that her daughter's physical condition interfered with bonding:

With Ellen I can remember even a few weeks after we got her, maybe it was a few days after we got her, talking to my husband and saying, you know, she is so sick, we were afraid, maybe, to bond. We kept calling her "the baby." We didn't even call her Ellen for a long time. She was just "the baby" and I can remember saying it's OK if we just take really good care of her for now. It's true and it was enough for us to take really good care of her. It might have taken six months before I was sure that I loved her. I'm sure that it happened before then. I just didn't know. It was a gradual thing with her, because also she smelled so bad. I think it was the formula they were giving her. They shaved her head, because they had lice there. I use to joke, "Don't worry, hair will help. Hair will help." I knew that she was getting what she needed in terms of care. I mean, I held her all the time. I was with her almost 24 hours a day. I would not let her sleep in the crib. I just carried her and eventually she started responding and she was so hungry.

Alongside medical requirements influencing bonding experiences were cultural concerns. The mothers who mentioned that Asian neighbors assumed some ownership of their children recognized the fragile negotiation that transpires. At Chinese restaurants this was brought to Peggy's attention, "Whenever we go out to eat to a Chinese restaurant and the Chinese people, I guess they assume she's Chinese, cause there's such an influx of Chinese adoptions in this area, pick her up and take her to the kitchen. She loves looking at Chinese faces or Asian faces, and you wouldn't think. She only spent six months in Korea, but she shows a big preference." Peggy explained with interest her daughter's affinity for Asian faces without it having a bearing on her sense that her daughter belongs with her. Meanwhile, Mary described her son's inability to respond appropriately to an elderly Korean woman at a picnic for Koreans and adoptive families with Korean children:

There's a lot of picnics and things with them [Koreans]. And they'd go up to my son and say something to him in Korean. This one time he sat in this really old lady's chair and he didn't know it was her chair, cause she was sitting at a table by herself at the picnic. And we all kind of went up and we were standing there, and he sat in this chair and she walked up to him and said something to him in Korean. He just kind of looked at her and didn't do anything. She kept standing there looking at him and then she said something else to him in Korean and, of course, he still didn't answer her. And finally I said, "I think you should get up; that might be her chair," 'cause in Korea you really respect your elders and he jumped up and she sat down and kind of looked at him like what's the matter with you, kid. There were chairs everywhere. I mean, it wasn't like it was the only chair in the place, but that was her chair. She wanted it. So, he was like, "I didn't know what she was saying." And I said, "Well, don't worry about it. I didn't know what she was saying either."

Although Mary relayed this story to me, she did not construct her son as belonging to another community other than her own, as exemplified in her response to her son not to worry because she did not understand the elderly Korean woman either. This response, instead, emphasized that her son was more like herself than like the Korean elder. Generally, the women with Asian children did not situate their children in the Asian community first. They acknowledged their children's "Asian-ness," but it did not preclude the children primarily belonging to them.

In contrast, mothers with Black and Biracial children, while maintaining a sense of ownership for their children, placed their children in another community. "Who am I to say who can love this child? He's not my possession. He's a gift. It is wrong not to share him." Remarks such as Sammie's were not uncommon among this group of women. Ownership was tied specifically to race as many of these mothers portrayed themselves as almost mothering for a community. In particular, their private mothering served another community to which their child belonged, and they did not. Indeed, throughout my conversations with Karen, she distinguished herself from her Black daughter. "She's different than me. Her skin is not my skin color and she knows she's Black. I've told her that she is Black. She knows it." Elaine responded to my question, "When did your daughter feel like your own?" in the following manner:

In one sense, always, since she came to the house when she was three months old, she's mine. Then I'm also aware that there are real differences in an adoptive situation and sometimes I feel that there's more responsibility because she's adopted. And I'm very aware of what has become a cliché —that African proverb that it takes a village to raise a child, especially because it's a transracial situation. I need Black people to help us give her a sense of identity, so because I feel I need the Black community to take her in, to help her with her sense of self, in that sense I feel she's not mine. She belongs to more people. So it's a very loaded question. I mean, in one sense I have, I'm sure, as deep as commitment to her as I would have to a biological child, but in another sense, because of the transracial, I'm aware of what I can't give her and what she needs, and so I'm very aware that I need the Black community to help.

Elaine exhibited a kind of quiet resolve that her daughter belongs both to her and elsewhere. At other times and for other women, as well, the notion of the child maintaining a kinship elsewhere could be uncomfortable. Carol, for example, spoke of waiting for the day her daughter would say something along the lines, "You don't understand because you're White." Even more vividly, Elizabeth envisioned a scene where she and her husband would arrive home only to find a "Go Home, Honkies" sign hanging on the door. As I detail later in this chapter, this fear is understandable because Black and Biracial children, as well as anonymous people on the street, often distinguish the White mother from her dark children.

Generating your sense of self as a mother from your children, however, crossed racial boundaries. Before closing this section, however, another narrative pattern must be introduced that does not correlate to racial groupings.

Regardless of race, many of the women simply felt good about themselves as mothers. "How do you feel adequate and inadequate as a mother?" elicited the following responses. Susan:

So when you asked about how do I feel adequate, and yes, I do because I feel like he's succeeding. So I have bad days, but I feel like overall this is a child . . . that he challenges the heck out of us sometimes, but when he gets in other environments, he gets along with the other kids. It's not just that he's intelligent and the teacher likes him, but he gets along with the kids and he respects.

Mary relayed an almost identical sentiment when she spoke of her Korean sons, "Well, all I have to do is look at them. They don't ever get in trouble.

They get good grades. They're good kids. They help around the house, so I know we're doing a good job. They're normal. Things seem to be going pretty well. I think that we have to be doing a good job if things are going that well." Echoes of a similar sort came from Carol who adopted transracially, "In our church Margaret is pretty much the oldest kid of the regular people that come. So pretty much everyone asks us for advice when it comes to parenting. It helps that she's turned out so well so far." In this quote, Carol acknowledged that she feels good about her mothering and parenting efforts because her daughter has turned out so well, leading others to respond favorably toward her.

It must be noted, however, that the women varied, to some extent, in how they chose to portray themselves. Certainly, all of the women were dedicated to their children, and this translated into their elevated sense of self-worth as mothers. There were women, however, who only wanted to share positive features of their mothering experiences. A couple of the mothers of Black children, in contrast, were overwhelmed with the racial difficulties they faced and openly shared their discouragement and sense of isolation. They remained, regardless, dedicated mothers. A final group gave a couple examples of when they felt stretched by the demands of motherhood and the added concerns of adoption, but stayed focused, by and large, on being devoted mothers.

Selected Feminists on Mothering "Fit-ly"

A multitude of things contribute to self-conceptions of the good mother and good parent. Sharon Hays, in her work, *The Cultural Contradictions of Mothering,* succinctly articulates the makings of a good mother. "In sum, the methods of appropriate child rearing are construed as child-centered, expert-guided, emotionally absorbing, labor-intensive, and financially expensive" (1996: 8). A dimension of appropriate child rearing of relevance here is the expert.

The "experts" play an important role in adoptive families because raising nonbiological children stands outside the norm. It is only in recent decades that so many White families have adopted children of another race and nationality, making this a relatively unfamiliar parenting experience. Of course, intra-race adoption has historically transpired informally. Latin and Black women have informally "adopted" children as their own without the aid of experts (Collins 1994). In these cases, the "expert" is the maternal figure found in the community. Of significance in the present context is whether experts contribute to the reliance on professionals to parent instead of intuitions and in addition, to women's self-alienation. Hays argues that parenting experts, among other factors, assist in the cultural understanding of mothering and parenting. Part of being a good mother is following expert advice, often at the expense of a woman's own intuitive sense to mother (Hays 1996).

Another feature of being a fit and good mother, according to cultural standards (Gordon 1994; Hays 1996), is intensive parenting. Most often, intensive parenting necessitates that the woman deny herself in order to meet the needs of her "priceless" child (Zelizer 1994). The child and his/her needs become the central focus of her life, relegating the woman's wants and desires to unimportance. In the past, children were wage earners and have evolved into precious beings, according to Zelizer (1994). Hays (1996) extends Zelizer's argument by asserting that the "priceless child" emerges at the expense of women. Women are supposed to discard themselves in order to provide the child with more than basic care; this sentiment is fueled by the underlying notion that there is no bad child. The women I interviewed certainly were intensive mothers. Mary shared with me that you cannot be selfish and be a mother.

The Women on Mothering "Fit-ly" according to Experts and Intensively

In our conversations fitness standards applied not solely to the birth mothers, as detailed in chapter 3, but to mothers and "parents" generally. I asked some of the women directly about their notions of "fit" and "good" mothers and parents. A couple of the women equated middle-class status with good parents, because, according to these mothers, members of the middle class spend time with their children. Pat and Mary, both mothers of Asian children, for instance, offered similar comments on this matter. Pat articulated the belief that parents need to be home to provide children with a sound family life:

I think you lose out in trying to parent without being around your kids all the time, but it's probably an old-fashioned viewpoint. But I really think that more people are coming around to feeling that they can't do everything and the tide is turning. People are realizing that it's really hard to keep working and spend time with your kids. But when my daughter was little, our neighbors across the street, they both work, and from the time their kids were born, they were in day care and they would all leave from the house at 7 in the morning and come back at 5 or 6 at night, and that's the norm for most people. A lot of people say that they don't have a choice financially and I think that's true for some people, but you can make the decision that you're going to drive your car until it has two hundred thousand miles on it and you're not going to go on vacations, and you can say well, that's because that's not as important as the way that we are going to set up our life. And so it's a whole value thing. There is no right or wrong, that's for sure. But sometimes I think that people have more choices than they think they have. But it's complicated. No question about it.

Mary uttered a similar sentiment when she spoke of rich and poor parents alike not giving their children the attention they require:

The biggest thing is you have to be there for them. You can be a poor parent who has to work 23 hours a day. You can be a rich parent who is climbing the ladder and thinks she has to work 23 hours a day, but you're not there for them either way. I don't care; you can't raise them if you're not there. So that's what I like about living here, everybody's kind of middle class and thinks they need to be home at night with their kids, but if you go too far east, then you get all these doctors and lawyers and they're never home and the kids are on their own all the time. Then you go back the other way and you can get the other extreme, where the kids are just running the streets, 'cause the parents don't care where they are, and this [her neighborhood] is just kind of middle-of-the-road.

Experts also figured into some of the women's narratives. Experts advised them about when to tell their children about adoption and helped them think about when to take their child to Korea. Interestingly enough, I found that the women with White and Asian children referred to experts more often than did those with Black and Biracial children. That is not to say the mothers with Black and Biracial children were totally inattentive to expert advice—this was not the case. Rather, experts were invoked less frequently in their narratives. Additionally, by and large, the mothers with Black and Biracial children were less likely to claim unconditionally that they were good mothers. It was certainly clear that the women with Black and Biracial children were less likely to participate in support groups than were the women with Asian children. Support groups offer a setting in which to share the latest adoption information and to gather expert advice. Yet, support group membership does not account for the difference because the women with White children also were not members. Instead, the women with Black and Biracial children faced more challenges and some of these women spoke openly of them such that their situations were not without racial difficulties entering the home whereas the other mothers placed racial concerns outside of the home.

Intensive mothering also surfaced in their narrations in association with the medically needy child. As I said in the previous chapter, medical concerns were predominantly associated with Asian children. What I failed to mention, however, was that few of these children had long-term and enduring problems. To reach a state of well-being required some of these mothers to frequent physicians and watch their children endure invasive surgeries. While children were going through the process of improving, these mothers were on constant duty. Take Andrea. Andrea, recall, was handed a baby with medical problems. It took a couple of years for Andrea's daughter to reach a healthy state:

She was full of infection. I never saw a child so infected. She couldn't open her eyes. She couldn't breath. I was furious for years that they even put her on the plane until I realized that if they hadn't put her on the plane, she probably would have died. She was really, really sick. She had spent all of her life in the hospital and hadn't really had a primary care giver, so she wasn't interested in making eye contact with anybody. She really was not interested. She was young enough that once she was given persistent care, she bounced back real fast, weeks and weeks and she was fine. Well, not fine, but she was making eye contact and smiling a lot, so it was very different. The first two years, the first year especially, we were in [with] the cardiologist or the plastic surgeon, so many doctors all the time, but she's way past all of that now. She's very healthy and we're very lucky. I don't plan to do it again. I'm glad I did it for her. I would do it for her again in a heartbeat, but it took too much out of me. I'm not willing to give that much again on purpose.

In a like manner, Deborah, confronted with her child's medical difficulties and more than the usual number of nights up, recognized that medical concerns affected the family, "Well, I guess having all the medical issues, we were different that way. Spent a lot of time at the doctors' offices. We have two doctor's appointments this afternoon. Do a lot of running back and that kind of thing. And that really does affect the family as a whole." Later in the conversation, Deborah talked about the possibility of adopting another child, but ruled out adopting another child with so many medical difficulties. Both Deborah and Andrea, who willingly gave of themselves to their children, recognized that they could not give so intensively again. The question that arises is how to understand these women with particular feminist arguments in mind.

Mothering Fit-ly and Intensively: A Response

Do notions of "good" mothers disregard women with medically demanding children? Could, contrarily, idealizations of the "good" mother be based in characterizations of the superhero or saintly mother who gives unselfishly? Given that the women often had been dubbed saints, I think otherwise. Intensive mothering standards indicate a norm of commitment whereby the mother is expected to give of herself, but is bound by expectations of the "normal" child—should she give too much, she may lessen her own personal gain. In other words, it could be said that too much exertion of maternal labor, decreases the value or gratification added to each unit of maternal work.

What of the expert in this context? In contrast to Hays's interpretation, the expert in the adoption setting maintains an ambiguous place. The expert may not simply malign women, but can be partly credited for making adoptions more open and less secretive. Many of the women acknowledged that adoption in the relatively recent past was shrouded in secrecy. According to Joanna, for example, it was secrecy that made adoption and adoptive children problematic in the past. Previously, adoptive parents hesitated even to tell their children they adopted them. Today, with the aid of expert advice, adoption has forsaken much of its dark shadows of concealment. Yet, the adoption experts had ulterior motives. Indeed, Yngvesson (1997) points to specific adoption experts, who, she says, sought to make adoptions more open in the hopes of luring White women to relinquish at a time when the availability of White babies was diminishing. Moreover, adoption experts assisted in originally making adoption a private and secretive transaction (Solinger 1992). Yngvesson explains that adoption experts during the 1950s sought to mimic biological families as much as possible and that secrecy helped achieve this goal. In this context, the experts sought to reproduce rather than to challenge the traditional family. In contrast, the Black woman who raised neighborhood children neither concealed that the children were not her biological own nor did she strive to replicate the traditional family (Yngvesson 1997).

Further complicating pronouncements of the expert in relation to adoption is that the expert may be neither the distant male figure nor the female social worker. The adoption industry is inundated by experts as witnessed by the number of references to physicians and attorneys in the women's narratives. But the "experts" are not just physicians and attorneys. They are also women and adoptive mothers. Hays's characterization of the expert as professional does not account for the number of adoptive mothers who write and talk about their mothering experiences to other mothers (Gilman 1987; Keefer and Schooler 2000; Wolff 1997). Unlike the expert woman and social worker who sought to alter maternal practices of poorer and darker women during the creation of the welfare state, this "expert" speaks to others empathetically (Gordon 1990). The "expert" then becomes the person with a unique viewpoint. She personally knows the family's experiences. Indeed, some adoption agencies are filled with workers who are adoptive parents themselves. The adoption world is not unique in this regard. It is, instead, part of a larger societal trend; drug rehabilitation programs, for instance, might be composed of workers who are themselves recovered. The thinking behind this trend is that only those with intimate knowledge can really "know" others' placement. Of import here is the signification of these experts for women.

This softer type of expert might be more insidious than the white-coated doctor, for she enlarges the scope of the Panoptic lens that Foucault envisioned (see chapter 1). This expert knows the day-to-day details of an adoptive mother's life and speaks openly of them. At the same time, it could be said that these experts signify liberation as some nonprofessional women are openly writing and talking to other women about their lives. The women's narratives bear out both statements. The women gathered comfort from other women who knew their experiences of infertility, for instance. Yet some of the women expressed self-doubt for not mothering in accord with how these "model" adoptive mothers write about their mothering (Wolff 1997).

On the whole, however, it is uncertain how much the expert contributed to these mothers' self-doubt as mothers. As noted, the women generally felt good about themselves as mothers. Although notions of goodness and fitness have their oppressive quality in that women reprimand themselves for not abiding by the experts, these women reaped the benefits of following expert advice and seeing results—that is, feeling good about themselves as mothers.[1] There is self-gratification for following the advice of experts, as well as gathering the accolades of others, be it professional "experts" or family members. Judith's own mother, for instance, was in the habit of telling her daughter that she was impressed with her mothering abilities. The women alluded to the power and respect that can be garnered from mothering work—something that Sara Ruddick, in "Maternal Thinking," recognizes.

Of course, it is essential to understand adoptive mothers' self-conceptions in correspondence with interpretations of the birth mothers. In the last chapter, when discussing the process by which these women became mothers, I pointed out that the White birth mother was often constructed as someone not ready or maybe not financially able to adopt. Solinger (2001) claims that the sentiment that only financially sound women should mother disparages poor women as unstable and unable to tend to their children. Solinger's focus is mostly on the birth mothers. What can be presently gathered is that the narratives, by and large, did promote the idea that the birth mothers were not ready and able to mother, because of their limited economic resources, among other factors. I might add that Solinger's work does not take into account something that surfaces in the interviews, namely, that the birth mothers do maintain some power as mothers [however slight it might be]. Several of the adoptive mothers felt relieved when the birth mother recognized them as the legitimate mother of the child. Adoptive mothers, faced with the cultural ethos that promotes biological ties as almost sacred, are, to varying degrees, vulnerable to the birth mothers' claims to the children (Gailey 2000). Katherine's narrative, for instance, pointed out the complicated position that both the adoptive and birth mothers hold as rightful and fit mothers. Katherine, remember, imagined that her son's birth mother would by chance catch her in a bad mothering moment, and that as a result his birth mother may regret that she placed the child in the wrong hands. With a biological, cultural, spiritual, and perhaps racial connection to the child, the birth mother has or is imagined to have the power to evaluate the adoptive mother's maternal capabilities (Modell 1997).

Lastly, it must be acknowledged that espying the presence of fitness standards in the women's words was not difficult even though it was not the intentional focus of many of the women and, as a result, most of the women did not consider fitness standards critically. It could be supposed that the birth and adoptive mothers both maintain a precarious position as legitimate and not-legitimate mothers. These adoptive mothers, for the most part, however, did not consciously locate themselves in a similar position with the birth mothers. Moreover, as I pointed out in chapter 2, what is most obvious is that many of the women do not characterize themselves as mothers, but rather as parents. In Pat's and Mary's narrative discussions that draw linkages between mothering and class, what is especially noticeable about their constructions was that they took the mother out of the picture through their emphasis on parenting. They disregarded the gendered expectations that usually require the woman to relinquish her outside work, if parents are to be home. In this sense, these mothers muffled gender. Yet, Mary, in particular, centered her parenting expectations on women. In a late moment in our conversation, she talked about a professional couple who ignored their child but, in the end, she faulted the mother, rather than both parents, for inattention. Following a larger narrative practice, many of the women mentioned political matters such as notions of fitness, but plucked these concerns out of their wider social and political contexts, and did not consider them in relation to their own families.

FATHERS

"He's a wonderful father and he's very involved."

"John Rosenmond yesterday was saying that in today's society fathers have become parenting aides. They do what they're told under supervision."

The women interviewed felt good about themselves as "parents," more so than as "mothers" per se, as I discussed in chapter 2. Many of the women did not distinguish and locate their child rearing experiences in maternity, irrespective of the race of the child. Rather, they described their voyage through "parenting" often in collaboration and juxtaposition with their husbands.

Through the use of parenting language they acknowledged their husbands' child rearing work, but more than paying respect to their husbands through this usage, they simply envisioned themselves as "parents" instead of "mothers." Even the two single mothers used parenting language. When the conversation was not tied to my mothering language, preference for the word "parenting" emerged. This was the case with Judith when she mentioned that her daughter learned about reproduction in the school lunch line, "Well, someone said something to her at school and then we had to, I had to tell her the correct story, because she was confused by what someone told her. It wasn't the right information in the lunch line in the cafeteria. So you have to just take a deep breath sometimes and go on as a parent, because you never know what's going to happen."

Beyond the women's natural inclination to use parenting language, there were other notable features of the conversations that related to fathers.

Race, in particular the race of the child, had little bearing on how the women talked about husbands and fathers. Of course, as was the case with fertility discussions, this was so because the women shared Whiteness with their husbands. Perhaps most noteworthy about the fathers and talk thereof is that up until this point they have lacked visibility in this work. I chose not to center attention on fathers because, among other factors, mothering experiences historically have been invisible. Of course, men traditionally have not been described as fathers first and have even gathered outside prestige and power from distancing themselves from their children.

With the central focus away from fathers, it might not be surprising that talk about the husband and fathers varied. Variability was built into the interview design. On most occasions, women were asked directly, "Reflecting on your family, do you have a 'traditional' relationship with your husband?" leaving the women to define "traditional." "In what ways do or do you not?" "How does this make you feel?" At other times, however, discussions about husbands and fathers emerged without my probing and, hence, were not contextualized by the label "traditional." As a result of the flexibility embedded into the interviews, patterns connecting the children's racial grouping to remarks about fathers were difficult to isolate. What I found, instead, was variability in the talk about the fathers that did not correspond to racial groupings. Variability even existed in the language the mothers used to talk about their husbands and relationships with them.

Some of the women used "we" to describe the laparoscopic surgeries performed on their bodies during infertility treatments. Others were in the habit of carrying out our entire conversations using the subject "I"— leaving the impression that they held the primary responsibility for infertility, adoption, and child rearing. Variability also emerged in how the women described their relationships with their husbands. Some of the women sometimes characterized their husbands as "parenting aides." Sammie even brought the "parenting aide" language to my attention when she said the following:

John Rosenmond yesterday was saying that in today's society fathers have become parenting aides. The mothers are the primary parent figures, and that it wasn't that way for previous generations, but that so much pressure has been put onto women to be the touchy feely, warm, self-esteem-based parenting style, which is embraced right now by psychology, that the family is the woman. The women are more sensitive and emotionally attuned, and they take more of that responsibility on and actually run interference between fathers who want to discipline the children. So fathers have become parenting aides. They do what they're told under supervision.

What surfaced with more certainty was that relatively few of the women acknowledged their husbands as parenting assistants, even when I asked directly. Even though Sammie, for instance, brought the above to my attention, she denied that it was applicable to her own family. Although some women did not talk about their husbands as parenting aides specifically, their words characterized their husbands as such: Primary responsibility rested with the mother, and the father helped out by playing with the child. Generally, moreover, regardless of the amount or quality of the father's efforts, the women were grateful for the father's participation. Leslie said:

I can plan and cook a meal a lot faster than he can, so I did that kind of stuff, but he did a lot of her care. During the night he use to get up all the time, cause she didn't want me, she wanted him. I do a lot more things. I plan a lot of their activities, but that's just what I do. It's just not something that he would normally think about. So, I think right now I would say maybe we're more traditional, probably. Like as they're growing older, I take more of the planning responsibility for them. But he's very involved with them. He's not a hands-off dad at all. He does everything, gives them baths. When I went to visit my parents, when my mother was in the hospital, I was gone for almost a week at a time, two times, he did everything and then people say, "Wow, he's such a good husband to do it." But it was like no question that he was capable of it.

Leslie's words resembled those of many other women, irrespective of the race of the child. Her relationship with her husband was described as relatively traditional. The woman took primary responsibility for the children, but it was to her liking or was a temporary arrangement while she stayed home with the kids or worked part-time.

A few of the women talked differently. Several expressed annoyance that their husbands were their child's playmate, while they disciplined and tended to basic upkeep. Elaine sounded like many of the other women when she said that she spends most of the time with her child. Unlike the other women, however, she was not completely pleased that the time spent with her child could not be as playful as it was for her husband:

He doesn't spend as much time with her as I do, so when he is able to spend time with her, he can focus 100 percent on her, which is the way she likes it. He will cater to her wishes and buy her things. You know, she wants to have candy, he'll let her have candy. If she wants to have soda, he'll let her have soda. I'm the one who says it's going to be too soon, you need to take a nap, or it's time to go to bed and you need to do this. And so I feel that I have to be more . . . I really can't just sit down and watch Sesame Street with her, and what he would do is just sit down and watch Sesame Street and call out for a pizza.

A small group of women expressed the sentiment that they were not in a traditional relationship. Tera, for example, expressed annoyance every time her father or someone else relegated her husband's fathering work to baby-sitting status or something like parental assistance work. When I asked her whether or not she lived in a traditional relationship she responded:

I'd say at this point in our lives right now, I'm working like one-third time; he's working two-thirds time. That's just because we made that decision to do it that way while the kids are little. I get upset with somebody, who says, "Oh, Ted's baby-sitting the kids." I'll say, "No he's not, he's being a father; that's what fathers do." I remember doing that to my dad. I went on a trip in January for a week, and while I was gone Ted was here with the kids, and I was telling my parents about going to this trip and my dad said, "Well, whose going to watch the kids?" I said, "Their father will; that's what fathers do, they watch their children when the mama's not around."

At other moments in the conversation, based on how she and Ted negotiated outside work, Tera did not characterize her relationship as traditional. This was a narrative practice employed by many of the women irrespective of whether or not they characterized their relationship as traditional. Outside work defined the parameters such that if the mother worked outside of the home more than did her husband, the relationship did not qualify as traditional. This was true for Carol when she ascertained whether her relationship was traditional:

Well, when you asked me that, how I interpreted that question is, do we have this male authority figure in the household, and I think I do defer to his judgment in a lot of stuff. But with me being the primary breadwinner, I think I get a whole lot more respect from him than some other women do. And I also get an unbelievable amount of help around the house. He totally does the laundry, 80 percent does the dishes, and probably does the cleaning, you know, and other women should have it so lucky. I think that we really have an egalitarian relationship, but I think that is really based on my income. And I think that there have been times before when that's not how things worked. When I took some time off, "Well, as long as you're at home, the house is yours, and I'm not gonna do anything." And I didn't agree with that, so now that we both work, we both have responsibilities.

While race proved inconsequential to how the women talked about their husbands and their fathering work, race filtered indirectly into the discussions about the birth fathers. In virtually all types of adoptions, the birth father was missing—this was particularly true for the Asian birth father. In the domestic context, however, the birth father exerted his presence through his absence. He, the Black or White birth father, refused to acknowledge paternity or simply was no longer present. He sometimes even interfered with the pace and progress of the adoption process by taking advantage of judicial protocol that requires a designated time to expire before paternal signatures are no longer necessary. The general tendency of the domestic birth father was to be absent, regardless of if he were Black or White. Yet, according to the women's words, the White birth father was more likely to be present if ever so briefly. Only two women mentioned that the birth fathers actively tried to stop the birth mother from relinquishing and in both situations the birth fathers were White, as were the children.

Maternal Silence

When extracting the political out of their family lives, many of the women deflate the import of gender by normalizing their mothering experiences. Here I consider whether neutralizing gender translates into maternal silence.

Originally, I counted maternal silence as a feature of mothering because White women historically have mothered in isolation (Bassin et al. 1994; Smart 1996). It is alone in the confines of the home that White mothers question whether or not they mother correctly by-the-book. Maternal silence has also meant that women have not narrated their own course through motherhood. Rather, they were evaluated and talked about by the male expert. Historically, the adoptive mother has also carried the burden of not living up to genetic expectations and having to hide her biological failings (Berebitsky 2000; Gailey 2000). Additionally, the mother living in a multiracial family often finds herself silently negotiating her own racial identity in juxtaposition as well as in correspondence with the racialization of her children (Ragoné and Twine 2000).

The extent to which these mothers mothered quietly, introspectively evaluating themselves, was unclear, especially given that they generally felt good about themselves as mothers. Most often I could not unravel the self-talk of these women as some of the women appeared intent on presenting the best face of their family life.

Equally difficult for me to discern was whether these women experienced maternal isolation. I got the sense that two of the mothers with Black daughters mothered without the companionship of other mothers in racially mixed families. I had this impression because they were confronted with difficult situations. Elaine's daughter, for instance, came home inquiring whether her mother loved her even though she was Black. Elizabeth's daughter used a class assignment to ask others to quit staring at her when she was with her parents just because they were White and she was Black. Elaine and Elizabeth confronted these racially charged scenarios without the companionship of other women; isolated, they engaged in self-questioning. But whatever isolation they may have experienced appeared temporary with the passing and resolution of difficult situations. At the same time, as will be discussed in the following chapter, isolation can prove empowering.

These mothers certainly did not endure the isolation and silence of the birth mothers, some of whom relinquished without ever telling close family members, according to the adoptive mothers. Additionally, the adoptive mothers, unlike the ones France Twine speaks of in her work, "Transracial Mothering and Antiracism: The Case of White Birth Mothers of 'Black' Children in Britain," overall, did not describe themselves as participating in "routine acts of everyday racism." Twine describes how the White birth mothers of Biracial children feel alienated from the White community and even see themselves as losing White privilege. For the most part, the adoptive mothers did not portray themselves similarly; they grounded themselves in the White community first.[2] It is easy to speculate that birth mothers of Biracial children may be more attentive to race, since they were not "saintly" for crossing racial lines to mother, but instead disparaged for breaking sexual taboos.

Silence and Parenting Language

Most often silence of a different sort pertained to the adoptive mothers. As I said, the women spoke often of themselves and other mothers as parents rather than as mothers. Of concern to me is whether emphasizing parenting may further silence maternal experiences—a point of discussion I took up in chapter 2. I do not want to repeat my earlier analysis of parenting language, but a few points deserve reiterating. There are some difficulties associated with parenting language. In light of the women's tendency to neglect gender, I think the difficulties with the term are pertinent.

"Parenting" language hides such facts as that the mother may feel such ultimate responsibility for the child that she does not leave the house alone to run errands (Hays 1996). Instead, she makes arrangements for the children to leave then. The father, in contrast, may withdraw, not thinking about who will tend to the children while he is gone (Hays 1996). I found, further, that with the ultimate responsibility for the children resting on the mother, she often feels overwhelmed and desires to be nurtured herself—a situation hidden by parenting language. Unfortunately, relatively few feminist works look at the implications of parenting language.

In her book, *Parents Who Think Too Much*, Anne Cassidy offers some insight into "parenting." Parenting, according to Cassidy, signifies the general movement toward and reliance on experts as opposed to insights and intuitions. She argues that the term "parenting" symbolizes the professionalization of child-rearing work in a gender-neutral manner. Cassidy, however, does not take into account race, class, or gender in her analysis of parenting. She appears to be addressing a White, middle- to upper-class audience alone.

Of course, the women interviewed were White and middle class. Many of the women did almost speak of themselves as "professional" mothers and what's more, gathered satisfaction from mothering efficiently. Yet, such intensive mothering did not come without costs. Recall that Sammie, like a good number of the women, portrayed herself as holding primary responsibility for the children, and for her, maternal demands necessitated that she be nurtured. Parenting language hides this situation because it neutralizes the unique role women hold in child rearing.

While I am aware of the difficulties associated with parenting language, I would like to avoid imposing a false consciousness on Mary and other women who chose to conceive of themselves as parents rather than as mothers, even when they talked about the "second shift" they encountered at home after work. How can I do so, moreover, when some of the women said that they liked the traditional gendered relations found in their families? I am also willing to recognize that parenting language may represent gender possibilities. Some of the women were not in traditional relationship and, for others who were, the fathers were active participants, which parenting language pays homage to by conjuring up images of family members sharing child-rearing responsibilities.

As I say in chapter 2, there are contradictions and inconsistencies associated with parenting language. What is certainly clear is that in the context of the interviews, most of the women negated the significance of their own gendered position—a narrative habit witnessed by the use of parenting language.

OTHERS' RESPONSES

"What I'm learning is how positive the stereotypes are of Asians. If you have to deal with a stereotype, I'd rather deal with a positive than negative one."

I highlight parenting language out of an interest in mothers. Fathers, as I said, generally were not the central focus of the conversations, even though I discovered slight patterns associated with race and the birth fathers. Others' responses to these women and their children were located prominently in the conversations. Maternal competence or the perception thereof is linked to ability to deal with responses both inside and outside of the family (Twine 1999). In part, at my instigation, significant portions of the interviews involved recounting stories and tales about how others responded to them. Of course, I intended to examine how responses altered as the child darkened. In addition, I configured "others" as the woman's family members, as well as strangers in the grocery store.

Irrespective of the race of the adopted child, these women overwhelmingly interacted with extended families. Extended family members played instrumental roles in adoption decisions as well as in ongoing interactions with the children and their mothers. I was struck by the tendency of many women to emphasize positive familial reactions, even though the degree and almost conditional nature of acceptance varied by race.

As might be expected, the White-on-White adoptions were unproblematic. Families waiting with anticipation for the arrival of a child filled their stories, as Jan recalled the special moment she first brought her child home:

It makes me cry thinking about this, too. When we came back with Mark and they [her family] met him it was just so exciting. I mean, they were just wonderful. Well, they were calling practically everyday, "When are you guys coming home? When are you coming home?" And then when we got there, they were standing there waiting at the door for us to pull up. It was really neat. It was really, really neat.

The children were accepted in part because they were considered to be of the family. One woman's own mother even attributed her adopted son's allergies to the adoptive father, only to be reminded that this would be impossible given that the boy was indeed adopted. In cases where discernible differences between the adopted child and the adoptive families existed, these were characterized positively, as when Joanna talked about her daughter's relationship with the rest of the family:

Everybody's accepted her. Dad has even said she's just refreshing, it's nice to have new blood in the family. 'Cause you do see your traits, and your stuff, kind of the negative stuff showing up, and Matilda is different from all of them. I don't know, I hate to say my family tends to be a little bit materialist, but I can see myself mortgaging my house to send this child to college and then she'll go on that Greenpeace ship or something, I can really envision that. She's extremely ecological, which is got to be hereditary, don't you think?

The child was portrayed as a welcomed addition to the family.

Similar language entered the conversations with women who adopted Asian children. They spoke of their families' total acceptance. Because the women talked about extended families' total support, there often was no story to tell, as when a mother responded to my probing about her family's reaction by saying, "Yeah, my family has been very supportive." Others, meanwhile, presented a more complicated narrative. Deborah's father-in-law, for example, intimated that he longed for grandsons of his own race to carry on his family name:

I don't think my father-in-law has any problem with it. He did make a comment that he wished, my husband has one other brother, and he has two daughters and right before he had his second daughter, I guess he had hoped they would have a boy to carry on the family name. These guys [her sons] are the only ones carrying on the family name. So I think that he may have a little regret there that he doesn't have a birth grandchild. I guess that's how you would say it.

Deborah portrayed her father-in-law's comment as a passing thought and not something she thought about:

I don't know how much it really bothers him. I think it was just a thought, and I think it's like you think these things, and then when you see how things can work out. He's real happy with our kids and seems to really like them, and I really don't think there's any problem. I don't think anything about it. It might have disturbed him, but I don't think it's a big concern of his now. Like I said, my mom didn't really want us to adopt an Asian child, and my son is just like her love of life. I mean, her whole world revolves around him. She'll do all kinds of things for him, you know, just loves him to death, so I think a lot of the things you think, when it comes to reality aren't really a problem, so once you know a name or once you know the child instead of just the idea of the child, it changes.

Deborah relegated to unimportance her mother, and father-in-law's initial reservations, given that they were "transformed" once the child arrived.

With more frequency, similar language or renditions of extended families' reactions surfaced in the women with Black and Biracial children's stories. Only one mother, Elaine, noted that her parents accepted the arrangement completely. More often it was the case that, at least initially, parents and often siblings showed hesitation. Phyllis's mother refused to hold her Biracial child until he was six months old:

Before we got the call about Anthony that fall when I talked to her [her mother], she said that she supported it, but she just thought it would make life really hard, and she didn't want me to see me have to go through that. What I find out later that actually were not her true feelings, because when we got Anthony she couldn't hold him. Isn't that bizarre? She wouldn't hold him for, like six months. And, you know, as a protective mother, I really watched her and I didn't want her to hold him, because she was so turned off by the fact that he was Biracial.

Phyllis chose to keep her child away from her mother to protect him from her mother's racism. Other mothers used a similar strategy, as did Elizabeth when she noticed that her father could not acclimate to her daughter's unruly hair and large stature. When Sammie's mother learned of her adoption plans she asked, "Couldn't you have adopted an Hispanic child?" and proceeded to announce publicly that the child was Latin rather than Biracial. Carol took offense when her father wanted to know if she was going to have her Black son tested for AIDS upon his arrival into her home. Despite recognition of these and other problems, the women played down the prejudice and bigotry in their families. They presented stories of their family members moving from initial hesitation to love, as did Karen when I asked her directly about her family's response:

My parents didn't want us to adopt a Black child, but then my father-in-law didn't either. My mother-in-law was fine. But my mother and father just said, "We don't think you should do it." Well, they just thought she would be better growing up with her own kind of people and they thought we would have problems . . . Oh, as soon as we brought Jessica home. Well, see when we got Jessica, my mom and dad were with us, so immediately there was a change, as soon as they saw her.

While some of the mothers spoke of a transformation, however, for others a note of uncertainty remained. Phyllis's brother continued to find it distasteful that his sister adopted a Biracial child rather than a Black one since he disapproved of Blacks and Whites mixing. In particular, in the two families composed of both Asian and darker children, a difference emerged. In-laws or even their own parents showed what these mothers interpreted to be preferences for the Asian child, with silkier hair and smaller stature.

It may not be surprising that mothers with Biracial and Black children, unlike the other sets of mothers, described family members as prejudiced. But while acknowledging prejudice, they also tended to disregard the significance thereof. There was a recognition that family attitudes were not perfect, but, at the same time, were not unmanageable. Leslie referred to the prejudice in her family. Here, she characterized the family's reaction first to her own daughter and then to her Puerto Rican niece:

I don't think I have an especially bigoted family and they're very accepting of people. Like right now my parents aren't doing well and they have a home-health-care person who lives in, and she's Jamaican. They have no problem with that. It was never an issue. My parents were never, I would never have someone who's Black in my house or anything like that. They just kind of accepted people. So, like I said, my family has changed a lot. My nephew, who got married last summer, his wife is Puerto Rican and they give him a hard time about it—certain members of the family. He loved her and she's really nice. Everyone likes her. I don't know if some people just feel like they're obligated to hang on to that bigotry. I think the era has changed. It's just more accepting. I always kind of kid 'cause when I was talking to my niece, the one that's Puerto Rican, and she was kind of hurt by some remarks, so I said something like, "Well, I think I've done my part. "Paul married you; you're Puerto Rican. I did my part by bringing someone who is Black into the family," So we just kind of turned it into kind of a joke. But the thing is, they'll say things behind someone's back, but they're very kind to them.

Leslie's narrative proves richly insightful. She disregarded family members' reactions. Her parents were accepting because they allowed a Black worker in their home, leaving unanswered the question of whether or not they would be so open to people of color who are of their same social and class standing. She created a joke out her Puerto Rican niece's concern. Her narrative pattern resembled some of the other women's in the Black and Biracial group in her tendency to acknowledge, but yet disregard, family bigotry. But she also understood that others may not relay their true feelings, but rather say things "behind someone's back." A couple of the other women with Black and Biracial children, in the face of family members' prejudice, had to act on their children's behalf. Phyllis and Sammie both attributed their mothers' unsettling reactions to the latter's weird personalities and own personal difficulties and had resigned themselves not to leave their children alone with their own mothers.

Similar patterns existed when the women talked about, what I call, "others' responses"—that is, how strangers reacted to them. All of the women, irrespective of their child's race, spoke of grocery store conversations and interactions. One might expect this, as the grocery store is one of the few public spaces found in suburbia. But additionally, it could be interpreted as a maternal space—a place that women frequent with their children—where other women observe her maternal skills, as witnessed by such acts as check-out-line stares assessing whether or not the mother on food stamps purchases healthful foods for her little ones. Not only did all of the women talk about grocery store interactions, but, generally, the women chose to accentuate the positive. As might be expected, this was particularly the case for those with White children.

At the grocery store, mothers decided if they should share with others that their child was not biologically theirs. As Jan explained:

It's really funny because in the store or anything, they don't know he's adopted. And they'll say, "Oh, he's so cute," "He looks just like you," or things like that, and it's really kind of fun. But some people I don't think are as ready to say that they've adopted. I mean, our story is just so wonderful I just want to tell everybody. One time in the store I did say he was adopted, and they said, "Oh, I just can't believe it. He just looks just like you." And he does kind of have resemblances of ours.

Even when the child did not resemble members of the adoptive family, interactions were unproblematic, according to these mothers.

Similar characterizations surfaced in conversations with the mothers with Asian children. Beyond the usual baby ogling, these women portrayed their experiences as overwhelmingly positive. Indeed, excessive positive attention at the grocery store was the problem. Mary ascertained that her baby-sitter and neighbor, with a baby herself, quit her child-care duties because her Asian baby got all of the attention:

The first thing that happened to us is so funny. Our next-door neighbor had a baby the same age, and she was adamant that she was going to baby-sit for Tim and I would go back to work. I really didn't want her to cause I thought that it would be too much. And she said, no, she could do it, she wanted to. It would be so easy on me to just run him next door and she was right, so finally I said, "You can do it." And after about five months, she said "I can't baby-sit for Tim anymore." And I said "OK, is it too much for you?" and she said, "Yeah." And that was when I had gone over there to get him. Her sister was over there with them. Her sister followed me home, and she said that the real reason was that whenever she would take them to the zoo or shopping or wherever she would take them both, Tim got all the attention, because he was different. And he was so cute, all this hair and he was really cute, and her baby was cute too, but her baby looked like all the other babies in the store. So everybody would stop and talk to Tim and ask all about Tim. And it really bothered her. So she didn't want to do it anymore.

Other women with Asian children mentioned similar experiences. Perhaps the only negative experience these women relayed was that their children were held to the high standards of positive stereotypes with the expectation that their children would grow up to be fine mathematicians or musicians. Andrea recognized that others assumed her son would be brilliant:

The only problem honestly has been positive prejudice because he's Asian. He'll be a genius. He's really a good kid. He's a very good boy. But he's a very good average student. We're very pleased with him academically, but he's not setting any records. And there does seem to be an expectation that he should be better than average. And that's not fair. I do have a friend whose kids are adopted. They're White. The kids are also White and one of them was a real behavior problem in Sunday School. And the Sunday School teacher told or started saying things that it's because he's adopted that he's a behavior problem. And that's awfully unfair. We've never had anything like that.

Andrea's story was like the others with Asian children not only because she said that they encountered only positive interactions, but in addition, she mentioned negative experiences as happening to people she knows, but "We've never had anything like that." Likewise Mary and Megan talked about uncomfortable scenarios happening elsewhere to other families. Megan never suffered the adoption attorney known for his thoughtless statements like "she's cute for a Chinese girl."

Keeping these "other" experiences in mind, some of the women speculated about a time when problems might arise. "Dating" might expose thoughts that families otherwise would not openly share. Deborah wondered about the dating prospects for her sons and even hoped that prospective dates' "fathers" would not share their true feelings, "I bet there's going to be some girls who are my sons' age that might end up dating my sons and their fathers will not want them dating an Asian, which I hope would be something that they just don't want, but they wouldn't say anything about." Several things stand out. The women with Asian children were so accustomed to purely positive reactions that they shelved the anticipation of racial difficulties until the distant future of dating. Racial differences and dynamics were not recognized as necessarily present and taking place within the family but elsewhere. Lastly, a silence and quiet quality permeated encounters that may be construed as racially fueled when they occur to the Asian child. Deborah, for instance, hoped that fathers would not let their feelings be known to her sons.[3] I found, in addition, that Asian children do not speak their minds in the manner that Biracial and Black children do, but instead withhold information from their parents (McRoy and Grape 1999).

The women with both Asian and White children shared a narrative practice that accentuated the positive and relegated uncomfortable situations to encounters with others, but there often was one experience that penetrated their narratives. For Peggy, there was the neighbor who slipped when he asked, "When did you buy her?" in reference to Peggy's Korean-born daughter; the work-related forms that asked the mother of White children to list her "natural children" separate from those who had been adopted; Joanna overhearing her daughter's new friend apologize upon learning that her daughter was adopted. What was curious about these stories was that the mothers chose to portray them as one-time events—the extraordinary rather than the ordinary. Yet, for mothers with Asian children, in contrast to those with White children, a relative uncertainty lingered about how others interpreted their "purple families."

Take Deborah. In our conversations she recalled grocery store trips where she and her children were the center of positive attention:

You are almost like the purple person, because people see my kids, they don't know who they are, they don't see me, they don't know who I am. But if they see us together, it's obvious, "Oh, it's that Caucasian women with the two Asian kids." They remember. But everyone at the grocery store knows us. I can't go in without them asking us something, and every checker knows them, they know them by name. In some ways it's nice, but in some ways they are used to so much attention.

Deborah, as did the others, experienced her children as members of the ideal minority. This was brought to Deborah's attention when her sister-in-law found the interracial portrayal of Cinderella objectionable:

It was funny because of the Cinderella video. Did you see that? I had one sister-in-law, who is very prejudiced against Blacks, call me and say that she was so disgusted and she wouldn't let her children watch it, because it had Whites and Blacks together. I was going. "You know, race is race and you are talking to someone who has a mixed-race family." And then she'd come back and say that Asians are different, and that's a weird thing to say. Why would it make a difference?

She continued by asserting that her sister-in-law made exceptions for her children because they needed homes, an equally unacceptable attitude to Deborah, "But then she tried to say that adoption's different; those children had to have homes. No, these kids are not charity cases. Yes, we did go for children who needed homes, but they're not charity. We benefited as much as they did, if not more. And then she tried to say that it was adoption." Deborah's interaction with her sister-in-law raised sentiments that the other women with Asian children either directly or indirectly mentioned. Racial exceptions were made for Asian children. According to Mary, her prejudiced aunts and uncles expressed racial anxieties about Blacks, but not about her Korean sons:

They'd [her relatives] never seen a Black person in their life, but they were all more prejudiced than anybody I'd ever seen. They were already prejudiced even though they didn't know anybody Black and my cousin, when he was 10 or 11 went to Chicago on a field trip and got beat up by four Black boys in one of the parks. I was like, oh, well! We'll never convince them any different. I could not believe that happened to him. No, they've never had any problem with our boys. It was just Black.

An Asian child's medical state added complexity to others' interpretations. Should the Asian child require medical attention, the woman would be elevated to sainthood status for nurturing the difficult—a sentiment Deborah, among others, found objectionable. Generally, however, the women enjoyed the favorable status granted their children. At times, however, as Deborah's interaction with her sister-in-law intimated, their status was uncertain. The question remained, moreover, whether these children enjoy heightened status because they resided in White homes.

Like the women in the Asian group, mothers with Black and Biracial children accentuated the positive. But, unlike the others, many of these women mentioned jarring experiences virtually from the onset of the interviews. At the start of our first conversation, Sammie recalled an elderly woman calling her White trash in the checkout line at the grocery store where she stood with her Biracial son. Carol recollected an encounter when her daughter was a baby and a car pulled up next to her in a parking lot. Once the woman in the other car saw her daughter in the back seat, the stranger yelled, "You bitch, nigger lover," and aggressively followed Carol in the car. Elaine noted a time that her husband was told that "those kind" like their Black daughter were not allowed toilet privileges on the premises. Karen felt uneasy when her family was seated in the back of an empty restaurant. Leslie continued to dislike the bagger at her local grocery store who insisted on asking, "Is she Black or White, what is she?" when encountering her Biracial daughter. Church members voted about whether to retain one mother and her husband as leaders in the church when they first adopted their Biracial child, eventually deciding in their favor.

More noteworthy than the content of these women's narratives was their descriptive style, which placed acts of overt racism, although vividly recalled, in the realm of the extraordinary. Often these acts occurred in rural locations where one would expect heightened racism as was true for Elaine and Karen's encounters. Or they were events in the distant past, not carrying the emotional weight they did at the time they occurred, as was the case for Carol and Tera. Indeed, Karen failed to remember jolting experiences even though in preparation for the interview she thought they might be relevant to our conversation. "There was another time I was trying to think of 'cause I just had a feeling that you were going to ask me this question. What was it? I have to think about it. I'll think about it, because there was something."

Even though overtly racist interactions were rendered relatively unimportant or infrequent, mothers with Black and Biracial children spoke of undertones. I heard about what the mothers perceived to be institutional practices that exclude children of color from frequenting local schools. Institutional practices spell *insidious*. With overt acts happening infrequently, the women questioned situations and scenarios for racial undertones. It was not uncommon for a woman to say, "If they thought something, they never said anything." Phyllis questioned and inferred that her neighbors were racist even though they never made any verbal gestures:

Two door[s] up, I would call them racist. I'd be careful with my boys with them. There's two boys on the corner, I wouldn't trust those parents, which means those boys probably. But we've never had . . . probably the fact that we've been here, and they lived here before us and we've gotten our boys and they'll walk up, but they'll never cross the street even though we live four houses down. If we were walking by somebody's that had kids, I don't know, I think we would cross the street and introduce ourselves. I think their isolation is probably purposeful and they've never said anything, but sometimes that has a lot of meaning.

The extent and degree that the women recognized undertones varied and, as I explain in the next chapter, contributed to whether they worked for change as those most attentive to the insidious were more likely to resist.

THE ADOPTIVE MOTHERS ON THEIR CHILDREN'S TALK

"Has my *Ebony* arrived?"

For many of the above women with Black and Biracial children racial dilemmas and unsettling situations were brought to the mothers' attention by the children themselves. Indeed, it was often by reference to the children's talk that the mothers assessed whether their children were well acclimated; overall, the women ascertained that, irrespective of race, their children were well adjusted.

The White children were most regularly portrayed as adjusting well to their adoptive families. Only one mother, Katherine, spoke of a passing time when her child would hit her every time she mentioned he was adopted and neither came from her stomach nor was breast-fed. Others, in fact, spoke so highly of adoption that they said their children's friends wished that they, too, could have experienced the adventurous route by which they entered their families.

One mother with Asian children, Andrea, expressed a similar sentiment. She recalled a time that her child felt sorry for his friend who was not adopted. According to Andrea, her son equated adoption with love. As I said before, however, what was most noticeable about the Asian children was the extent to which they did not share their feelings, especially in comparison to the Black and Biracial adoptees. Three of the seven mothers with Asian children mentioned times when their children were called "Chinese boy" or "girl." These episodes were brought to mothers' attention after long bouts of name-calling. Andrea learned that her daughter was being called "Chinese girl" all school year long only after it became unbearable to her daughter:

So we haven't encountered any problems with them being Asian. Qualify, until this morning when my daughter came out of kindergarten and said that there was a boy in her class that keeps calling her "Chinese girl," and it's not in a friendly way. It's making her feel sad. She feels like he's picking on her. I've waited eight and a half years. I've embraced and readied for this moment, and today she said that this has been going on all school year. She never said anything before today. Today she was in tears about it. That's why I got this equal book out that I got. It's about getting teased. Well, she'll be fine with it. She had a substitute teacher today and I think it's possible that the substitute teacher didn't handle it as well as her regular teacher does and maybe that's why it bothered her.

Kathy, meanwhile, found out from her Latin daughter that her Korean son was being teased by boys on the school bus. These two cases involved youngsters still in primary school. Mary's middle-school adoptee also apprised his mother of his ongoing battle with teasing. All of these episodes were constructed as devoid of race. Mary, for instance, wondered why being called *Chinese* bothered her son, "Like John getting upset because people call him "Chinese," but the next-door neighbors may have a problem because they call their kids "four eyes" so what's the difference? To me it's the same thing. Everybody has something that can be made fun of or teased if somebody wants to do it. No matter what it is." Clearly, equating "Chinese" and "Chink" encounters to disparaging remarks garnered about wearing glasses dismissed race as the relevant focus. Later, in another conversation, Mary assessed that her son's personality contributed to him receiving such kidding. She reached this conclusion in part because her older son with a strong personality and physical build had not informed her of similar difficulties. From what I gathered, the children and parents were not distinguishing themselves from one another racially, which encouraged the sentiment that being called "Chinese boy" lacked racial significance. Because of this, race was perceived to be unproblematic within the home environment and, therefore, outside the home as well. Indeed, almost from the start of the second interview with Mary, she shared with me that her son, the one called "Chinese boy," had fallen into a deep depression requiring her to seek professional help for him. Mary did not tie his depression to racial and identity difficulties, but chose instead to link it to genetic causes.

In contrast to this stood Black and Biracial adoptions. Mother after mother with Black and Biracial children discussed their children's awareness of their race, often without prodding or recognition from the mothers. In these scenarios, racial encounters did not reside outside the home, but within. The racial dynamics of the family itself were challenged by the children. On several occasions, I heard something to the effect, "She knows she's Black, I didn't have to tell her." Children were portrayed as not only recognizing their distinct skin color, but also vocalizing their racial difference from their White mothers, saying such things as "Look Mommy, they're Black like me!" Often this recognition was expressed in the physicalness of being Black and ignited an expressed desire on the part of the child to have White features or simply to be White. "He wishes we were all the same race," Phyllis shared with me. Elaine cringed recalling her daughter's inquiry, "Do you still love me even though I'm Black?" Elizabeth started a subscription to *Ebony* magazine for her daughter after she noticed the daughter's habit of biting her lips in order to make them smaller and less Black. Black hair was a topic that arose in our conversations particularly for those with Black and Biracial girls. I heard comments such as, "She's got loose curls" or "She's got that typical Black hair." Should the child have "typical Black hair," it was an issue. Elizabeth talked about her daughter as a five-year-old wearing long scarves to simulate long flowing blond hair. Cheerleading uniform and dress requirements presumed White hair with their insistence that the girls wear ponytails. Large portions of the mothers' time were dedicated to hair treatments. But more than simply tending to Black hair, the child verbalized disapproval of his or her hair. Phyllis remembered the time that her son cried for the straight, stringy hair of his friend's:

He was crying one day and I said, "What are you crying about?" And he said, "Well, I want hair like Josh's." "Well, Josh's got really stringy, straight, blond hair, which I don't think is attractive personally." I think that he's got gorgeous hair. It's beautiful. So I said, "Well, bottom line is God made you like you are and this is the hair you always will have and you can cry that you want Josh's hair, but you're not going to get it." And I said, "Not only that, I've got a perm in my hair. My hair is like Josh's and I have to go get a perm just to have a little bit of curl in it." We talked about it a little while longer and we have a really good friend who's Black. But he is just as handsome as he could be and Anthony kind of resembles him a little bit, and I said, "You think Hubert's handsome, don't you?" And he's said, "Yeah." And I said, "Well, think about your hair and Hubert's hair." And he goes, "Yeah, my hair looks like his." I said, "Yeah. He's a very handsome man." That was it. He was off playing. So things that come up just get talked about and then they're off doing something else.

Phyllis constructed the hair interaction as manageable and rather unproblematic given that her son was quickly off playing and thinking about something else. Yet, Phyllis also pointed out the ironies of a White culture that loathes those things Black such as extremely kinky hair, but desires them as well in the form of Whites perming their hair. Elaine used a similar strategy when her daughter complained about her dark coloring, saying that Whites tan themselves to reach a similar hue. Elizabeth, perhaps more so than any other mother, constructed her nine-year-old daughter, Nicole, as vocal about race. Nicole, when asked to express her wishes in a class assignment requested that others stop staring at her when she was with her parents just because they were White and she was Black. In a White beauty salon, Nicole questioned out loud why none of the stylists were Black and why no photos of Blacks adorned the salon.

Of greatest import here was how the mothers responded to their children's verbalizations or lack thereof. I found, for instance, that when the Black and Biracial children distinguished themselves from their mothers racially, the women followed suit or even initiated the idea that they belonged to different racial categories. Karen, for instance, was in the habit of saying "Jessica's Black, I'm not." Two of the women with Biracial children chose to accentuate their shared racial similarity with their children. Leslie, olive skinned herself, compared her skin color with that of her daughter's and asserted their likeness even though the daughter pointed out their dissimilarities:

Sometimes kids notice her being different in her coloring, and kids are very accepting, but sometimes they'll say, "Is that your daughter?" I guess that is what adults probably think. With me, you see, I don't really see a difference in her compared to me. Now Tori sees a difference because she'll say that her skin is brown, and not that she says "Why is my skin brown and you're . . . She says that my skin is gold.

For Phyllis, her son's being Biracial meant that he resided in her community as well as in the Black community with which he identified:

Anthony's got a Black identity. Like we were going down Main Street the other day and there were a bunch of Black men on the sidewalk standing outside the store. And he says, "Mom, how come there's so many of my people standing there?" And I looked at him and I said, "Well, first of all you need to know that I'm also your people, OK." And I wasn't offended, but I want him to understand that he's not just Black, not that I don't value. If he was just Black, then I wouldn't have said anything, but he's got more than just Black heritage in him.

All of the mothers above talked about the need to provide their children with a racial education, be it subscribing to *Ebony* magazine or looking into diversity in the local schools, neighborhoods, or churches. Attention to diversity did not necessarily mean, however, that these mothers were living and raising their children in diverse settings. Indeed, only one mother, Tera, lived in a diverse environment, as well as sent her children to a predominantly minority school. Attention to diversity did mean, in any case, that some of the mothers frequented schools complaining about lack of diversity in the either all or predominantly White settings. In addition, some of the women with their children attended racially mixed churches or gathered educational materials that helped their children understand their racial heritage. As I said, their understanding of what their children needed stemmed partly from their children's initiatives and partly from others' responses, which aided their own racial understanding of their child. Karen, for instance, took instruction from others. In this particular case, she listened to a Brazilian woman who contributed to Karen's feeling that her son could pass for almost any race and, therefore, did not need a Black identity and education:

She [the Brazilian woman] asked me if he was Hispanic and I said, "Well, he's supposed to be Black and White." And I said, "I've seen the mother and I know the mother is White, blond hair, beautiful and he looks just like her except he has the dark hair, the darker skin. But she said to me, "Well, if you had not said that, I would have thought he was Hispanic." And he does, he looks just like her son. The only thing that you could give him would be just constant self-esteem and try make him proud of whatever he is. You can't because you don't know what can you give him, just love. I do have girlfriends that I worked with that were Black and the one friend, she said, "Oh, she could see it right away that he was Black," but since I guess there aren't any features that stand out. I think with Jessica you can look at her. I mean, you know she's as Black as Black can be, you know. But with him you never would be able to tell. Always tell my husband, well, he's going to go through life, he can pass for anything he wants to be because of the skin color. He could be anybody. If he told somebody he was White, he'd be White. If he told somebody, he was Hispanic, he looks Hispanic and then if he wanted to pass for Black, I guess he could pass for Black.

Karen interpreted her son as not Biracial to such an extent that she did not count him among the number of minority people in her neighborhood.

As I noted above, the Asian child's race was generally not negotiated or challenged, as was true for Karen's experience with her Biracial son. With this in mind, concern for diversity in the schools was mentioned by only one mother with an Asian child. Despite what I would call a racial leveling of Asian children, whereby the importance of race was erased, these women, more so than mothers in any other group, were active support group members dedicated to providing their children with a Korean cultural education. In collaboration with members of the Korean community, potlucks celebrating Korean food and classes teaching the Korean language were all part of the repertoire of activities available to both the adoptive mother and her adopted children. Culture rather than race became the focus. Kathy elucidated her perspective about educating her children:

I do feel like they have to know about their birth country and a little bit of their history and culture to help them know who they are. But I think the other thing that we do is we appreciate all cultures. We may go see a program at the museum or whatever that looks interesting, and it may be about a different country, but we may go to that. Because we want them to love and respect all cultures.

These mothers followed expert advice to educate their children about their birth country.

As might be expected, neither culture nor race figured into the conversations with mothers with White children. Yet, similar to the women with Asian children, they practiced conscious parenting. Educational materials and expert assistance helped them to acquaint their children with and to celebrate adoption. Through these efforts, they followed modern adoption experts who suggest being as open as possible with your children. With such an intention, these mothers created scrapbooks that chronicled their child's entry into their homes to encourage a sense in their children that they were always loved.

Situated in the Political

The political, as defined in the previous chapter, links wider arrangements with individual situations and surfaces throughout the women's narratives. I mentioned the political earlier in relation to adoption processes. Of course, political features of their narratives surfaced in a variety of topics ranging from their descriptions of infertility treatments to their handling of racially charged episodes. As mentioned throughout, the works used to ground this project are attentive to a variety of political matters. They include Elaine Tyler May who, in her work, *Barren in the Promised Land*, uncovers the historical habit of blaming women for infertility problems. Katz Rothman (1994) argues that women who participate in infertility treatments are victims, at the same time criticizing those women who participate in NRTs for perpetuating the medical industry's practice of disembodying women. Raymond (1993) situates international adoptions within a global market for babies. And Herrmann and Kasper (1992) espy eugenic and racial sentiments in adoptions. Amid these critical assessments, some mothers of Asian, and Black and Biracial children encountered a sentiment of a different sort. People in the community elevate the transracial and/or transnational adoptive mother to saint status for raising children that others perceive to be too troublesome because of their skin color, physical condition, or both.[4] Attentive to the above, I characterized the mother who adopts Black, Biracial, and Asian children as occupying an uncomfortable space—a position akin to the "damned if you do and damned if you don't" dilemma.

In the previous chapter, I gathered pieces of the women's narratives where they spoke of the ideology of capitalism. By and large, however, the women were inclined to remove adoption from its controversial context, even when the political entered their homes. Recall Mary, a mother of Asian children. When her son came home complaining that he was called "Chinese boy," she consoled him by saying that the child down the street who wears glasses also gets teased. She, along with other women, mentioned the political, but neutralized its importance in preferring to accentuate their family's relative likeness with other families. This is not to say that the women, particularly those who adopted transracially and transnationally, did not recognize their differences from other families. "Differences," however, did not preclude being similar to any other family. Kathy, an international adoptive mother, expressed this sentiment. You may recognize that the following quote is one I used in an earlier chapter to point out Kathy's preference for parenting over mothering language:

There are differences in parenting a child of a different race, but they're manageable. It's just an extra step that you have to work through. And it's the same with adoption. You have adoption issues, and if you chose to adopt transracially then you have those issues on top of your normal parenting issues. It is hard. It is more of a challenge, but I think that it is all manageable, and I wouldn't trade it for anything.

Again, Kathy, like some of the other women, accepted and acknowledged differences, but chose to depreciate their importance. In doing so, she recognized the political relevance of transnational adoptions, but did not fully engage it. On the whole, these women, unlike the ones Twine (1999) highlighted, did not lose their White privilege through their adoptions.

The Political: A Response

Day-to-day evaluations of adoptive mothers, perhaps, witnessed their racial privilege since several of the women were thought to be saintly for adopting transracially and/or transnationally. An evaluation of this sort may add to the women's feeling that their adoptions are not politically significant. With this being the case, I am left questioning the appropriateness of superimposing the political on their lives, given that the women mentioned political things, such as saint labels, in an apolitical manner. More often, they spoke of their lives in a religious tenor. Equally curious to me, then, is whether religiosity contributes to veiling race, class, and gender from their narrations of adoption. For those women who were "traditional Christians," religiosity, I believe, occludes politics.[5] I elaborate on this thought in the following section.

Race and Culture, Too? The Women Talk about Race

As I have repeatedly written, I found that many of the women leveled the significance of race. This was not, however, the complete picture.

Virtually all of the women recognized and agreed that adopting Black and Biracial children is the most challenging form of adoption. As might be expected, those women with Black and Biracial children accentuated race with more regularity than did the others.

These women expressed preferences for darker skinned children. Some women spoke of moments when they were more attentive to race than were their children. Tera recognized that her notion of beauty altered with the adoption of her Biracial children:

seeing all my friends with their White kids and thinking, "Oh God, these kids look so gross and sick and pale. These poor kids need some sun." Then seeing a friend that had an Oriental baby, an Asian baby, and thinking, "Well, this kid looks a lot more healthy," not even thinking these things, but just flipping through your mind realizing that my idea of a good-looking child now is my child.

Tera knew that her view of race changed with adoption, something she acknowledged when asked directly, "Pay more attention to it [race], done a lot more reading and talking to people about it that kind of thing than I think I've ever done just because I need to. Before it was a luxury I didn't have to. I could just live my life and not worry about it."

Deborah, a mother of Asian children, meanwhile, intimated that she experienced not just a greater awareness of race, but, also an altered sense of her own racial placement. Deborah, as noted above, spoke of herself and her family as the purple family, "You are almost like the purple person. Because people see my kids, they don't know who they are, they don't see me, they don't know who I am. But if they see us together, I mean, it's obvious, 'Oh, it's that Caucasian women with the Asian kids.' "

Deborah interpreted her "purpleness" positively as it brought her and her family positive attention. But what is curious about her characterization of herself as the purple person is that she lost her traditional White coloring and took up some sort of hybrid racial positioning—purple.

The women with White children also took notice of race. Unlike other White women who have children biologically, these women were required to make deliberate choices about the race of their children.[6] Given the dearth of available White children, they had to decide whether they would raise a child of another race and/or nationality. They thereby contemplated race only to decide against adopting transracially. In some sense, the mothers with White children complied with the National Association of Black Social Workers' (NABSW) historic stance. Recollect that in the past NABSW argued against transracial adoption in favor of intra-community adoptions or Black- on-Black adoptions. Some of these mothers said that they could not provide Black children with the kind of situation they would like. Eleanor and her husband decided not to adopt transracially because they felt that they could not provide a Black child with the proper environment. Once the child reached these women's homes, however, they, like so many other White families, had the luxury of deciding when and if they thought about race. Race could be discarded once the child arrived.

In the above, I have pointed out ways that the women integrated race into their narratives. Yet, many of the women practiced an odd narrative habit of acknowledging prejudice but not racialism or any way of thinking that makes race a significant category. A case in point was Leslie's description of her family's prejudice presented earlier in this chapter:

I don't think I have an especially bigoted family and they're very accepting of people. Like right now my parents aren't doing well and they have a home-health-care person who lives in, and she's Jamaican. They have no problem with that. It was never an issue. My parents were never, I would never have someone who's Black in my house or anything like that. They just kind of accepted people. So, like I said, my family has changed a lot. My nephew, who got married last summer, his wife is Puerto Rican and they give him a hard time about it—certain members of the family. He loved her and she's really nice. Everyone likes her. I don't know if some people just feel like they're obligated to hang on to that bigotry. I think the era has changed. It's just more accepting. I always kind of kid 'cause when I was talking to my niece, the one that's Puerto Rican, and she was kind of hurt by some remarks, so I said something like, "Well, I think I've done my part. "Paul married you, you're Puerto Rican. I did my part by bringing someone who is Black into the family," so we just kind of turned it into kind of a joke. But the thing is, they'll say things behind someone's back, but they're very kind to them.

Recall Leslie was a mother of a Biracial girl. Most of the women who chose to reduce the significance of race, however, were the mothers of

Asian children. Culture, not race was their focus. The suggestion was made that culture, not race distinguished these women from their children. These women worked to provide their children a culturally sensitive upbringing emphasizing Korean culture, but they talked about doing so, most often, without overtures to race. As I noted above, moreover, women with Asian children did not racially distinguish themselves from their children as the women with Black and Biracial children were in the habit of doing.

Culture weaves in and out of importance for the other women. The women with White children slighted culture as well as race because they simply shared the child's race and, additionally, in some cases, the birth mother's religion. These mothers, thus, adopted within community in the broadest sense.[7] The women with Black and Biracial children also used race to define culture. Yet, for some of these mothers, because their child's race differed from their own, their culture did as well. For many of the women, moreover, their understanding of race and culture, and the intersection between the two was mediated by religion.

As mentioned earlier in this chapter and elsewhere, most of the women were religious, and their religiosity was expressed in their language as well as in their commitment to their religious communities. Yet, how they expressed this religiosity differed. A good number of the women were traditional Christians, which meant that they frequented church, subscribed to their religious liturgy, and expressed devotion to God in their narratives. Another set of women were what I would call spiritual. They frequented, perhaps, the Unitarian church or more traditional religious settings, such as synagogues, but they did not, in the context of our conversations, express devotion to God or to a particular religious persuasion. Through religion, the former group of women lessened race. These women were less likely even to employ the word "racism," but instead speak of bigotry and prejudice—words that connote attitudes and practices that are less insidious than are racism or racialism. This narrative style can be further explicated through an example.

Recall Kathy's situation. Kathy's Latin daughter, Betti, came home wanting to be called "Chinese boy" like her Korean brother, who had been so dubbed by boys on the school bus. Here was Kathy's response:

"Ok, Betti, first of all, nobody's Chinese in our family. And Michael, you need to correct them." First of all, our policy at home is that we call each other by our names, that's why we have names, and so I said, "To whosoever is calling you "Chinese boy," you need to tell them what your name is and then you need to tell him that you are not from China, that he's close, but you are from a place close to China, but you are really from Korea." But we just approached it like that. But Betti felt just so left out because she wasn't Chinese.

Knowing Kathy to be a devout Christian, I perceived Kathy's response to be very Christian. Race was not her focus since her response excluded race or racism as a factor in reacting to the name-calling. She instead took the opportunity to kindly teach others about her son's country of origin instead of labeling those doing the name-calling. Similar to other women who spoke of God and their church life, Kathy chose to think that all people are created equal regardless of race. Through their religiosity, some of the women, regardless the race of the child, demonstrated "color blindness." They did so by asserting that they did now and had always believed in racial equality.

Selected Writers on Race and Color Blindness

In her article, "Analyzing Ethical Conflict in the Transracial Adoption Debate," Janet Farrell Smith alludes to color blindness. Such an orientation holds "that color or race does (or should) not matter" (Smith 1996: 14). Smith implies that such thinking fails fully to appreciate the extent to which racism or racialism defines social relations and has done so historically. Sandra Patton (2000) argues that a color-blind orientation, especially to understanding transracial adoptions, does not acknowledge the saliency of race, and further, runs counter to the experiences of transracial adoptees who have difficulty sorting out their racial identities. Michael Kimmel succinctly explicates this point when he says, " Inequality is structural and systemic, as well as individual and attitudinal. Eliminating inequalities involves more than changing everyone's attitudes" (Kimmel 2002: 48). By contrast, Peter Hayes to a certain extent uses a color-blind approach to promote transracial adoptions. He argues that opposition to transracial adoptions, based in distinguishing the races, represents an antihumanist movement, "The refusal to recognize humanism as a viable alternative philosophy with which to raise transracially adopted children is indicative of the claim that the objective of instilling a strong sense of ethnicity and awareness of cultural heritage in minority children has an incontestable, total, and exclusive validity" (Hayes 1993: 308). Hayes, unlike the women in this study, based his humanism in the civil rights movement. As noted, many of these women gathered their humanism from their religion. A color-blind brand of humanism, however, stands in contrast to the brand of humanism grounding this work that is espoused by Kimmel and Patricia Hill Collins in *Black Feminist Thought*.

Kimmel calls for making visible the invisible. In his estimation, "privilege needs to be visible," and normalcy needs to questioned. "We always think about inequality from the perspective of the one who is hurt by the inequality, not the one who is helped" (Kimmel 2002: 44). Privilege itself is thereby under scrutiny, not those unable to enjoy privilege. With a focus on privilege itself, individual attitudes become secondary to recognizing the structural arrangements that enable the White and middle class to be constructed as normal. Working to overcome structural inequalities, then, requires large-scale social movements that are collective in nature.

Collins (1991) seeks to promote Black women's self-actualization. Her humanism does not assume that progress moves in a linear fashion nor is imminent, in contrast to the some of the religious humanisms mentioned above. The humanism she defends is in a constant state of incipience, rather than already realized. Situating Black women's unique experiences in a history and legacy of racism, she aims to achieve racial progress, not by erasing race, but rather through the process of working to realize Black and other racial groupings' autonomy. Her vision is expressed well in her definition of Black feminism: "Black feminism is a process of self-conscious struggle that empowers women and men to actualize a humanist vision of community" (Collins 1991: 39). Her struggle is situated in acknowledging the significance of race rather than diminishing its force. Collins does not address directly transracial adoptions, but one can extrapolate her humanism onto the subject matter. She might regard domestic White, as well as transracial and transnational adoptions that occur without contextualizing the larger racial climate to be antihumanist. Indeed, it is my intention to extend Collins's thoughts to adoption, and by doing so regard adoption as part of an ongoing struggle for racial social justice, and not a politically neutral endeavor.

Race: A Response

Of significance to me, as well as to Smith and Hayes, is whether stepping out to adopt a child darker than oneself can signify racial progress. Is religious humanism that decreases the significance of race, enough? This is hotly debated in the adoption literature. Supporters point out that Black and Biracial adoptees do well in White homes and also argue that transracial adoptions represent a reduction in racial strife (Macey 1995). Those opposed to transracial adoption allude to the oft-quoted phrase "cultural genocide" to say that transracial adoption is merely another artifact of racism (Abdullah 1996).

The difficulty I face is figuring out the relevance of this debate to the women's narratives given that most of the women simply did not engage it. Only a couple of the women said directly that transracial or transnational adoptions with Whites crossing the racial divide to nurture children darker than themselves, signified racial progress. There often occurred, however, the indirect or implicit suggestion that transracial adoption and, moreover, color blindness equals progressiveness.

I, then, negotiate two types of humanism. I, along with other feminists, subscribe and, moreover, try to integrate Kimmel's and Collins's humanist project into my daily life and work. Yet, many of the women subscribed to a different form of humanism, the religious one. I face a dilemma. Both I and the women try(ied) to uphold moral standards—standards that, in some sense, do not differ terribly, since we both would like to see racial equality. We differ, however, in our understanding of the significance of race and racialism and, correspondingly, our evaluation of the current racial landscape. We also differ in our understanding of what racial equality means or at least in what achieving it involves. Many of the women feel that their own color blindness reflects larger and wider societal sentiments that racial parity exists or is on its way to being fulfilled.

Instead of working from religious humanism, as noted previously, the unruly task of disciplining two types of humanisms, religious and feminist, has been attempted. Some effort has been made to bridge the two by simply labeling the women's religious faith a humanism. Of course, immense liberty has been taken to label the women's religiosity a humanism, especially in relation and juxtaposition to the humanism articulated by Kimmel (2002) and Collins (1991). The content of religious and feminist humanisms differs markedly while sharing in common that they both offer a moral blueprint for conduct for followers.

Attentive to the above, I remain committed to Kimmel's and Collins's brand of humanism that centrally locates race and racism in our society and culture instead of seeing it as an intervening variable. From a position that envisions racism as not solely individually experienced and acted out, but also institutionally bound, adoption as a potential space promoting the "actualization of a humanist vision of community" is considered (Yngvesson 1997).

SUMMARY

In this final section, narrative details are reviewed, and thoughts pertinent to answering whether or not transnational and transracial adoptions challenge hierarchies are presented.

The women talked similarly as well as differently. Regardless of the race of the child, for virtually all of the women being a mother meant participating in a two-parent family. The women generally chose to accentuate their positive relationship with their husbands even while also acknowledging that ultimate responsibility for the child rested with themselves. Overall, these women felt good about themselves as the primary care providers. A majority of the women also chose to highlight the positive, or rather depreciate the negative, in talking about public responses to them and their children—mention was made of, perhaps, one jarring interaction but the weight of that experience was lessened.

Of course, their narrative talk also differed by race. Part of becoming a mother entailed feeling some ownership of the child, which differed according to race. The women with White children felt total ownership of their children, even if there were moments of fear or threats from the birth mother. Race did not intervene. Similarly, race did not interfere with mothers of Asian children feeling ownership of their children, even when faced with challenging situations where Koreans in the United States claimed ownership of their children. In contrast, the women with Black and Biracial children usually did not claim total ownership of their children. Instead, their children belonged also in another community in which they, their mothers, did not necessarily associate.

The responses the women received from others, often strangers, also differed by race, even though the women chose to accentuate the positive regardless of race. The women with White children focused on comments from others that assessed whether or not the children looked like the rest of the family. Asian children and their White mothers gathered positive attention from others. The women with Black and Biracial children had more jarring stories to tell, as their children apprised them of difficult and tense situations at school. Race thus entered the home of mothers with Black and Biracial children. In contrast, Asian children endured difficult encounters silently. These mothers discarded race in preference for culture. Race and culture, meanwhile, remained absent for those with White children, the implication being that racial similarity spelled cultural likeness between mother and child.

Throughout the chapter, documented racialized details have been juxtaposed to particular feminist discussions in order to relate the thoughts that initiated this project to the women's words and to consider the "potentials" of transnational and transracial adoptions to challenge racial, gendered, and class hegemonies. The women, for instance, applied fitness standards to themselves as well to the birth mothers. The adoptive mothers mothered intensively, often driven by expert advice, and reaped the benefits of doing so as witnessed by their own and others' assessment of them as good mothers. Interestingly enough, however, some of the women referred to the power that the birth mother holds over them as they wondered out loud whether the birth mother would approve of their mothering. Overall, these adoptive mothers did not mother silently or in isolation. Instead, silence entered these women's narratives in a different manner. By and large, the adoptive mothers degendered their mothering experiences through parenting language, and thereby obscured the gendered expectation that women spend their time raising children regardless of their financial standing. Lastly, most of the women lessened the significance of race through their emphasis on prejudice and individual behaviors rather than on racism and racialism—their racial vision called on people to be color-blind, in opposition to an orientation that views our society as fundamentally defined by race, class, and gender.

Essentially, placing the women's words inside a certain feminist dialogue is an effort to find potentials in multiracial families. Do these adoptions, and the women who mother in them, challenge class, gender, and racial hierarchies? As I explain in the following chapter, I believe those women who positioned themselves outside of their natural communities

[White and middle-class], challenged hierarchies the most. I will further delve into this thought in the next chapter.

NOTES

1. Oddly enough, I believe that only two women, mothers of Black girls, both, seriously questioned if they were doing a good job. In our conversations, they did not make overtures to the "experts." Yet, more relevant than expert advice to their sense of selves was the fact that their daughters had challenged them about race.

2. Of course, some of the women were acutely aware of their altered racial positioning. Deborah, a mother of Asian children, coined for herself the expression "purple person." It is hard to accurately say if the women with Black and Biracial children also described their racial positioning as changed with adoption. Some did, whereas others talked more about their children belonging to another racial community.

3. Notice Deborah talks in a very traditional gender manner. It is the girls' fathers who will protest if their daughters date boys to their displeasure.

4. Specifically, most of the women who mentioned being labeled "saints" had adopted children with disabilities from overseas.

5. I derive an understanding and definition of "traditional Christians" from the interviews themselves. Those women whom I would characterize as traditional Christians spoke of their devotion to their religion and God in our conversations. In addition, they participated in their religion in an organized fashion by frequenting church. Many of the women spoke of going to church, but those I would categorize as "traditional Christians," most often Baptists, also mentioned their devotion to God in our conversations.

6. The extent to which the women with White children had to make deliberate decisions about the race of their adoptive children was indicated by their recognition that they may be criticized for adopting White children rather than "special needs" children. One mother and social worker shared with me that others had been openly critical of her for not adopting the latter.

7. The mothers with Black, Biracial, and White children who, in particular, described the birth mother as belonging to a different class, in most cases lower class, intimated that a cultural difference existed between themselves and the birth mothers based in class. With little to no information about the Asian birth mother, characterizations of her class status were made relatively less frequently.

CHAPTER 5

Location, Resistance, and Potentials

As was noted at the beginning of this book, works that explore adoption traditionally avoid linking adoption to wider concerns about race, class, and gender. This is not surprising since, as Yngvesson (1997) notes, judicial and legislative mandates promote adoption while failing to engage difficult questions about race, class, and maternity. In contrast to the sentiment that adoption promotes a universal good and, therefore, deserves unchallenged support, Yngvesson, along with Patton (2000) and Solinger (2001), argues that adoption policies and practices are imbued with ideologies of race, class, and motherhood. This book concurs and begins from the premise that adoption implies much about the status of women, racial minorities, and families (Berebitsky 2000). Accordingly, a magnified inspection of adoptive mothers' narratives of their lives can offer insights into broader social relations. More than offering insight, moreover, the intention throughout this work has been to listen for potentials to challenge race, gender, and class hierarchies (Mahoney and Yngvesson 1992).[1] Do these mothers in their everyday lives challenge hegemonic notions of race, as Twine (1999) argues that White birthmothers of Biracial children do? By inhabiting a particular position, location, or identity, are these mothers inclined to resist? Answering these questions requires listening.

Maureen A. Mahoney and Barbara Yngvesson, in their article, "The Construction of Subjectivity and the Paradox of Resistance: Reintegrating Feminist Anthropology and Psychology," articulate the importance of listening, ". . . listening is at the heart of emotional engagement, shaping the capacity of the other to speak. Whether the listener may be experienced as friend or enemy, it is in this dialogue that the disjunctures and conjunctures of culture are reshaped into the subjective forms of desire, empowering subjects who are not only complicit but capable as well of resisting relations of domination" (Mahoney and Yngvesson 1992: 70–71). This work practices "listening": to the women's words, naturally, but, in addition, to surrounding sounds—my own and those of academic inclinations.[2] Through listening, the cultural imprints that mark the women's narratives can be discovered (Rosenwald and Ochberg 1992). According to Mahoney and Yngvesson, the importance of listening is that through it, possibilities and potentials to confront rigid conceptions of race, gender, and family are created.

The possibilities that can be uncovered in this work went unmentioned in previous chapters, as the women's words and renditions thereof were pieced together in kaleidoscopic fashion. Their words, categorized according to race and maternity, were approached from different angles and presented against different backdrops, the women's and academic settings. Some of the piecemeal construction reflects a writing and analytical style that details, but it also bears witness to the complexity of the women's lives and their portrayals of them. I found that some of the women sometimes downplayed the significance of race, and others always did. Thick description, therefore, avoids simple renditions of these women as people who long to mother or as exploiters who ignore larger contexts in order to mother. It is within thick description, moreover, that possibilities reside.

I will unearth potentials by returning to the original research questions that motivated this book. The central question was whether maternal identity depends on the child's race. This book has shown that mothering challenges intensified as the child darkened and, correlatively, that a woman's sense of herself as a mother wavered more with a darker child than it did with a lighter one. A second initial research question was whether adoption enhances relations among women. In particular, I concentrated on whether adoption is an opportunity for women to relate as legitimate and illegitimate mothers. As was stated in the introductory chapter, the urge to investigate this issue comes from thinkers like Chandra Mohanty, who, in her work "Women Workers and Capitalist Scripts," unravels the ideological frameworks that place women in comparable work globally. At the end of this work, it is clear that most of the women did not draw larger or universal connections between themselves and the birth mothers.

Based in the women's talk, this concluding chapter attempts to answer and confront the following two questions and possibilities: Do transracial and transnational adoptions offer the possibility of disputing racial hierarchies that assume Whiteness as the standard of normality? And can adoption, generally, oppose maternal restrictions that equate good mothering with biological motherhood relations or with "fitness" standards that privilege certain middle-class, White women?

The search for possibilities begins with a general discussion of identity and resistance in order to subsequently relate these concepts to the women's talk. In particular, in the following section I review the accounts of identity found in Mahoney and Yngvesson (1992), Naples (1998), Remennick (2000), and Twine (1999), and in order to apply their thoughts to adoptive mothers.

LOCATION, IDENTITY, AND RESISTANCE

An unspoken feature of the interviews is the extent to which the women used "identity talk" throughout the conversations, most notably when they described the shifts to becoming mothers. I, however, do not thoroughly recognize the women's talk as "identity talk" nor analyze it accordingly. I have not engaged identity discussions out of my own unfamiliarity with the depth and breadth of the psychoanalytical works of Lacan, Freud, Chodorow, and Kristeva that delve into such matters as the formation of an active and independent self (child) distinct from the mother. A small number of works about identity, meanwhile, consider the development of the self in the midst of inequality (Mahoney and Yngvesson 1992; Remennick 2000; Twine 1999). This approach to interpreting identity and resistance is applicable to a project dedicated to listening.

Mahoney and Yngvesson claim that oppression and silence create a landscape in which change and resistance emerge.[3] They concern themselves with how self-dislocation results in self-determination (Mahoney and Yngvesson 1992: 48). Mahoney and Yngvesson also "argue for a theory of agency in which dependence is a condition of independence and inequality is a condition of resistance" (Mahoney and Yngvesson 1992: 63). According to their notion of agency, for example, the Black woman may experience social life as someone "who should be acted on and active only in disobedience" (Mahoney and Yngvesson 1992: 64). The Black woman encounters the social world as both "like and not like" at the same time. In the midst of social alienation, Mahoney and Yngvesson strive to show that there occurs "a point of disjuncture or contradiction [moments when the invisible woman recognizes her insecure positioning] that moves a previously 'invisible' subject to activity . . . " (Mahoney and Yngvesson 1992: 68). "Activity" occurs within everyday practices and social relations, and is not necessarily marked by thunderous or extraordinary events. Mahoney and Yngvesson's thoughts about resistance are relevant to adoptive mothers.

Twine offers, further, insights directly relevant to transracial and/or transnational adoptive mothers. In her article "Transracial Mothering and Antiracism," she asserts that White birth mothers of Biracial children participate daily in antiracist acts because of their unstable location between the White and Black communities. So located, the self-evaluation and competency of White mothers of Biracial children, Twine found, is tied to both their ability to protect their children from their own family's racism and to their success in winning the approval of women from the Black community. These mothers, moreover, lose some of their White privilege as they negotiate multiple communities and are unable to transfer the advantages of being White to their children.

Whereas Twine focuses on women whose racial transgressions are hypervisible, Remennick (2000) concentrates on women whose failure to meet mothering imperatives is invisible, and queries whether or not these women choose to resist. In "Childless in the Land of Imperative Motherhood: Stigma and Coping Among Infertile Israeli Women," Remennick distinguishes between infertile women who cope and those who resist. She argues that in the Israeli context, where pronatalism, or the moral and religious imperative to reproduce, dominates, resistance to the stigma infertility is virtually nonexistent. With this in mind, she maps out what constitutes resistance such that a woman may move from simply coping with a stigma to overtly challenging it. Remennick, along with Mahoney and Yngvesson and Twine, offers insight for ascertaining whether or not adoptive mothers resist.

What bearing do the above works have on the current one? Are identity and resistance embodied in adoptive mothers' renditions of their lives, even though many of the women neither aspired to resist nor thought of themselves as silenced through invisibility?[4] Much of Mahoney and Yngvesson's characterization of the emergent subject does not apply, given that "relations of domination" did not overwhelmingly mark the women's situations. Yet, subtleties surfaced in their narratives that coincided with Mahoney and Yngvesson's interpretation of identity and resistance. While some mothers went to great lengths to portray themselves as like other mothers, others understood themselves to be both "like and not like" typical mothers. They knew that, with the adoption of their child, their social location altered. Often, moreover, "relations of domination" did appear in their portrayals of their children's lives, which required these mothers to respond.

Twine's analysis of White birth mothers with Biracial children also provides a basis for interpreting these adoptive mothers. Similar to the birth mothers Twine addresses, some of the adoptive mothers, particularly those with Black and Biracial children, spoke openly of assaults to their maternal identity directly tied to their inability to meet their children's racial/ethnic needs. The same women also thought about and tried to win the approval of Black women. Unlike the experiences of Israeli women detailed in Remennick's work, these mothers virtually never spoke of being stigmatized. Yet, although stigmatization was not widely thematized in the women's narratives, a few of the women did experience a process of self-determination that involved the recognition that their social positioning changed with the adoption of their children, and which required them to act. All of these observations are elaborated later in this chapter, in particular, by drawing on examples from the narratives. Before doing so, however, something more must be said about location and resistance.

The aforementioned writers share the belief that a person moves toward resistance when situated in a socially awkward or disparaged position. Nancy Naples, in her works, *Community Activism and Feminist Politics* and *Grassroots Warriors*, further considers the "politics of positionality" by examining the link between a woman's social location and how she responds to social problems. In Naples's estimation, a person's standpoint is both a location and an achievement. As a result, building a social location is an ongoing and constantly in-flux process. In *Grassroots Warriors*, Naples specifically ties a gendered location "to enacting change" (1998: 132). She focuses on minority, urban women who view their community work as akin to mothering (1998: 129). Indeed, these women, according to Naples, draw on the power granted them as mothers to assert power in the larger community. These mothers, along with women who are not mothers, regard their community activism as mothering the community. All of these women activists recognize the fluidity of their positions in the community and, through such recognition, generate and assert power in their ever-changing location in the social landscape. Through such recognition, the very notion of community is also redefined. "As a dynamic process, the social construction of community offers the possibility for redefinition of boundaries, for broadened constituencies, and for seemingly unlikely alliances" (Naples 1998: 337). Of course, the low-income women with whom Naples conversed were attentive to the relations of domination that marked their communal and maternal lives and that required them to build "unlikely alliances." They were keenly aware that they mothered "their" children along a "fault line" (Ragoné and Twine 2000). In contrast, the adoptive mothers I interviewed hesitated by and large to recognize fault lines of domination and inequality in their maternal lives and selves. Through the women's talk of maternal identity, however, I discovered that the possibility exists to defy racial standards even if most of the adoptive mothers interviewed here chose not to realize these potentials. In the following section, the women's narratives are considered in relation to the potential to defy racial hierarchies.

LOCATION, RESISTANCE, AND RACE

The women with children of a different race and/or nationality were the most likely to experience identity alterations and, correspondingly, were the most likely to resist. Of course, all the women shared the identity shift associated with mothering itself—a welcomed and longed-for position for all the women regardless of the race of the child. Yet, a greater identity shift accompanied adopting a child of a different race; recall that Deborah, with her Asian children, regarded herself as a "purple person," and that Tera knew that ignoring racial concerns was a luxury she could no longer afford with the adoption of her Biracial children. For these women, and Deborah in particular, not only did their racial awareness change, but additionally their racial location became muddled.[5]

While Deborah, with her altered racial identity, moving from White to purple, signified heightened racial awareness, it was the women with Black and Biracial children who found themselves most challenged, and spoke openly of these challenges, and were most likely to move toward resistance. Recall also that, unlike the other sets of women, several of the women with Black and Biracial children constructed themselves almost as joint owners of their children, sharing responsibility and the child's allegiance with the larger Black community. For mothers with Black and Biracial children who did not construct themselves as joint owners, there was the intimation or even outright recognition that their children were both of them and not of them. This was particularly true for Karen, who was in the habit of telling her Black daughter that she was Black unlike her adoptive mother. In contrast, recall that the women with White children did not mention racially awkward situations and the effect of these situations on their identity. Meanwhile, some of the women with Asian children were confronted with situations that could have affected their identities, but most often they did not leave encounters, particularly with Asians living in this country, feeling unsettled. Remember Mary's response to her son's interaction with the Korean elder: At a Korean-American social function, Mary's Korean son was approached by a Korean elder who spoke to him in Korean and demanded that he offer his seat to her. Her son, gathering from Mary's description, felt slightly sheepish about the encounter because he could not understand the Korean spoken by the elderly woman and, as a result, did not respond appropriately. Mary allayed her son's apprehension by remarking to the effect, "Don't worry, I didn't understand either." Mary's reaction revealed the extent to which her identity, as her child's rightful mother, remained stable despite her son's uneasiness and the Korean elder's assumption that her child was Korean and would understand Korean and follow traditional Korean customs and manners.

In contrast, Elaine and Elizabeth, two of the mothers with Black daughters, took instruction from their daughters to take notice of their children's race and to respond to the children's racial needs. More so than any of the other mothers, Elizabeth and Elaine articulated in our conversations the adversities facing their daughters and how these difficulties influenced their own maternal identities. Elaine's daughter, remember, asked her whether or not Elaine still loved her "even though" she was Black. Elizabeth's daughter, meanwhile, asserted Elizabeth was merely her stepmother and asked to meet her "real mother."[6] Of course, these women may have faced more troubles than did Tera, the mother of Biracial children, because they, unlike Tera, did not place their children in predominantly minority schools, but instead in White settings: Unlike some of the women with White children, moreover, Elaine and Elizabeth did not unquestioningly describe themselves as adequate mothers. It was both this questioning self and being driven by their daughters that motivated these women to act. These women reinforced Gailey's idea that transracial adoptive mothers view motherhood as something learned whereas other adoptive mothers do not (Gailey 2000: 34).

I have chosen to focus on Tera, Elaine, and Elizabeth because each consciously acted to combat racial hegemonies, whereas other women with Black and Biracial children spoke of combating racism to a limited extent. Several of the latter did, however, mention participating in antiracist acts when contending with their family's racism. Phyllis chose not to leave her sons with her own mother because she was uncomfortable with her mother's racism. Sammie tried to make sense out of her mother's habit of telling others that her grandson was Latin when he was in fact Biracial. Although these women negotiated their family's racism, they did not portray these racial demands as infringing upon their maternal identities to the same extent as did Elaine and Elizabeth. This could partly be due to the fact that some of the women's children in the Black and Biracial group, at the time of the interviews, were infants. A few women in this group, however, while recognizing their child's racial differences from themselves, disregarded the significance of race and, as a result, were not inclined to act.

Working from the narratives themselves, the women, particularly those with Black and Biracial children, appeared to resist racial hierarchies to varying degrees and on various levels. Of course, I maintain that some mothers with Black and Biracial children, like Leslie, did not resist at all because they chose to make a joke out of or ignore the racial difficulties that surfaced in their own families. Sammie and Phyllis, meanwhile, combated their mothers' racism by choosing not to leave their children alone with their mothers, but in our conversations they decided to discount the weightiness of such difficulties and to present themselves as simply managing uncomfortable situations. The question surfaces, Are these women resisting, as Twine maintains, when they do not perceive themselves to be? Certainly, Sammie and Phyllis, among other women with Black and Biracial children, performed daily antiracist work. According to Mahoney and Yngvesson, Naples, and Remennick, however, the greatest levels of resistance require greater self-recognition that one is defying relations of domination. Borrowing from the above thinkers; resistance, in the context of this work, means that the women recognize themselves to be dislocated and use their self awareness and their very location to enact change. To a certain extent, the very narrative practices the women employed revealed the degree to which they resisted, as those most willing to share maternal difficulties were more likely to resist.

Yngvesson and Mahoney (2000) maintain that cohesive identities and narratives are central to feeling authentic and whole. We all need a center, a point of origin, and a story. They apply this thought to the identities of transnational and/or national adoptees who occupy a space of "belonging and not belonging." Fractured narratives serve to legitimize and strengthen those who appear to have whole, faultless identities. Adoptees, in contrast, find themselves "not belonging anywhere but with others who don't belong" as they live out the "arbitrariness of their identities and their constructedness" (Yngvesson and Mahoney 2000). In this unstable location, adoptees attempt to create cohesion where it is lacking by trying to piece together their own narratives. Much of what Yngvesson and Mahoney say about the identities of transracial and/or national adoptees' can be applied to the mothers of these children as they try to create order in both their own maternal identities and the identities of their children.

For many of the women interviewed, creating narrative order meant presenting tidy views of their lives, especially when they were asked a series of questions requiring that they consciously portray themselves. For those who were least inclined to resist, narrative order was paramount; correspondingly, they chose to portray their lives as unhindered by problems, racial or otherwise. Most of the women—particularly transnational and/or national adoptive mothers—practiced a habit of recognizing difficulties but shelving their poignancy. A few, Elaine and Elizabeth in particular, used the interviews to confront the dislocation their children experienced; more than the other mothers, moreover, they used the interviews to sort out maternal difficulties. Elaine and Elizabeth, along with the other mothers who did not ignore, but instead narratively engaged problems, resisted.

Elaine fought vigorously to keep her daughter in a predominantly White school with achievement-oriented students, even when the school, according to Elaine, more or less deliberately tried to rid itself of minority children. She was forced to juggle the importance of race in relation to class and ultimately decided that class difficulties were more important than race in the school setting. Indeed, she constructed herself as defiantly battling the intimations and direct acts of others that told her to keep her daughter with "her own kind" in a school where students lag academically. Here, she described her battle with local public-school officials:

I would not have let it drop and I think they [school administrators] knew that. I suspect because I was raising such a stink in so many different areas, making it public. I mean, "a key administrator" at one point said to me, "If you'll keep quiet, I'll get her in somehow," and then I kind of repeated that back to him and he backtracked on that. But I think he knew there was going to be trouble. I would have gone public. I would have gone to the newspaper. I would have gone to the county board of education, and they don't want any more friction.

Even with her determination and will to prevail, Elaine understood that she acted in a manner that was, prior to the adoption of her daughter, foreign to her, "My parents took everything sitting down. They were very passive, so I'm not so sure that it's a bad thing. It's not my personality to be confrontational like that, and so I found it very stressful, very difficult." Despite the stress, Elaine's resolution to "win" did not cease with her daughter's acceptance into the school. Rather, she worked to establish a scholarship fund for other minority children to attend the "White" school.

Elizabeth, perhaps not as dramatically as Elaine, also took action. She built a relationship with school officials by regularly complaining to them that they needed to diversify. At the time we met, she was helping to organize her community's Martin Luther King celebration.

Mindful of Elaine and Elizabeth's actions, transracial adoption can be characterized as a potential space—a space and landscape where racial assumptions can be made problematic. The equation is rather simple. The women who adopted transracially, placed their children in predominantly White settings, and recognized the adversities their children faced experienced the greatest affronts to their sense of selves as mothers. Tera avoided some of the difficulties facing Elizabeth and Elaine since she and her husband were raising their children in a predominantly minority setting. As a result, however, Tera confronted, more than the others, minority women's evaluation and appraisal of her mothering skills.

Of course, through comparing Elaine and Elizabeth with Tera, some of the complexities associated with resistance surface. Who are actually the defiant ones? It remains questionable whether the battle and effort to place minority children in White environments is worth the racial identity costs it may bring both mother and child. By contrast, Tera, and not her children, may have carried the brunt of identity difficulties that accompanies raising Black children in a minority community. Much of the controversy around transracial adoption questions the soundness of placing Black and Biracial children in uncomfortable White landscapes (Abdullah 1996; Howe and Kennedy 1998; Kallgren and Caudell 1993). Entering this discussion, if ever so briefly, I would suggest that making more room for minority children in White, privileged settings is an act of resistance and creativity. Elizabeth and Elaine resisted by forcing White settings to not be so White. Don't schools, with a legacy of academic achievement associated with the White and upper-middle class, have an obligation to educate less financially secure minority children? Tera, meanwhile, resisted perhaps more fully by submerging herself in Black and Latin communities that ordinarily would not be her own, thereby, catering to her children's identity needs first. Rather than digressing further into a discussion about who resisted more or about how to evaluate the correctness of placing minority children in White settings, let me remain focused on the difficult decisions that faced these mothers and on how racial demands impinged upon their maternal identities.[7] As witnessed by their actions, all of these mothers recognized that their racial location changed with the adoption of their children, requiring them to act differently than they did before adopting—be it Tera who immersed and dedicated herself to a minority environment, or Elizabeth and Elaine who recognized and challenged the racism present in their predominantly White landscapes.[8]

Tera, Elaine, and Elizabeth shared a practice of confounding race by viewing themselves as incomplete owners of their children. While these mothers were deeply committed to their "own" children, they understood that their children also belonged elsewhere. Recall that Elaine spoke to this eloquently in response to the question when her daughter felt like her own:

I'm very aware of what has become a cliché, that African proverb that it takes a village to raise a child, especially because it's a transracial situation. I need Black people to help us give her a sense of identity, so because I feel I need the Black community to take her in, to help her with her sense of self, in that sense I feel she's not mine. She belongs to more people. So it's a very loaded question. I mean, in one sense, I have, I'm sure, as deep as commitment to her as I would have to a biological child, but in another sense because of the transracial I'm aware of what I can't give her and what she needs, and so I'm very aware that I need the Black community to help.

Elaine's private mothering demands required her to turn to the larger Black community. In some sense, Elaine, like some of the other mothers of Black and Biracial children without a well-defined ownership of their children, could be construed as "other mothers." Other mothers, according to Patricia Hill Collins, participate in broad-based mothering and, in the process, "help build community institutions and fight for the welfare of their neighbors" (Naples 1998: 115). Unlike Elaine, however, Collins's other mothers act out of a concern for the larger community, not simply to meet their private mothering needs. In contrast, Elaine and Elizabeth's private demands led them to reach out to their daughters' "other" community, even if they did not see themselves as fully part of that community. For Elaine and Elizabeth, meeting their daughters needs was their first priority, and this eventually pushed them to work for wider change. Tera, meanwhile, living and working in a minority setting of which her children were a part, practiced mothering in a fashion more strictly aligned with what Collins had in mind and committed herself to promoting the good of the wider community.

What can be gathered from the above discussion is that a position of "other mothering" offers possibilities. When a mother looks beyond the demands of her private mothering experiences and places her life and those of her children into a wider context, she is more likely to resist.

LOCATION, RESISTANCE, AND MATERNITY

Although Elaine and Elizabeth confronted race through their own maternal distress, they did not use their adoptions as a space to confound limited notions of maternity that configure only certain women as able mothers. In fact, Elaine and Elizabeth, more so than some of the other women, feared meeting the birth mother and hesitated to talk and share information about the birth mothers with their daughters. Of course, part of their hesitation was tied to the extent to which their status as rightful mothers had been challenged. Correspondingly, both of them quivered at the thought of having an open adoption.

As mentioned above, my attention to the women's attitudes toward the birth mothers arose from an effort to unearth universal connections drawn by the adoptive mothers to women, generally, and to the birth mothers specifically. Universal connections mean that women are appreciative of racial and class differences among women but also recognize similarities among them, for instance, that both adoptive and birth mothers share legitimate and illegitimate claims to the children. I ask, Did these women see themselves as connected to the birth mother not only through the child, but as women defined by their shared work as mothers and "not mothers" (Mohanty 1997)?

Most of the women sympathetically related to the birth mother, but that did not necessarily mean identifying with her as a member of a community of women tied together by Mohanty's (1997) notion of shared work. On most occasions, she, the birth mother, was not conceived as a coinhabitant in a web of social relations that defines all women as mothers or not mothers. Most often, then, larger connections were not drawn between the adoptive mothers' own identities as mothers and not biological mothers to the birth mother's identity as both mother and not mother. "Localized" interpretations of the birth mother surfaced when the women were asked to compare themselves to the birth mothers.[9] Many of the women noted the birth mother's age or personality as the defining difference with themselves—those women who knew almost nothing about the birth mother withdrew from comparing and contrasting themselves because, they had nothing to say. In my estimation, the focus on personality obscures the wider context in which the adoptive mothers become mothers and the birth mothers relinquish. Not drawing larger connections between one's own maternal situation and others' locations, moreover, distracts from questioning fitness standards that mark certain women alone as able mothers.

An argument could be made, however, that simply by adopting the women contradicted sedentary notions of maternity. The women defied traditional notions of mother and child by nurturing someone who was not their biological own. It is hard to gauge the extent to which biological and genetic connections continue to define ideal family relations. Christine Ward Gailey, in her article, "Ideologies of Motherhood and Kinship in U.S. Adoption," argues that genetic relations, as witnessed by legal precedents, remain the ideal standard for the creation of families. Adoption, says Gailey, violates "the norms of nonmarital procreation and marital nonprocreation" (Gailey 2000: 22). In the end, she asserts, adoption choices, for example, pursuing " blue-ribbon" White babies or working through public agencies show "parents' weddedness or lack thereof to dominant ideologies" (Gailey 2000: 54).

In contrast to Gailey's diagnosis, the women, in their narratives, were, by and large, not interested in confronting dominant ideologies. They were instead concerned with normalizing adoption. Many of the women could barely remember a negative comment by others about adoption per se, and, in their estimation, adoption no longer carries the stigma it once did. Although this may well be the case, the sentiment that adoption is less than ideal surfaced subtly, or not so subtly, in their words, and is also widespread in the popular media. Joanna heard her daughter's friend apologize when the friend learned that her daughter was adopted, for example. For a time, Katherine's son became angry every time she mentioned he was adopted. Even on a *Seinfeld* television episode, the Elaine character started to wonder whether her boyfriend, an adoptee, was a mass murderer after Kramer alerted her to the "fact" that all mass murderers are adopted. Still, given the mixed evaluations of adoption, all of the women resisted traditional notions of legitimate families and ways of forming a family simply through their participation in adoption.

Of course, because most of the women did not seek to undercut fitness standards, but in fact realize them, the mere fact of adoption does not undercut assumptions about maternity. As Yngvesson (1997) points out, moreover, adoption has historically replicated and reinforced the ideal family as a unit composed of male and female parents. Thus, although adoption offers the theoretical possibility of resistance against rigid conceptions of the family and maternity, it does not guarantee such resistance, especially in the midst of bureaucratic and structural arrangements that promote maternal ideals (Gailey 2000; Yngvesson 1997). Even within bureaucratic and attitudinal constraints, however, some signs of resistance exist.

RESISTANCE, MATERNITY, AND OPEN ADOPTIONS

The possibilities of confronting gender strictures in the adoption context are conditioned by the placement of the birth mother. The birth mother was often characterized as physically experiencing secrecy and isolation. Who cannot be struck by Phyllis' interaction with her son's birth grandmother? Having what Phyllis described as an open relationship with the Black birth mother of her Biracial child, Phyllis called the birth mother's home only to reach the birth grandmother. Upon identifying herself, the birth grandmother let it be known that she had no idea she had a grandchild:

One day I called down there. She [the birth mother] lived, at this time, with her mother. Called down there and I was asking for her and I explained who I was and the mother says, "Why you calling here?" I said, "Well, I just wanted to invite your daughter and, of course, you're welcome to come, too, for dinner and I just wanted to touch base since we hadn't. . . ." Well, a long story short, she [the birth mother] had not told anybody she was pregnant and had placed him. His grandmother was extremely angry. One of the funny things that she said was, "So you going to give him back to us?" And I said, "Oh, no ma'am."

Phyllis tried to make light of the situation with the birth grandmother and did not concentrate on the birth mother's lot, or the scene the birth mother endured when she returned home the day that Phyllis called. At other moments, Phyllis referred sympathetically to the birth mother's attempt to keep quiet. Most of the women did not mention as directly as did Phyllis that the birth mother relinquished in secrecy. But there was the intimation that the birth mother endured pain silently. Many of these mothers recognized that their own joy came at the expense of someone else's pain. They contended with this dilemma by hoping that the birth mother's pain subsided with time, by asserting that she made the correct choice in relinquishing, or like Phyllis, by participating in "open" adoptions—even if these relationships were not devoid of secrecy.

Yngvesson (1997) argues that open adoptions offer a setting for confounding maternal fitness standards by creating the opportunity for the birth mother no longer to be buried under shame and secrecy. Instead, she can maintain an official and formal position and relationship vis-à-vis the child and the adoptive family. The birth mother of Tera's children, for example, felt relieved to know that her children were well cared for and that her decision to relinquish was a good one. Moreover, Tera, like the other mothers in open adoptions liked her relationship with the birth mother. Through this relationship, a complex understanding of the birth mother developed that portrayed her neither as the martyr who made the ultimate sacrifice nor as a villain who carelessly relinquished, but as someone trying to manage a difficult situation.

Despite positive experiences with the birth mother such as Tera's, Yngvesson found that open adoptive situations are not idyllic and may in fact both reinforce gendered stereotypes of fit and unfit mothers and suggest that only married and financially secure women can mother well and be recognized as legitimate maternal figures by the larger society. Racial differences between the adopting family and relinquishing mother only add complexity to "open" relations. Even if an adoption is designated as "open," Black birth mothers, choose not to be present as frequently as do White birth mothers, as in Phyllis's situation. In my interviews, I found that difficulties arose in families with two Biracial children when the child with a White birth mother, but not the child with a Black birth mother, had regular contact with its birth mother. Given the overall unwillingness of Black birth mothers to participate in open adoptions, the potential of open adoptions to challenge gender hegemonies perhaps is negligible in these situations. Indeed, the gulf between White and Black communities may be too great, at this particular time, to hope for "open" relations between Black birth mothers and White adoptive parents who live in predominantly White settings.[10]

Yngvesson, while recognizing the shortcomings of open adoptions, maintains the belief that open adoptions offer the possibility for "evolving" maternal identities. Yngvesson well articulates the complex relations that surface and "evolve" in open adoptions:

The "openness" of open adoption is suffused with risk and enabled by restraint, by the silences that surround it, and by the fragile space that open adoption provides. The mothers that are made in this process are not simply given in the biological connection of mother to child or made as a "code for conduct" in the legal family. Rather, they are created, over time, in the evolving relations between mothers [of various kinds] in "legal" families and the "other" mothers who in relinquishing their children have unsettled this family in the very act of making it "whole" (Yngvesson 1997: 75).

Yngvesson recognizes that open adoptions are always in the making and constantly negotiated. Indeed, Grotevant and McRoy (1998) describe open adoptions as relationships that fall along a continuum of degrees of openness as decided by adoption agencies, birth mothers, and adoptive parents.[11] In the process of creating an open relationship, adoptive and birth mothers contribute to new understandings of open adoptions—they help set precedent. In the end, it is hoped that, similar to the women on which Naples focuses, "unlikely alliances" will develop that aid in transforming static notions of maternity through the process of creating open relationships. Evolving maternal identities allow mothers the freedom to relate legitimately to their children from a number of locations, be it as birth or adoptive mother. I add that this is most likely the case in either in White-on-White adoptions or transracial situations with a White birth mother.[12] Tera recognized the potentials in open adoptions to a certain extent by noting that open adoptive families signify alternative family relations comparable to stepperson relations:

Yeah, my mother said to me when we were talking about doing all this stuff [open adoption], "Well, won't that be so confusing." I said, "It's not going to be any more confusing than three-fourths of the rest of the kids out there who have divorced parents, remarried parents, stepfamilies." One of my nephews has a stepfamily, and he lives with his mother most of the time. The interesting thing is trying to explain the difference to my son about the differences between my nephew and his father and their relationship, and his relationship with his birth father. The divorced family versus the adoptive family trying to sort all that out. It's hard to do.

Tera, while mindful of varying family compositions, fails to acknowledge that in most instances "other family" configurations mimic traditional families with their usual gendered relations. At the same time, the rise in diverse family situations may well allow for greater flexibility in families and, thereby, as Yngvesson (1997) insists, affect the positionality of women. Through open adoption, for instance, maternity need not be confined to the "woman of the house." Instead, a "shared" maternal position might emerge akin to that of the Black neighborhood woman who cared for the area children without thinking about the absence of a biological lineage between herself and them (Glenn 1994; Yngvesson 1997). Maternity could become and can be a flexible location available to those who desire it, and not confined to those who meet biological, financial, and marital, among other, conditions.

In my own work I discovered, moreover, that all of the women in open adoptions relished and gathered deep satisfaction and enjoyment from their open relationships with the birth mothers. Phyllis, recall, was pleased that she did not pursue an international adoption because it lacked the prospect of being open. "See, if we adopted like that [from an Asian country], our adoptions wouldn't be open and so we wouldn't have all these other benefits." In *Openness in Adoption: Exploring Family Connections,* Harold Grotevant and Ruth McRoy find some indication that birth mothers experience less grief if they participate in open adoptions. Judging from the reactions of adoptive and birth mothers, open adoptions offer a glimmer of hope of mending many of the difficulties surrounding adoption. It certainly appears that open adoptions have the potential of undercutting the habit of "individualistic societies of legally binding the separation of children from their birth parents" (Grotevant and McRoy 1998: 5). Perhaps through open adoption, moreover, maternal positions can become occupied by "other mothers" so that the child is surrounded by caring individuals added to his/her life rather than having such individuals sub-tracted from it. Ideally, the birth father would also participate in open adoptions; in such a case, "mothering work" could further defy gendered expectations, and parenting language could truly connote gender neu-trality (Ruddick 1997).[13]

I have tried to reveal the possibilities in open as well as transracial adoptions generally while remaining mindful of the dilemmas these re-lationships face. The immense detail gathered from the interviews make inconsistencies more apparent; these women are not uniform in their re-sponses to their children or in their narrations. Some of the women with Black and Biracial children challenged racism in their families daily, but did not necessarily view themselves as doing so. Those mothers keenly aware of their antiracist work were the ones more likely consciously to resist. Generally, most of the mothers did not confound gender and crit-ically regard mothering imperatives that designate only certain women as legitimate mothers. The possibility of breaking down barriers between the adoptive and birth mothers, however, surfaced for those women in very open adoptions who had regular in-person contact with the birth mother. Of course, as noted, open adoptions are complex relationships; the Black birth mothers, recall, were unwilling to participate in open re-lationships.

In the brief conclusion that follows, I focus on complexities and dilem-mas. In particular, I magnify unresolved research difficulties associated with this project such as making women visible in order to look at pros-pects for future studies that examine adoption with listening in mind.

NOTES

1. It must be noted that listening is my own intention and not necessarily one of the women.

2. Listening can be thought of not simply as a way of uncovering potentials in individuals or, in this case, in research findings, but additionally as a way of think-ing about research that challenges rigid notions of knowledge production.

3. Defining resistance is, at a minimum, difficult. Indeed, its designation is more easily articulated in reference to specific actions. Resistance requires self-recognition; a woman can resist only if she is cognizant of the relations of domi-nation amid which she resides. It is the very domination, moreover, that affords an opportunity for change.

4. The conclusion revisits the question of whether White adoptive mothers are invisible. The arguments made in this chapter assume that they do experience invisibility at least to some degree.

5. There are works that explore adoptees' racial identities (Patton 2000; Simon and Altstein 2000). It would be interesting, however, to study adoptees' racial identities in relation to and in juxtaposition with their adoptive parents' racial identification.

6. As was noted in previous chapters, Black and Biracial children were more

vocal about race than were Asian children. Black and Biracial children let their mothers know almost immediately when something said at school or elsewhere displeased them. In contrast, the Asian children were in the habit of not telling their mothers about kidding until it became unbearable to them maybe after a year had past. Another hint of a pattern emerged that intimated that Black and Biracial girls are more vocal than Black and Biracial boys. Of course, it cannot be fully known whether or not this is the case from the limited focus of this work.

7. This very brief discussion of who resisted more does not reflect the extent to which I have thought long and hard about what is the right course of action—send adopted Black and Biracial children to schools where the students are college-bound or consign them to predominantly minority schools where financial resources are lacking and many children do not come from families that can afford college. Although the child may be more likely to achieve by going to the "White schools," he/she may suffer greater identity difficulties in the process of reaching these goals. I ask instead, What do we want in the long run? Which practices further racial segregation or promote integration? Certainly, it is true that the type of integration we have now and in the past comes at the expense of children of color.

8. Only Tera, along with one other mother of minority children, was not raising her children in a predominantly White setting. Interestingly enough, many of the women with Black and Biracial children, when asked directly about diversity in their neighborhoods, expressed guilt that they were not raising them in a mixed community or talked about in the future moving to a mixed race neighborhood. Only one mother with Asian children talked about looking for diversity in her children's schools or neighborhoods.

9. The potential exists to use local understandings to build wider connections. Indeed, one mother related to birth mothers because she had relinquished a child years before adopting. She was the same women who quit her volunteer work at an adoption agency because she felt they equated good mothering with the possession of healthy finances.

10. It would be interesting to discover whether Black birth mothers also hesitate to have open relations with either Black adoptive families or White families who live in predominantly minority communities.

11. I found this to be the case in my interviews. Four of the women had very open relationships with the birth mothers with regular and ongoing direct contact with them. Other women said that they had semi-open relationships even though they did not have in-person contact with the birth mother. They corresponded through letters negotiated by the adoption agency. Then there was Phyllis who called her relationship with the Black birth mother open even though it was clear that the birth mother was not open about relinquishing.

12. The possibilities arising from open relationships with Asian birth mothers are difficult to gauge given that adoptive parents often choose Asian adoptions at least in part to avoid dealing with birth parents (Gailey 2000).

13. I am not sure how much I support Ruddick's effort to degender mothering work. It is undeniable that the more men participate in mothering work, the more societal value may be granted to such work. Yet, women also maintain and gather a certain amount of power through their work as mothers, which could be lost with the deletion of gender. Lovabond (1994) argues, moreover, that taking gender out of specific work tasks does little to overcome structural inequalities.

Conclusion

The possibilities to confront racial, gender, and class hierarchies are pursued not only through the women's words, but also in the research act itself by virtue of a conversation with selected feminist scholars. In this short conclusion, gaps in the feminist dialogues used in this book are reviewed, the benefit of making women's lives visible is disputed, and the virtues of reflexivity as promoted by many feminists are celebrated. These matters are considered so as to enhance the prospect that feminist research is a forum where listening occurs.

OVERSIGHTS, DILEMMAS, AND POSSIBILITIES

Interest in uncovering possibilities in open as well as transracial and transnational adoptions gathers energy and force from feminist discourse. Through feminist dialogue, the words become available even to question adoption practices. But the reflexivity found in so many feminist works allows the critical gaze to turn not only on a variety of subject matters such as adoption, but also on the methodological and theoretical assumptions driving feminist efforts (Naples 1996). In this section, my gaze concentrates on the feminist works that aided in creating and carrying out this project (Abramovitz 1994, 2000; Blee 1993; Collins 1991; Gluck and Patai 1991; Harding 1991; Katz Rothman 1994; Naples 1996, 1998; Oakley 1981; Raymond 1993; Reinharz 1992; Rich 1976; Ruddick 1997; Solinger 1992, 2001; Twine 1999; Yngvesson 1997).

An Oversight: Religion

As was noted in earlier chapters, the very act of writing and talking about the women was confounded by my political understanding of adoption, which was at odds with the apolitical orientation of many of the women themselves. I entered the work thinking as a feminist humanist, while many of the women, as noted earlier, described and experienced their family lives religiously. Of course, my sample of women might have been particularly religious because of the adoption social workers with whom I worked. In any case, most of the women and I worked from different humanisms. With the insight of hindsight, it is hard not to wonder whether this work would have been better served by being grounded in the women's religious humanism.

The similarities and differences between the two "humanisms" have been accentuated earlier in the book in the hope of emphasizing the extent to which feminist efforts need more fully to consider the importance of traditional religion. Religion provides the social context in which many people act. Religion contains a social morality that drives, as a matter of fact, creativity and constraint—a morality that, on the one hand, promotes maternal ways of being, which preclude abortion, but, on the other hand, advises on racial matters. A broader sociological understanding of religion may well discard counting how many times a person attends church as its sole focus, and examine the interface of religion with race, class, and gender as an integral feature of social stratification. Religion, thereby, is no longer factored into the equation as a contributing variable, and instead becomes an identifying marker that associates people with particular social practices and notions about the stratified world. It may even be possible to consider a person or group's religious orientation as a standpoint—that is, both a location and an achievement (Naples 1998). In the foregoing book, religious location was linked to how women narratively reacted to social problems. A few of the women, as mentioned in an earlier chapter, for example, were not "traditional" Christians, but remained religiously inclined and even used their religion to question racial hierarchies. Efforts need to be made, then, in feminist and wider literature, to distinguish a "religiosity" that hides the poignancy of race from those religious practices that do not. I now realize that it is essential to think about religion as an elemental feature of stratification and to appreciate that American society is a religious one.

Maternal Gratification: A Dilemma

It needs to be mentioned once again that another phenomenon that is relatively absent in the feminist discourse that grounded this work is the sense of gratification that, for many women, accompanies motherhood. A good number of the women interviewed here, as noted in chapter 4, found their mothering work far more satisfying than their other work outside of the home. Maybe part of some feminists' hesitation to emphasize women's desires to nurture is a reaction to the patriarchal habit of defining all women by their ability and desire or lack thereof to mother (Rich 1976). Equally problematic, however, is ignoring the satisfaction and gratification that accompany mothering, as well as the need and desire that many women have to nurture. Sarah Ruddick articulates the shortsightedness of portraying maternity solely as an oppressive state:

> to suggest that mothers are principally victims of a kind of crippling work is an egregiously inaccurate account of women's own experience as mothers and daughters. Although one can sympathize with the anger that insists upon and emphasizes the oppressive nature of maternal practices, an account that describes only exploitation and pain is itself oppressive to women. Mothers, despite the inevitable trials and social conditions of motherhood are often effective in their work (Ruddick 1997: 585).

Ruddick balances the social, and often oppressive pressures that drive so many women to mother with the tremendous joy that accompanies mother work—a joy not available in other endeavors. This book has sought to do the same. The pleasure and self-assurance that many of the women gathered from mothering cannot be ignored. Who cannot feel some satisfaction upon hearing Judith's characterization of herself as an "excellent mother?"

> Oh, I think I'm an excellent mother. I feel very good about myself as a mother. It's the most favorite thing I've ever done. I've wanted to be a mother more than anything and I felt comfortable with it right off the bat.
>
> I hear people saying, "Oh, well, it took us a little bit of time to get in the swing of things." It was just immediate for me and for us that's just what we wanted for so long and we just went with it, and it was wonderful. I never felt incompetent or shaky or how are we going to do this; it just fit.

The trick or challenge confronting this work has been to acknowledge Judith's and the other women's joy, while also placing it in larger contexts such as in relation to the birth mothers and to racial and class hierarchies.

Visibility: A Dilemma

The difficulties understanding maternal gratification and religion in the adoption context stem, in part, from the odd placement of adoptive mothers as both legitimate and illegitimate mothers, as well as reflect the problems that generally confront efforts to make people's lives visible. Works such as Collins's (1991) seek to make visible people and their knowledge that otherwise would be relegated to unimportance, in particular, Black

women and other members of minority groups. The thought is that the
Black woman, historically, has not charted her own unique experiences.
Making visibility more generally significant is a theoretical and methodological procedure for giving voice to those who normally are made insignificant. The work, in particular, the women's experiences as both
visible and invisible people, problematizes the concept of visibility as
White, middle-class women who, by and large, are not marginalized. This
implies that visibility is also problematized more generally as a tool for
giving voice to the oppressed. The concern, in particular, is that in-depth
interviews are too in-depth and only encourage Panoptic invasion.

Throughout this work I have struggled with the relevant fact that I have
not studied the "oppressed." Correspondingly, I have wondered whether
feminist research suggestions apply to these White, middle-class women.
These are women of privilege whose experiences are relatively known and
visible. Indeed, it has traditionally been the case that White, middle-class
women uphold standards and ideals of femininity and maternity as is
apparent in public discussions and policies dealing with poor women
(Gordon 1990, 2000). Yet, in this work, it was discovered that these women
occupy an odd position as both visible and invisible.

The women with children of another race and nationality are physically
visible. Deborah, recall, felt herself to be the "purple person" because
visual differences attracted people's attention when she was in the company of her children. She received the overwhelmingly positive attention
granted the Asian child, especially in contrast to some of the disparaging
remarks made to the White mother with Black and Biracial children. This
hypervisibility that accompanies being physically different from others
did not necessarily translate into greater understanding of the women's
daily lives. Deborah, for instance, objected to the label "saint" being applied to her. She also alerted me to the awkward possibility that positive
attitudes toward Asian adopted children and their mothers may result, in
part, from the heightened status that minorities experience when in the
company of Whites. Complicating matters, however, was the fact that
some of the women, including Deborah, felt slightly, but not thoroughly
misrepresented in their hypervisibility. They objected to the saint label,
but, at the same time, most of the women with Asian children welcomed
the positive attention; for many of the women with Black and Biracial
children, the attention they received in public went unnoticed or was inconsequential after a time. With the oddity of feeling hypervisible, the
elemental question of whether or not her visibility or the lack thereof
matters surfaces again.

I would argue that her visibility matters because of her unique placement between White and minority communities, and the insights that can
be gathered therefrom. Through the women's own impressions, it can be
seen that visibility/invisibility is not a dichotomous matter but instead

constitutes a spectrum that allows for varying mixes of the two. Visibility and invisibility are experienced in degrees and under most conditions; one is neither completely visible nor invisible. Thinking of visibility/invisibility in this way avoids moral parables about whose experiences are thought to be worthy of making visible, given that visibility and invisibility are not static states. Additionally, acknowledging visibility and invisibility as matters of degree recognizes the power that can accompany various mixes of them.

More than bringing attention to the peculiar visibility and invisibility of the White adoptive mother, the difficulties associated with the effort to make women's lives visible, particularly those of disenfranchised women, need to be recognized again. Collins (1991), in her discussion of the outsider/within, recognizes the power that resides in the positioning of the Black woman domestic who knows both the White person's world and her own in the Black community. If, perhaps, only in passing, Collins alludes to the power of invisibility. It can be asked, however, Does not making visible the invisible undercut some of the power that resides in the knowledge held as an outsider/within? There is immense value in making experiences visible to enhance the position of Black women and gays, among other groups. Yet, is there a point of too much visibility? Was not the welfare mother too visible, too monitored (Gordon 1990)? In-depth interviews have the benefit of providing intimate detail in the women's own words (Naples 1996). Research techniques that provide an ethic of care may have the unintended effect of opening the doors to Panoptic invasion, as the woman interviewee reveals things to the sympathetic researcher she would not share with the pollster. Through so much sharing, she, the interviewee becomes intimately known by a wider academic community—a community, on most occasions, that is not her own—and, thereby, opens herself up to scrutiny. Essentially, I am trying to say that there are different kinds of visibility, some bad, and that becoming more visible in one way might lead to becoming more invisible in another. The effort to make women's lives visible is not opposed here. Instead, the potential hazards should be reflected on in an effort to avoid further objectification of those with whom we speak.

Reflexivity: A Virtue

Reflexivity, found in so many feminist works, has provided the space for the above discussions. Reflexivity is, in this context, a methodological and theoretical practice of attending, not only to the women "participants," but additionally to the wider context in which the words are gathered—noticing, for instance, the power dynamics between myself and the women with whom I spoke (Smith 1990). As a research strategy, reflexivity also involves critically looking back on the research process.

Uncertainties and dilemmas associated with reflexivity were pointed out in chapter 2. There it was recognized that reflecting back on the research process might encourage the generation of objective results (Gould 1989), the scientific standard some—but not all—feminists are trying to avoid (Harding 1986; Smith 1990).

In this conclusion I want to mention the virtues of reflexivity. Reflexivity, as a way of going about research, provides a framework for critically regarding research—not only in particular interviews or in specific circumstances, but more fundamentally in guiding aims of, for instance, making women's lives visible. Reflexivity also grants space for the researcher to talk honestly about her work and the perils and gratifications that reside therein (Borland 1991; Naples and Sach 2000).

In my own case, as might be painfully obvious, I have written with the women in mind. I could be accused of "hyperempiricism," or of trying too hard to follow the lead set by the women. With the focus on the women's words, my own will moves in and out of focus and clarity. Part of the difficulty stems from my own inexperience and discomfort with interviewing women who do not share my interest in studying race, class, and gender (Blee 1993). Although I tried to extend an ethic of care to all the women I interviewed, I found that my empathy and sympathy varied. I sympathized with all of the women some of the time, but with some of the women only some of the time. Specifically, I sympathized with all the women's need and desire to nurture, even as some of the women's habit of brushing aside racial concerns was uncomfortable and even at times objectionable to me. Unlike Raymond (1993), however, I could not completely disregard the women who tossed aside race because, through the venue of the in-person interviews, their understanding of race was accompanied by profound maternal emotions. The above facts are relayed not simply to be self-disclosing, but more importantly to note my feelings as a relevant feature of this work that influenced the writing of this document. Reflexivity, then, is an important avenue along which strengths and weaknesses of this work are exposed and room is created to offer suggestions for future work delving into adoption.

SOME SUGGESTIONS

Increasingly, studies and works are surfacing that critically regard adoption to unravel the racial, gender, and class ideologies that surround it (Berebitsky 2000; Patton 2000; Solinger 1992, 2001; Yngvesson 1997). Future works need to continue this trend. For adoptive relationships to reach their true potential to challenge hierarchies, difficult questions about them must be engaged. A wide assortment of works, for instance, have focused on the racial identities of adoptees, but I think that these works would be enhanced by widening the focus to look at these identities in light of those of the adoptive parents. Further, much can be gathered about the racial and class positioning of and between Latins, Blacks, Asians, and Whites through studies that regard the dynamics of race and class in adoptions. Continued efforts need to be made to regard gender critically in adoptions especially those that build links between adoptive parents and poor women. Future studies might also look at fathers [birth and adoptive] who are relatively absent from this work.

As was mentioned in chapter 1, these suggestions are made in the hope that this and future projects boost an understanding of mothering work as an act of peace (Ruddick 1994). I return again to Sara Ruddick's concluding thoughts in *Thinking Mothers/Conceiving Birth*, "to become a mother, whatever one's particular relation to individual acts of birth, is to welcome, shelter, protect, and nourish birth's bodies and thus to undertake a work of peace" (Ruddick 1994: 44). I would add that, in the process of recognizing and practicing mothering work as an act of peace, adoptive relations can fulfill their potential to counteract racial and maternal restrictions.

Bibliography

Abdullah, Samella B. 1996. "Transracial Adoption is Not the Solution to America's Problems of Child Welfare." *Journal of Black Psychology* 22(2) (May): 254–261.

Abramovitz, Mimi. 1994. "Challenging the Myths of Welfare Reform from a Woman's Perspective." *Social Justice* 21(1) (spring): 17.

———. 2000. *Under Attack, Fighting Back: Women and Welfare in the United States.* New York: Monthly Review Press.

Afshar, Haleh, and Mary Maynard (eds). 1994. *The Dynamics of "Race" and Gender: Some Feminist Interventions.* London: Taylor and Francis Press.

Alexander, Jacqui M., and Chandra Talpade Mohanty (eds). 1997. *Feminist Genealogies, Colonial Legacies, Democratic Futures.* New York: Routledge.

Allen, Sheila. 1994. "Race, Ethnicity and Nationality: Some Questions of Identity." In *The Dynamics of "Race" and Gender: Some Feminist Interventions,* edited by Haleh Afshar and Mary Maynard, 85–105. London: Taylor and Francis Press.

Altstein, Howard. 1993. "Adoption, Intercountry." In *Encyclopedia of Childbearing: Critical Perspectives,* edited by Barbara Katz Rothman, 10–12. Westport, CT: Oryx Press.

Altstein, Howard, and Rita J. Simon (eds). 1991. *International Adoption: A Multinational Perspective.* Westport, CT: Praeger.

Bartholet, Elizabeth. 1991. "Where Do Black Children Belong? The Politics of Race Matching in Adoption." *University of Pennsylvania Law Review* 139(5) (May): 1163–1256.

———. 1995. "International Adoptions Should Be Encouraged." In *Adoption: Opposing Views,* edited by Andrew Harneck, 178–187. San Diego, CA: Greenhaven Press.

Bassin, Donna, Margaret Honey and Meryle Mahrer Kaplan. 1994. *Representations of Motherhood*. New Haven, CT: Yale University Press.

Bates, Douglas. 1993. *Gift Children: A Story of Race, Family and Adoption in a Divided America*. New York: Ticknor and Fields.

Bayerl, J. A. 1977. "Transracial Adoptions: White Parents Who Adopted White Children and White Parents Who Adopted Black Children." Unpublished dissertation. University of Michigan.

Berebitsky, Julie. 2000. *Like Our Very Own: Adoption and the Changing Culture of Motherhood, 1851–1905*. Lawrence: University Press of Kansas.

Blee, Kathleen. 1993. "Evidence, Empathy, and Ethics: Lessons from Oral Histories of the Klan." *The Journal of American History* 80(2): 596–606.

Blumer, Herbert. 1966. "Sociological Implications of the Thought of George Herbert Mead." *The American Journal of Sociology* 5: 535–544.

Borland, Katherine. 1991. "That's Not What I Said: Interpretive Conflict in Oral Narrative Research." In *Women's Words: The Feminist Practice of Oral History*, edited by Sherna Berger Gluck and Daphne Patai, 63–75. New York: Routledge.

Bowles, Gloria, and Renate Duelli Klein (eds). 1983. *Theories of Women's Studies*. London: Routlege and Kegan Paul.

Bunjes, Lucile A. C. 1991. "Born in the Third World: To School in the Netherlands." In *Adoption: International Perspectives*, edited by Euthynia Hibbs, 279–287. Madison, WI: International University Press.

Cassidy, Anne. 1998. *Parents Who Think Too Much*. NewYork: Dell Publishing.

Chodorow, Nancy. 1978. *The Reproduction of Mothering*. Berkeley: University of California Press.

Chowdry, Geeta. 1995. "Women in Development (WID) in International Development Regimes." In *Feminism/Postmodernism/Development*, edited by Marianne H. Marchand and Jane L. Parpart, 26–41. Boulder, CO: Westview Press.

Collins, Patricia Hill. 1991. *Black Feminist Thought*. New York: Routledge.

———. 1994. "Shifting the Center: Race, Class, and Feminist Theorizing about Motherhood." In *Representation of Motherhood*, edited by Donna Bassin, Margaret Honey, and Meryle Mahrer Kaplan, 56–74. New Haven, CT: Yale University Press.

Cotterill, Pamela. 1992. "Interviewing Women: Issues of Friendship, Vulnerability, and Power." *Women's Studies International Forum* 15(5): 593–606.

Crittenden, Ann. 2002. *The Price of Motherhood: Why the Most Important Job in the World is Still the Least Valued*. New York: A Metropolitan Book.

Cullum, Carol. 1995. "Gays and Lesbians Should Have the Right to Adopt Children." In *Adoption: Opposing Viewpoints*, edited by Andrew Harneck, 117–125. San Diego, CA: Greenhaven Press.

Curtis, Carla M. 1996. "The Adoption of African American Children by Whites: A Renewed Conflict." *Families in Society: The Journal of Contemporary Human Services* 77(3) (March): 156.

Davis, Molly. 1992. "Transracial Adoption." *The Crisis* 99(8) (November–December): 20–22.

Dinnerstein, Dorothy. 1976. *Mermaid and the Minotaur: Sexual Arrangements and Human Malaise*. New York: Harper & Row.

Ehrenreich, Barbara, and Deirdre English. 1973. *Complaints and Disorders: The Sexual Politics of Sickness*. New York: The Feminist Press.

Escobar, Arturo. 1995. *Encountering Development: The Making and Unmaking of the Third World*. Princeton, NJ: Princeton University Press.

Fausto-Sterling, Anne. 1987. "Society Writes Biology/Biology Constructs Gender." In *Learning about Women: Gender, Politics, and Power*, edited by J. Conway et al., 61–77. Ann Arbor: University of Michigan Press.

Forde-Mazrui, Kim. 1994. "Black Identity and Child Placement: The Best Interests of Black and Biracial Children." *Michigan Law Review* 92(4) (February): 925–967.

Foucault, Michel. 1965. *Madness and Civilization: A History of Insanity in the Age of Reason*. New York: Vintage.

———. 1978. *The History of Sexuality, Volume I: An Introduction*. New York: Vintage Books.

———. 1979. *Discipline and Punish: The Birth of the Prison*. New York: Vintage Books.

Fulton, Kaye E. 1995. "Bringing Home Baby." *McClean's* 108(34) (August): 34–39.

Gailey, Christine Ward. 2000. "Ideologies of Motherhood and Kinship in US Adoption." In *Ideologies and Technologies of Motherhood: Race, Class, Sexuality, Nationalism*, edited by Helena Ragoné and France Winddance Twine, 11–55. New York: Routledge

———. 2002. "Race, Class, and Gender in Intercountry Adoption in the USA." In *International Perspectives on Intercountry Adoption*, edited by Peter Selman. London: Skyline House.

Gans, Herbert J. 1995. *The War against the Poor: The Underclass and Antipoverty*. New York: Basic Books.

Gilligan, Carol. 1982. *In a Different Voice: Psychological Theory and Women's Development*. Cambridge, MA: Harvard University Press.

Gilman, Lois. 1987. *The Adoption Resource Book*. New York: Harper & Row.

Glaser, Barney G. and Anselm L. Strauss. 1967. *The Discovery of Grounded Theory: Strategies of Qualitative Research*. Chicago: Adline Publishers.

Gluck, Sherna Berger, and Daphne Patai (eds). 1991. *Women's Words: The Feminist Practice of Oral History*. New York: Routledge.

Goddard, Lawford L. 1996. "Transracial Adoption: Unanswered Theoretical and Conceptual Issues." *Journal of Black Psychology* 22(2) (May): 273–281.

Gordon, Linda. 1990. *Women, the State, and Welfare*. Madison: University of Wisconsin Press.

———. 1994. *Pitied but Not Entitled: Single Mothers and the History of Welfare, 1890–1935*. New York: Free Press.

———. 2000. *The Great Orphan Abduction*. Cambridge, MA: Harvard University.

Gould, Stephen Jay. 1989. *Wonderful Life: The Burgess Shale and the Nature of History*. New York: Norton.

Grotevant, Harold D., and Ruth G. McRoy. 1998. *Openness in Adoption: Exploring Family Connections*. London: Sage.

Groze, V., and J. A. Rosenthal. 1991. "A Structural Analysis of Families Adopting Special-Needs Children." *Families in Society: The Journal of Contemporary Human Services* 72: 469–481.

Haizlip, Shirlee Taylor. 1994. *The Sweeter the Juice*. New York: Simon and Schuster.

Hammersley, Martyn, and Paul Atkinson. 1990. *Ethnography: Principles and Practice.* New York: Routledge.

Hammonds, Evelynn M. 1997. "Toward a Genealogy of Black Female Sexuality: The Problematic of Silence." In *Feminist Genealogies, Colonial Legacies, Democratic Futures,* edited by M. Jacqui Alexander and Chandra Mohanty, 170–182. New York: Routledge.

Hansen, Elaine Tuttle. 1997. *Mother without Child: Contemporary Fiction and the Crisis of Motherhood.* Berkeley: University of California Press.

Harding, Sandra. 1986. *Science Question in Feminism.* Ithaca, NY: Cornell University Press.

———. 1991. *Whose Science? Whose Knowledge?* Ithaca, NY: Cornell University Press.

Harneck, Andrew. 1995. *Adoption: Opposing Viewpoints.* San Diego, CA: Greenhaven Press.

Hayes, Peter. 1993. "Transracial Adoption: Politics and Ideology." *Child Welfare* 72(3) (May–June): 301.

Hays, Sharon. 1996. *The Cultural Contradictions of Motherhood.* New Haven, CT: Yale University Press.

Hermann, Valerie Phillips. 1993. "Transracial Adoption: 'Child-Saving' or 'Child-Snatching?'" *National Black Law Journal* 13(1–2) (spring): 147–164.

Herrmann, Kenneth J., Jr., and Barbara Kasper. 1992. "International Adoption: The Exploitation of Women and Children." *Affilia* 7(1) (spring): 45–58.

Hibbs, Euthynia D. (ed). 1991. *Adoption: International Perspectives.* Madison, WI: International University Press.

Hirschman, Mitu. 1995. "Women and Development: A Critique." In *Feminism/Postmodernism/Development,* edited by Marianne H. Marchand and Jane L. Parpart, 42–55. New York: Routledge.

Hollingsworth, Leslie Doty. 1997. "Effect of Transracial/Transethnic Adoption on Children's Racial and Ethnic Identity and Self Esteem: A Meta-Analytic Review." *Marriage and Family Review* 25(1–2): 99–130.

Howe, David. 1998. *Patterns of Adoption: Nature, Nurture, and Psychosocial Development.* Malden, MA: Blackwell.

Howe, Ruth-Arlene W. and Randall Kennedy (facilitated by Lise Funderburg). 1998. "Who Should Adopt Our Children?" *Essence,* January (28): 64.

Hubbard, Ruth. 1990. *The Politics of Women's Biology.* New Brunswick, NJ: Rutgers University Press.

Hunt, Scott, and Robert D. Bedford. 1994. "Identity Talk in the Peace and Justice Movement." *Journal of Contemporary Ethnography* 22 (4): 488–517.

Ives, Edward D. 1989. *The Tape Recorded Interview: A Manual for Field Workers in Folklore and Oral History.* Knoxville: University of Tennessee Press.

Jones, Merry Bloch. 1993. *Birthmothers: Women Who Have Relinquished Babies for Adoption Tell Their Stories.* Chicago: Chicago Review Press.

Kallgren, Carl A., and Pamela J. Caudill. 1992. "Current Transracial Adoption Practices: Racial Dissonance or Racial Awareness?" *Psychological Reports* 72(2) (April): 551.

Katz, Jeffrey. 1993. "Special Needs Adoption." In *Encyclopedia of Childbearing: Critical Perspectives,* edited by Barbara Katz Rothman, 13. Westport, CT: Oryx Press.

Keefer, Betsy, and Jayne E. Schooler. 2000. *Telling the Truth to Your Adopted or Foster Child: Making Sense of the Past.* Westport, CT: Bergin & Garvey.

Keller, Evelyn Fox. 1987. "Women Scientists and Feminist Critics of Science." In *Learning about Women: Gender, Politics, and Power,* edited by J. Conway et al., 77–93. Ann Arbor: University of Michigan Press.

Kenison, Katrina, and Kathleen Hirsch (eds). 1996. *Mothers: Twenty Stories of Contemporary Motherhood.* New York: North Point Press.

Kichen, Ian. 1995. "Long Journey, Happy Ending: Adopting a Foreign Child." *Business Week,* 12 June: 102–104.

Kimmel, Michael. 2002. "Toward a Pedagogy of the Oppressor." *Tikkun* 17(6) (November/December): 42.

Kingsolver, Barbara. 1996. "Quality Time." In *Mothers: Twenty Stories of Contemporary Motherhood,* edited by Katrina Kenison and Kathleen Hirsch, 151–164. New York: North Point Press.

Kitzinger, Shelia. 1978. *Women as Mothers.* New York: Vintage Books.

Knoll, Jean, and Mary-Kate Murphy. 1994. *International Adoption: Sensitive Advice for Prospective Parents.* Chicago: Chicago Review Press.

Koven, Seth, and Sonya Michel. 1993. *Mothers of a New World: Maternalist Politics and the Origins of Welfare States.* London: Routledge.

Lather, Patti. 1986. "Research as Praxis." *Harvard Educational Review.* 56(3): 257–277.

Lewis, Oscar. 1968. "The Culture of Poverty." In *On Understanding Poverty,* edited by Daniel Moynihan, 107–201. New York: Basic Books.

Lifton, Betty Jean. 1998. "Bad/Good, Good/Bad: Birth Mothers and Adoptive Mothers." In *"Bad Mothers": The Politics of Blame in Twentieth-Century America,* edited by Molly Ladd-Taylor and Lauri Umansky, 191–197. New York: New York University Press.

Lovette-Tisdale, Marilyn and Bruce Anthony Purnell. 1996. "It Takes an Entire Village." *Journal of Black Psychology* 22(2) (May): 266–269.

Lovibond, Sabina. 1994. "Maternalist Ethics: A Feminist Assessment." *The South Atlantic Quarterly* 93(4): 779–804.

Lynthcott-Haims, Julie C. 1994. "Where Do Mixed Babies Belong? Racial Classification in America and Its Implications for Transracial Adoption." *Harvard Civil Rights-Civil Liberties Law Review* 29(2): 531–558.

Macey, Marie. 1995. "'Same Race' Adoption Policy: Anti-Racism or Racism?" *Journal of Social Policy* 24(4): 473–492.

Mahoney, Maureen A., and Barbara Yngvesson. 1992. "The Construction of Subjectivity and the Paradox of Resistance: Reintegrating Feminist Anthropology and Psychology." *Signs* 18(1): 44–73.

Marchand, Marianne H. and Jane L. Parpart (eds). 1995. *Feminism/Postmodernism/Development.* New York: Routledge.

Martin, Emily. 1987. *The Woman in the Body: A Cultural Analysis of Reproduction.* Boston: Beacon Press.

May, Elaine Tyler. 1995. *Barren in the Promised Land: Childless Americans and the Pursuit of Happiness.* Cambridge, MA: Harvard University Press.

Maynard, Mary. 1994. "Race, Gender and the Concept of Difference in Feminist Thought." In *The Dynamics of 'Race' and Gender: Some Feminist Interventions,* edited by Haleh Afshar and Mary Maynard, 9–25. London: Taylor and Francis Press.

Mbilinyi, Marjorie. 1989. "I'd Have Been a Man: Politics and the Labor Process in Producing Personal Narratives." In *Interpreting Women's Lives: Feminist and Personal Narratives*, edited by the Personal Narrative Group, 204–227. Bloomington: Indiana University Press.

McMahon, Martha. 1995. *Engendering Motherhood: Identity and Self Transformation in Women's Lives*. New York: Guilford Press.

McRoy, Ruth G. 1999. *Special Needs Adoption: Practice Issues*. New York: Garland Publishing.

McRoy, Ruth G., and Helen Grape. 1999. "Skin Color in Transracial and Inracial Adoptive Placements: Implications for Special Needs Adoption." *Child Welfare* 75: 673–675.

Melina, Lois Ruskai. 1986. *Raising Adopted Children: A Manual for Adoptive Parents*. New York: Tapestry Books.

Mendenhall, Tai J., Harold D. Grotevant and Ruth McRoy. 1996. "Adoptive Couples: Communication and Changes Made." *Family Relations* 45: 223–229.

Mies, Maria. 1989. *Patriarchy and Accumulation on a World Scale: Women in the International Division of Labor*. London: Zed Books.

Mink, Gwendolyn. 1990. "The Lady and the Tramp: Gender, Race, and the Origins of the American Welfare State." In *Women, the State and Welfare*, edited by Linda Gordon, 92–122. Madison: University of Wisconsin Press.

Modell, Judith. 1992. "How Do You Introduce Yourself as a Childless Mother?: Birthparent Interpretations of Parenthood." In *Storied Lives*, edited by George C. Rosenwald and Richard L. Ochberg, 76–94. New Haven, CT: Yale University Press.

———. 1994. *Kinship with Strangers: Adoption and Interpretations of Kinship and American Culture*. Berkeley: University of California Press.

———. 1997. "Where Do We Go Next? Long-Term Reunion Relationships Between Adoptees and Birth Parents." *Marriage and Family Review* 25(1–2): 43–66.

Mohanty, Chandra Talpade. 1997. "Women Workers and Capitalist Scripts: Ideologies of Domination, Common Interests, and the Politics of Solidarity." In *Feminist Genealogies, Colonial Legacies, Democratic Futures*, edited by M. Jaqui Alexander and Chandra Talpade Mohanty, 3–29. New York: Routledge.

Moosnick, Nora Rose. 1993. "The Significance of the Construction of Race in the Life Histories of African Americans from Three Generations." Unpublished thesis. University of Kentucky.

Naples, Nancy. 1996. "A Feminist Revisiting of the Insider/Outsider Debate: The 'Outsider Phenomenon' in Rural Iowa." *Qualitative Research* 19(1): 83–106.

———. 1998a. *Grassroots Warriors: Activist Mothering, Community Work, and the War on Poverty*. New York: Routledge.

——— (ed.). 1998b. *Community Activism and Feminist Politics: Organizing Across Race, Class, and Gender*. New York: Routledge.

Naples, Nancy, and Carolyn Sachs. 2000. "Standpoint Epistemology and the Uses of Self Reflection in Feminist Ethnography: Lessons for Rural Sociology." *Qualitative Sociology in Rural Studies* 65(2): 194–115.

Oakley, Anne. 1981. "Interviewing Women: A Contradiction in Terms." In *Doing Feminist Research*, edited by Helen Roberts. London: Routledge.

Omi, Michael, and Howard Winant. 1986. *Racial Formation in the United States*. New York: Routledge.

———. 1994. *Racial Formation in the United States: Second Edition*. New York: Routledge.

Patton, Sandra. 2000. *Birthmarks*. New York: New York University Press.

Pertman, Adam. 2000. *Adoption Nation: How the Adoption Revolution Is Transforming America*. New York: Basic Books.

Phoenix, Ann. 1996. "Social Constructions of Lone Motherhood: A Case of Competing Discourses." In *Good Enough Mothering?: Feminist Perspectives on Lone Motherhood*, edited by Elizabeth B. Silva, 175–190. London: Routledge.

Phoenix, Ann, and Anne Woollett. 1991. "Motherhood: Social Construction, Politics and Psychology." In *Motherhood: Meanings, Practices and Ideologies*, edited by Ann Phoenix et al., 13–27. London: Sage Publications.

Phoenix, Ann, Anne Woollett and Eva Lloyd (eds). 1991. *Motherhood: Meanings, Practices and Ideologies*. London: Sage Publications.

Plath, Sylvia. 1965. *Ariel*. New York: Harper Colophon Books.

Polakow, Valerie. 1993. *Lives on the Edge: Single Mothers and Their Children in the Other America*. Chicago: University of Chicago Press.

Porter, Bruce. 1993. "I Met My Daughter at the Wuhan Foundling Hospital." *The New York Times Magazine*, 11 April: 24.

Punch, Maurice. 1994. "Politics and Ethics in Qualitative Research." In *Handbook of Qualitative Research*, edited by Norman Denzin and Yvonna Lincoln, 83–97. Thousand Oaks, CA: Sage Publications.

Ragoné, Heléna, and Frances Twine (eds.). 2000. *Ideologies and Technologies of Motherhood: Race, Class, Sexuality, Nationalism*. New York: Routledge.

Rank, Mark. 1994. *Living on the Edge: The Realities of Welfare in America*. New York: Columbia University Press.

Raymond, Janice. 1993. *Women as Wombs: Reproductive Technologies and the Battle Over Women's Freedom*. San Francisco: Harper Collins Publishers.

Reddy, Maureen. 1994. *Crossing the Color Line: Race, Parenting and Culture*. New Brunswick, NJ: Rutgers University Press.

Register, Cheri. 1991. *"Are Those Your Kids?" American Families with Children Adopted from Other Countries*. New York: The Free Press.

Reinharz, Shulamit. 1992. *Feminist Methods in Social Research*. Oxford: Oxford University Press.

———. 1993. "Neglected Voices and Excessive Demands in Feminist Research." *Qualitative Sociology* 16(1): 69–76.

Remennick, Larissa. 2000. "Childless in the Land of Imperative Motherhood: Stigma and Coping Among Infertile Israeli Women." *Sex Roles: A Journal of Research* 431 (11/12): 821.

Rensberger, Boyce. 1994. "Racial Odyssey." In *Physical Anthropology*, edited by Elvio Angeloni. Guilford, CT: Dushkin Publishing Group.

Rich, Adrienne. 1976. *Of Woman Born*. New York: Bantam Books.

Roseneil, Sasha, and Kirk Mann. 1996. "Unpalatable Choices and Inadequate Families: Lone Mothers and Underclass Debate." In *Good Enough Mothering?:*

Feminist Perspectives on Lone Motherhood, edited by Elizabeth B. Silva, 191–210. London: Routledge.

Rosenwald, George C., and Richard L. Ochberg (eds). 1992. *Storied Lives*. New Haven, CT: Yale University Press.

Rothenberg, Karen H., and Elizabeth J. Thomson (eds). 1994. *Women and Prenatal Testing: Facing the Challenges of Genetic Technology*. Columbus: Ohio State University Press.

Rothman, Barbara Katz. 1994a. "Beyond Mothers and Fathers: Ideology in a Patriarchal Society." In *Mothering: Ideology, Experience, and Agency*, edited by Evelyn Nakano Glenn, Grace Chang, and Linda Rennie Forcey, 139–157. New York: Routlege.

———. 1994b. "The Tentative Pregnancy: Then and Now." In *Women and Prenatal Testing: Facing the Challenges of Genetic Technology*, edited by Karen H. Rothenberg and Elizabeth J. Thomson, 260–270. Columbus: Ohio State University Press.

Ruddick, Sara. 1994. "Thinking Mothers/Conceiving Birth." In *Representations of Motherhood*, edited by Donna Bassin, Margaret Honey, and Meryle Mahrer Kaplan, 29–45. New Haven, CT: Yale University Press.

———. 1997. "Maternal Thinking," In *Feminist Social Thought: A Reader*, edited by Diana Tietjens Meyers, 584–603. New York: Routledge.

Rush, Sharon. 2000. *Loving Across the Colorline*. Lanham, MD: Rowman & Littlefield.

Russell, Audrey. 1972. Position paper: Transracial Adoption. National Association of Black Social Workers. New York.

Sacks, Karen Brodkin. 1989. "What's a Life Story Got to Do with It?" In *Interpreting Women's Lives: Feminist Theory and Personal Narratives*, edited by the Personal Narrative Group, 85–95. Bloomington: Indiana University Press.

Scanlon, Jennifer. 1993. "Challenging the Imbalances of Power in Feminist Oral History: Developing a Take-and-Give Methodology." *Women's Studies International Forum* 16(6): 639–645.

Schneider, Phyllis. 1987. "What It's Like to Adopt." *Parents' Magazine*, November: 167–179.

Schooler, Jayne E. 1993. *The Whole Life Adoption Book*. New York: Tapestry Books.

Shapiro, Vivian B., Janet R. Shapiro and Sabel H. Paret. 2001. *Complex Adoption and Assisted Reproductive Technology*. New York: Guilford Press.

Silva, Elizabeth Bortolaia (ed.). 1996. *Good Enough Mothering?: Feminist Perspectives on Lone Mothering*. London: Routledge.

Simon, Rita J. 1992. *Adoption, Race, and Identity*. New York: Praeger Publishers.

Simon, Rita J., and Howard Altstein. 1977. *Transracial Adoption*. New York: John Wiley Sons.

———. 2000. *Adoption Across Borders: Serving the Children in Transracial and Intercountry Adoptions*. Lanham, MD: Rowman & Littlefield.

Simon, Rita J., Howard Altstein and Marygold S. Melli. 1995. "Transracial Adoptions Should Be Encouraged." In *Adoption: Opposing Viewpoints*, edited by Andrew Harneck, 197–204. San Diego, CA: Greenhaven Press.

Sklar, Kathryn Kish. 1993. "The Historical Foundations of Women's Power in the Creation of the American Welfare State, 1830–1930." In *Mothers of a New*

World: Maternalist Politics and the Origins of Welfare States, edited by Seth Koven and Sonya Michel, 43–93. London: Routledge.

Smart, Carol. 1996. "Deconstructing Motherhood." In *Good Enough Mothering?: Feminist Perspectives on Lone Motherhood*, edited by Elizabeth B. Silva, 37–56. London: Routledge.

Smith, Dorothy. 1990. *The Conceptual Practices of Power: A Feminist Sociology of Knowledge*. Boston: Northeastern University Press.

Smith, Janet Farrell. 1996. "Analyzing Ethical Conflict in the Transracial Adoption Debate: Three Conflicts Involving Community." *Hypatia* 11(2) (spring): 1–33.

Solinger, Rickie. 1992. *Wake Up Little Susie: Single Pregnancy and Race Before Roe v. Wade*. New York: Routledge.

———. 2001. *Beggars and Choosers: How the Politics of Choice Shapes Adoption*. New York: Hill and Wang.

Taylor, Robert Joseph, and Michael C. Thorton. 1996. "Child Welfare and Transracial Adoption." *Journal of Black Psychology* 22(2) (May): 282–291.

Thompson, Becky. 2000. *Mothering without a Compass: White Mother's Love, Black Son's Courage*. Minneapolis: University of Minnesota Press.

Thurer, Shari L. 1994. *The Myths of Motherhood: How Culture Reinvents the Good Mother*. Boston: Houghton Mifflin Company.

Tisdale, Sallie. 1991. "Adoption Across Racial Lines: Is It Bad for Kids?" *Vogue* 181(12): 251.

Trolley, Barbara C., Julia Wallen and James Hansen. 1995. "International Adoption: Issues of Acknowledgement of Adoption and Birth Culture." *Child and Adolescent Social Work Journal* 12(6) (December): 465.

Tsing, Anna Lowenhaupt. 1990. "Monster Stories: Women Charged with Perinatal Endangerment." In *Uncertain Terms: Negotiating Gender in American Culture*, edited by Faye Ginsburg and Anna Lowenhaupt Tsing, 282–299. Boston: Beacon Press.

Twine, France W. 1999. "Transracial Mothering and Antiracism: The Case of White Birth Mothers of 'Black' Children in Britain." *Feminist Studies* 3(25) (fall): 729.

Versluis-den Bieman, Herma J. M. and Frank C. Verhulst. 1995. "Self Reported and Parent Reported Problem in Adolescent International Adoptees." *Journal of Child Psychology and Psychiatry and Allied Disciplines* 36(8) (November): 1411–1429.

Vitillo, R. J. 1991. "International Adoption: The Solution or the Problem?" *Social Thought* 13(3): 16–24.

Wasserfall, Rachel. 1993. "Reflexivity, Feminism and Difference." *Qualitative Sociology* 16(1): 23–41.

West, Candace, and Sarah Fenstermaker. 1995. "Doing Difference." *Gender and Society* 9(1): 8–37.

West, Candace and Don H. Zimmerman. 1987. "Doing Gender." *Gender and Society* 1(2): 125–151.

Wolff, Jana. 1997. *Secret Thoughts of an Adoptive Mother*. New York: Tapestry Books.

Woollett, Anne. 1991. "Having Children: Accounts of Childless Women and Women with Reproductive Problems." In *Motherhood: Meanings, Practices and Ideologies*, edited by Ann Phoenix et al., 47–65. London: Sage Publications.

Yngvesson, Barbara. 1997. "Negotiating Motherhood: Identity and Difference in
    'Open' Adoptions." *Law & Society Review* 31(1): 31–80.
Yngvesson, Barbara, and Maureen A. Mahoney. 2000. "'As One Should, Ought
    and Wants to Be': Belonging and Authenticity in Identity Narratives." *Theory, Culture and Society* 17(6): 77.
Zelizer, Viviana A. 1994. *Pricing the Priceless Child: The Changing Social Value of
    Children.* Princeton, NJ: Princeton Unversity Press.

Index

About the Author

NORA ROSE MOOSNICK is an independent scholar and writer.